In New Guinea, fire ants, poisonous spiders, and other insects land on a sleeping man and, like vampires, suck out his body fluids. If the intense heat, the wildlife, or the many varied diseases fail to kill a person, the razor-sharp blades of grass standing seven feet high, capable of cutting a man open as easy as a bayonet, might. Little light penetrates the thick canopy during the few times the rain ceases, and when the sun appears, the area turns into a vast suffocating sea of steam which rots the clothes right off a man's back. This was the place from which MacArthur would defend Australia. He was hell-bent on preventing the Japanese from reaching their goal.

THE GREAT COMMANDERS OF WORLD WAR II

Volume III: THE AMERICANS

BY CHARLES E. PFANNES AND VICTOR A. SALAMONE

ZEBRA BOOKS
KENSINGTON PUBLISHING CORP.

ZEBRA BOOKS

are published by

KENSINGTON PUBLISHING CORP.
475 Park Avenue South
New York, N.Y. 10016

Second printing: August 1985

Printed in the United States of America

FOR JOHN MILLS:
    WHO STARTED THE WHOLE THING

Table of Contents

Volume III of our Great Commander series brings us to the Americans. As with the Germans and the British, our choices have been limited to six. Of the six, Patton, Bradley, Eisenhower, and MacArthur are obvious. Given a choice, readers would expect them. The selection of Alexander Patch might appear arbitrary to some. Perhaps it is. The authors, however, feel justified in including Sandy Patch in this volume. His steadiness in the field and his ability to wield his army from August 15, 1944 to war's end highly qualifies him as a great commander. 'Vinegar' Joe Stilwell is a highly controversial person. The authors feel that Stilwell's ability to conduct himself in the Byzantine courts of Chiang Kai-shek's government places him in the forefront of American commanders.

We are delighted to present this third volume. There are a number of people we would like to thank. Again we want to thank all the people at Zebra for allowing us to bring this series to print. We want to thank all the readers who have encouraged us to continue with it. We would particularly like to thank our children, Tom Pfannes, John Pfannes, Jennifer Pfannes, Charles Salamone, and Victor Salamone. Thank you, kids, for putting up with your absent fathers. We would like to give a special thanks to our inspiration, our wives, Lillian Pfannes and Susanne Salamone. Book writing is time-consuming and our wives have helped us immensely in providing us with the time and the atmosphere conducive to writing.

Charles 'Chuck' Pfannes
Cold Spring, New York

Victor A. Salamone
Poughkeepsie, New York
September 1981

Cross Channel Versus Mediterranean Strategy

On June 6, 1944, a combined British, Canadian, and American military force invaded the coast of Normandy, France. D-Day, as this operation is universally known, was the culmination of two and one-half years of discord and debate among the American and British military chiefs. The foremost spokesman for the Americans was General George C. Marshall, Chief of Staff, while the British cause was championed by General Sir Alan Brooke, Chief of the Imperial General Staff. This introduction is their story, a history of their arguments, debates, and points of view. Cross-Channel attack versus the Mediterranean strategy is a tale of high-level conferences involving decisions that ultimately determined the future history of the entire world. The commanders whose careers are discussed in this volume were all affected in one way or another by the decisions reached during these meetings. The story begins in North Africa.

On November 8, 1942, American and British forces waded ashore at three different North African beaches, Algiers, Oran, and Casablanca, leading the Americans into an involvement in the Mediterranean area that continued until May 1945. With a marked reluctance, the U.S. Chief of Staff, General Marshall, accepted the British plan known as Operation Torch. Actually, this plan was spawned in the fertile mind of Sir Winston Churchill who persuasively convinced President Franklin D. Roosevelt not to heed the military counsel of Marshall, who was opposed to Torch. The origins of this plan had their roots in the Arcadia conference held in Washington shortly after the Japanese attack on Pearl Harbor and Germany's declaration of war on the United States. The British were of the opinion that a North African undertaking would cause few casualties and require relatively little effort. It would also produce some beneficial effect, such as the prevention of Axis penetration into the French North African colonies, the securing of the Mediterranean line of communications so dear to the British, and the installation of potential bases for an entry into southern Europe.

The American Chiefs of Staff saw the positive benefits that could be derived from a North African invasion, yet they opposed it on strategic grounds. In short, they were concerned lest this venture dissipate Allied strength in what was generally felt to be a secondary theater. The Americans, and in particular Marshall, favored instead a major concentration of force in the United Kingdom (Operation Bolero) to be used for a massive attack against western Europe as early as possible. In the American view, the enemy was Germany and only by fighting in Germany itself could the enemy be defeated. Thus, any talk of a North African venture was, for the time being, tabled.

The British accepted the American view that a cross-Channel attack was inevitable, but felt that this should take place at a later date. They had been fighting the Axis since 1939 and remembered too clearly the blood bath of the First World War and the slaughter associated with the amphibious invasion at Gallipoli. The English Channel running red with blood was a distinct British fear. They further felt that it would be folly to hit the Germans when they were at their strongest. Instead, it would be better to wait until the enemy had been significantly weakened by peripheral attacks along the perimeter and until their forces were dispersed. Then, a cross-Channel attack could be launched as a *coup de grace*, rather than as a heavily contested battle.

Such peripheral strategy came naturally to British leaders. They had followed it so often in earlier wars against continental powers that it had become deeply embedded in England's military tradition.[1]

North Africa was therefore stressed by Churchill and Brooke. They emphasized its benefits, the economy of life, and the possibility of bringing France back into the Allied fold.

The American chiefs, however, were not desirous of peripheral actions. Germany had to be defeated so that more attention could be focused on the Japanese. Pre-war strategy had already been discussed well before the bombing of Pearl Harbor. Hypothetically, it was accepted that if America found itself in a two-ocean war, the European enemy would be the more dangerous and should thus be the primary target. This was known as the Rainbow 5 plan. In the United States' opinion, an attack across the Channel offered the shortest and quickest route to the very heart of Germany with the potential of ending the war in Europe earlier, thereby allowing them to turn their full force against the Japanese.

And so the lines were drawn. The British discussed a plan for North Africa (Gymnast, the predecessor of Torch) and the Americans planned for Bolero (a concentration of troops in the United Kingdom), Sledgehammer (an emergency landing in 1942 in the event the Russians crumbled), and Roundup (a mas-

11

sive invasion of northwest Europe in the Spring of 1943). The Americans felt this program offered the best hope of defeating the Axis while giving maximum support to the Soviet Union.

Though Churchill was open to the American view, Marshall could readily see that he held reservations about completely accepting it, as did Brooke. In April 1942, however, Bolero was approved by the British with one important stipulation: "it was not to interfere with Britain's determination to hold its vital positions in the Middle East and the Indian Ocean area."[2]

Soon after, the British began to express doubts about the availability of sufficient resources for an early cross-Channel operation. Would there be enough landing craft and would the landing crafts themselves prove adequate? This alone made the British apprehensive about launching a premature cross-Channel attack. On top of this was their fear that an early operation would be staffed predominantly by British troops whereas, in time, more and more trained American troops would become available.

In June 1942, a second Washington conference was held. Once more the major principals were present and again the prime order of business was the American desire to push through plans for a cross-Channel attack. The British clung tenaciously to their North African proposal.

The latter were distinctly cool to Sledgehammer, their contention being that an emergency invasion in 1942 to aid Russia would "slow down preparations for landings in 1943."[3] Furthermore, it should only be attempted if the Germans were demoralized by failure against Russia.

Since the British had cooled to any invasion across the Channel during 1942, President Roosevelt, who was anxious to commit American troops to combat against the Germans somewhere, asked his military advisors about the possibility of resurrecting the Gymnast Plan for North Africa. General Marshall and Secretary of War Stimson both opposed such a proposition. So the June meeting ended with the Bolero, Sledgehammer, and Roundup plans still intact.

By June 1942, however, the British had suffered serious setbacks in the desert at the hands of the Axis formations led by the indomitable Desert Fox, Erwin Rommel. In light of this, Churchill adamantly insisted that a premature cross-Channel attack would result in disaster. The Prime Minister again emphasized the importance of a North African operation for it would afford, he said, the sole means by which the United States would be able to strike at Hitler in 1942. If the President, he went on, decided against Gymnast, then it would appear that nothing could be done in 1942. In this opinion, Churchill was backed to the hilt by Brooke.

Reluctantly, the American Joint Chiefs conceded there were problems connected with Sledgehammer. Unfortunately, landing craft construction was lagging and the German U-boats were wreaking havoc on the buildup plans in England. Even so, Marshall and Admiral King, the Chief of Naval Operations, remained committed to Sledgehammer and insisted on continuing to plan for that as well as Roundup, which was slated for 1943. In their enthusiasm for a cross-Channel operation, both Marshall and King shot off a memo to Roosevelt indicating their advocacy of a Pacific plan should the British fail to back them up. In other words, the American Chiefs were threatening to turn their backs on Europe and concentrate on wiping out the Japanese. Roosevelt, however, failed to agree with his chiefs, but remained determined to send American forces against the Axis before the end of the year, even if it meant in North Africa.

As we have already seen, now more than ever Churchill was convinced that North Africa could provide the Allies with the greatest chance of success. A victory there would open up vast vistas for the Allies and lead to the liberation of Morocco, Algeria, and Tunisia, the return of the French to the war, and the freeing up of the Mediterranean. It would require the Germans and Italians to overextend themselves. The British leader did stress, though, that this did not rule out the possibility of launching Roundup in 1943.

The American chiefs continued to hold out for Sledgehammer, fearing that a North African campaign would divert Allied strength to a secondary front. They also feared that a commitment to the Mediterranean in 1942 would indeed rule out Roundup for 1943.

Roosevelt was unhappy with the deadlock. He desired action so he sent instructions to his representatives in London, directing that some agreement for action in 1942 be made on one of the following:

1. A British-American operation against French North Africa (either Algeria or Morocco or both).
2. An entirely American operation against French Morocco (Gymnast).
3. Combined operations against northern Norway (Jupiter).
4. The reinforcement of Egypt.
5. The reinforcement of Iran.

This sealed the fate of Sledgehammer, and Marshall and King knew it. Not wanting to send American troops to the Middle East or Norway, they accepted Gymnast (now renamed Torch) with great reluctance.

The American chiefs, however, tacked a stipulation on to the agreement. Roundup was to remain intact. Thus it was the pressure applied by the U.S. President which sealed the fate of Sledgehammer and jeopardized the life of Roundup.

With the decision finally made, Anglo-American cooperative planning was finally restored. It was, however, the two political leaders who made it possible. But the big question remained unanswered. Where would the Allies' major effort be: in the Mediterranean or across the Channel? Though he reluctantly accepted Torch, Marshall was determined not to give up his relentless pursuit of Roundup.

Was the decision to choose Torch over Sledgehammer proper? In retrospect, it was indeed. First of all, there was a critical shortage of landing craft which would have seriously hampered a large-scale landing in France in 1942. In addition, the Germans were at their strongest at that time and probably would have inflicted severe casualties on the invaders and thrown them back into the sea. Furthermore, knowledge of how to conduct large-scale amphibious operations were seriously lacking in the Allied camp. This know-how could only be gained by conducting successful operations on a smaller scale.

The question can be further examined and expanded. Should Torch have prevented Roundup in 1943? This is even more difficult to answer and its consequences would be far more important.

The successful assault against North Africa was launched on November 8, 1942. When 1943 dawned, the Allies found themselves bogged down in Tunisia where the Axis had managed to develop a strong defensive position. Now the big question for the Allies was where to go from there. Would Roundup take place or would the British, who generally advocated bold thrusts in the Mediterranean, continue to lobby for a continuance of operations after North Africa into Sicily, Italy, and the Balkans? The American chiefs became suspicious of British motives, feeling that their allies forever intended to sidetrack or indefinitely postpone the invasion for the completion of a Mediterranean strategy.

Roundup, however, was doomed. 1943 was a year of major conferences at Casablanca, Washington, Quebec, Cairo, and Tehran. Each meeting dealt with global strategies, but the underlying issue of the cross-Channel operation versus the Mediterranean strategy stood out sharply. The Mediterranean concept continued to win out at Casablanca. Sicily was demonstrated by the British to be the next logical target and with Mussolini's fall on July 25, 1943, new vistas of conquest were opened in Italy. Then there existed the possibility of invading the Balkans.

Never once did the British deny the importance of a future cross-Channel operation; they merely continued to lay down logical reasons for its delay. With 1944 looming large on the horizon, an important conference was scheduled to be held in Cairo and continued at Tehran. At the latter, for the first time, Stalin joined Roosevelt and Churchill for serious discussions. General Marshall was determined to make this meeting of the 'Big Three' the decisive one for pinning the British down to accepting a firm date for the cross-Channel attack in 1944 once and for all.

Because a cross-Channel attack was not attempted in 1943, numerous historians have debated whether or not the boat had passed the Allies by. One recent book (*1943 The Victory That Never Was* by James Grigg) severely criticizes the fact that no attack occured during that year. If it had been successful, it could have saved millions of lives in occupied Europe and would have beaten the Russians to central Europe.

The British, however, would not accept that thought at the time for they continued to cling to the theory that the same objectives were obtainable by exploiting the Mediterranean theater. The problem appears to boil down to this conflict: the British felt that if the Americans had placed as much emphasis on the Mediterranean as they desired to put into the cross-Channel operation, the war there would not have been fought hampered by the shortages of men and material which were, instead, husbanded for the cross-Channel attack. Without this handicap, all of Italy could have been taken and the Balkans entered, thereby allowing the Allies to move into central Europe long before the Russians.

That is how the British viewed the debate. As for the Americans, they questioned the British motive. To them, it smelled too much like traditional British imperialism. Again and again the Americans insisted that the way to defeat Germany was by a direct stab into the heart of western Europe. Armed with that opinion and short on patience, the Americans travelled to Cairo in November, 1943, ready to do battle with their British counterparts.

It had now been a year since the North African diversion and still no firm decisions regarding the cross-Channel operation were forthcoming, except for the fact that it was tentatively scheduled for sometime in the spring of 1944. The Americans were determined to call a halt to any further peripheral operations. Indeed, to many of the American planners, it seemed as if the British were afraid to meet the German Army on equal terms. In a letter to the President, Stimson said:

We cannot now rationally hope to be able to cross the channel and come to grips with our German enemy under a British commander. His Prime Minister and his Chief of the Imperial Staff are frankly at variance with such a proposal. The shadows of Passchendaele and Dunkirk still stand too heavily over the imagination of these leaders of his government. Though they have rendered lip service to the operation, their hearts are not in it and it will require more independence, more faith, and more vigor than it is reasonable to expect we can find in any British commander to overcome the natural difficulties of such an operation carried on in such an atmosphere of his government. There are too many natural obstacles to be overcome, too many possible side avenues of diversion which are capable of stalling and thus thwarting such an operation."[5]

At Quebec the previous summer, the British had accepted in principle the cross-Channel operation (Overlord as it was now called), but did not say too much about it. The situation in Italy worsened and the British spoke of the dire consequences should the Allies suffer a defeat there. They advised a retention in Italy of the all important LSTs (Landing Ship, Tank-landing craft for amphibious assault) required for Overlord in order to attempt a circumvention of the German's vaunted defensive line around Cassino. Therefore, they advised a postponement of the May 1, 1944 target date for a cross-Channel attack. Overlord again appeared to get the short end of the stick.

At Cairo, the Americans found the British eager to pursue their viewpoint. Churchill declared,

It is certainly an odd way of helping the Russians to slow down the fight in the only theatre where anything can be done for some months.[6]

Again and again the British insisted that they were prepared to carry out the cross-Channel invasion attempt, but only when the German strength in France was diluted enough to insure success. More positive action in the Mediterranean, they insisted, would determine this.

Meanwhile, other problems and obstacles to Overlord were discussed at Cairo. To that city came Chiang Kai-shek and with him the multiple problems of the China-Burma-India theater. The U.S. had a special interest in China and was desirous of initiating an amphibious operation (Buccaneer) to expedite the defeat of the Japanese in Burma and open the lines of communication to China. That, however, would necessitate a further delay of Overlord since some of the landing craft slated for the latter would naturally have to be sent to India. This created an embarrasing situation for the American chiefs, for now their own desires hampered a May 1 target date for Overlord. And so the first Cairo conference ended with the British calling for additional Mediterranean activity while accepting Overlord in principle and the Americans insisting upon priority for Overlord and Buccaneer. No firm decisions were reached. Final verdicts would have to wait until the Russians indicated their pleasure at Tehran. Boarding planes, the American and British chiefs, along with the President and Prime Minister, embarked on the voyage to Iran.

During the opening session at Tehran on November 28, 1943, Roosevelt noted that Overlord might have to be postponed for one, and possibly two or even three months. He then spoke of various Mediterranean

19

operations that could draw German pressure away from the Eastern front. He did, however, emphasize that Overlord would draw away more German formations than any of the Mediterranean operations.

Churchill then presented the British case, with particular emphasis on the promising opportunities in the eastern Mediterranean without in any way taking away from Italy and Overlord. He then asked Stalin about his feelings towards a two-month delay of Overlord.

Stalin's abrupt reply was like a bombshell dropping in the British camp. He said that the entire Mediterranean program appeared to him to involve an excessive diversion of forces. Overlord should be the basic operation for 1944. He went on to say that any other operation would cause nothing more than a delay. The only Mediterranean operation he saw of any note was an invasion of southern France.

Marshall was overjoyed with Stalin's response. The primacy of Overlord for 1944 was now assured. The British, for all their persuasiveness, were forced to accept the Soviet-American decision. The attack would be set for sometime in May with an invasion of southern France either preceding it, in conjunction with it, or immediately following. As for Buccaneer, the British pressed for cancellation. What gave force to the British insistence on this was an earlier Stalin admission that once Germany was defeated the entire might of the Soviet Union could be turned against the Japanese. With Soviet aid, Chinese help against the Japanese did not seem as important. Furthermore, the British felt that the cancellation of Buccaneer would allow the Allies more landing craft which could be used for possible additional Mediterranean operations without weakening the primacy of Overlord. As it was, the combined Chiefs had already agreed to allow some

LSTs to remain in the Mediterranean. This was necessary to outflank the Gustav (strong German defensive live in Italy around Cassino) Line via a landing at Anzio. In addition, these very same landing crafts could then be used for the proposed invasion of southern France, Operation Anvil. The British, however, were also casting glances at Rhodes in the Aegean Sea, a target greatly coveted by them.

But they were to be disappointed in regards to their aspirations for Rhodes. The Tehran conference ended with many questions left unanswered. The Overlord operation was to take place in May, but that date was seen by the British as too early. Their opinion was based on the fact that many of the LSTs were to be retained in the Mediterranean until January. Therefore, the British Chiefs proposed that the invasion be postponed until at least six weeks beyond the May 1 date. They also expressed some doubts about Anvil. These issues were tabled until their return to Cairo, out of the reach of Stalin.

Overlord and Anvil were the primary operations slated for 1944. After debate, the issue was finally settled; Overlord would proceed sometime in late May or early June, depending on the moon and the weather. As for Anvil, it was finally set for August 15, more than two months after Overlord and much too late to be of any significant assistance to the success of Overlord. In the months following Tehran, the Anvil operation came perilously close to being abandoned in favor of additional exploitation of Italy and perhaps even the Balkans. The widespread demands to strengthen the Overlord operation, the slow progress of the Italian campaign, and the lukewarm attitude of the British all conspired against Anvil. In the end, the U.S. insisted upon it and so it was scheduled for August.

Thus, on June 6, 1944, after two and one-half years of debate, General Marshall's great plan for the defeat of Germany, Operation Overlord, crashed ashore on the Normandy coast. The once reluctant British put their whole heart and soul into this great venture. In less than a year following this historic endeavor, the Germans went down in bitter defeat.

The years have passed and historians have had a field day expounding on and exposing the many defects in Allied strategy. This two and one-half year Allied debate has filled endless volumes and will probably fill many more in years to come. Whether the cross-Channel attack should have been launched in 1943 deserves special note. The British theory also had its good points. The exciting thing about history is that we can look back and say what could or should have been. We are most fortunate that our own decisions do not involve the lives of millions of people.

Chapter 1

In the fall of 1945, America's generals began returning home to the adulation of a grateful country. The war had ended in September and the achievements of these men were hailed and glorified while their personages were cheeered and honored. Only MacArthur chose to remain abroad, but he too was lavished with praise. Patton soon perished tragically in an auto accident. Eisenhower was elevated to Chief of Staff and eventually rode on the coattails of his victory to the White House. Bradley, Halsey, Spruance, and Clark were rewarded with promotions and prestigious positions. Nothing seemed too good for the leaders who had brought the United States through one of her most trying ordeals, the horror of World War II.

One general whose contribution rivaled those of his more illustrious peers was not destined to share the post-war rewards. Lt. General Alexander Patch succumbed to pneumonia on November 25, 1945, in a manner typical of his wartime career, without fanfare but with dignity.

Patch's war record was unique in that he was one of the few American generals to have won major victories in both the Pacific and European theaters. J. Lawton (Lightning Joe) Collins was another. Ironically, the latter's introduction into the war was as a divisional commander under Patch.

Alexander McCarrell Patch was born on November 23, 1889, at a cavalry post, Fort Huachucna, Arizona territory. His father was an officer commanding a detachment of horse soldiers. Growing up on the frontier during that period was an exciting experience for a young boy. The cavalry was still the prestigious and glamorous service glorified in recent years by Hollywood. In the evenings, the fort's troopers regaled the impressionable lad with tales of past exploits and the heyday of the service during the Civil War. Excursions against hostile Apache Indians were a way of life and young Alexander eagerly greeted returning patrols, anxious to hear a blow-by-blow description of the latest expedition. As far back as he could recall, there was little doubt in the youth's mind that he too would eventually become a soldier. There was never a thought for any other profession.

As soon as he was of age, Alexander took the exams for the United States Military Academy at West Point and shortly afterward received the cherished appointment.

In the summer of 1909, he traveled east to the banks of the Hudson River where he joined the corps of cadets. Although their academic careers overlapped, Eisenhower, Bradley, and Simpson, were students during Patch's term at West Point. Devers and Patton had graduated two months prior to his enrollment.

During his four years at the academy, Patch was an unspectacular student who did not attract an unusual amount of attention. As graduation time approached, Patch found himself torn between sentiment and practicality for a choice of careers. The cavalry had been responsible for inspiring his choice of the army for a career, but modern military technology was rapidly making the horse obsolete on the battlefield. After much soul searching, Patch opted to cast his lot with the queen of the battlefield, the infantry. So it was that in 1913, Alexander M. Patch was commissioned a 2nd Lieutenant of Infantry.

A series of routine assignments followed at various army posts. The year after Patch's graduation was marked by the outbreak of World War I in Europe. America declared her neutrality, publicly announcing her intention not to become involved in the political and military problems abroad. Most high-ranking officials knew better. They were certain that United States participation in the war was merely a matter of time. Accordingly, training was intensified and recruiting stepped up in anticipation of the inevitable demand. Patch found himself instructing troops in the art of using the machine gun, the very same weapon that had written finis to the career of the cavalry and the gun that dominated the battlefields of Europe.

On April 6, 1917, three months after Germany began unrestricted submarine warfare, America declared war. The Selective Service Act was passed the following month and the ranks of the army began to swell with recruits replacing the troops being readied for overseas operations.

On June 25, American troops began landing in France under the command of General Pershing. Among this contingent was 1st Lt. Alexander Patch. The Allied commander, Marshal Foch of France, was reluctant to use the raw Americans in battle. Thus, the newly-arrived allies trained and grumbled in rear areas or on quiet fronts for their first few months in France. After the Cambrai battle in late November and early December, the entire front settled down to await the arrival of spring when suitable campaigning weather could be expected.

Patch was restless. He had not crossed the Atlantic Ocean to guard supply depots and rail centers. He therefore requested his commanding officer to reassign him to the machine gun school as an instructor. Since his credentials were impressive, his request was quickly granted. Thus, he spent the winter of 1917-18 in this capacity.

When spring arrived, bringing suitable weather, the final battles of the Great War began to unfold. March witnessed the beginning of the Third Battle of the Somme. At the end of May, the Third Battle of the Aisne erupted and continued through the first week of June. At the end of that month, American marines wrote another chapter in their glorious history during the Battle of Belleau Wood. For 4 days in mid-September, the opposing forces slugged it out at the Battle of St. Mihiel. Finally, at the end of that month, the Battle of the Meuse-Argonne heralded the beginning of the German collapse. Through it all, Patch led his men with courage and intelligence.

Trench warfare in World War I was a miserable existence. Men lived and died for months on end in squalid, muddy ditches stretching the length of the battlefield. Attacks were launched en masse with troops leaving their trenches, making their way forward through barbed wire to conduct a front assault on a dug-in enemy. Casualties were usually high for the attackers as enemy artillery and well-sighted machine gun fire raked their ranks. Officers were expected to lead their attacks, so an unusually high rate of casualties occurred in the ranks of company, battalion, and regimental officers. Then, of course, there was the ever present danger of poison gas attacks. In addition to being encumbered by a field pack, a weapon, and spare ammunition, troops were required to carry gas masks at all times.

Patch was a popular officer. His courage and skill were evident to all who fought under his command and he was greatly admired and respected. Unlike some officers, Patch did not believe in feeding his men into a meat grinder, although occassionally he was left with little choice. His theory of command was that you could not win battles without troops to do so. If these soldiers were foolishly sacrificed, the battle would be lost. Nevertheless, he never hesitated to lead the charge personally whenever orders called for his unit to go over the top.

Patch's bravery and fighting spirit was not lost on a member of Pershing's staff. One George C. Marshall marked Patch down as an officer whose career should be closely observed with the prospect of greater things to come.

At the conclusion of hostilities, American troops began to make their ways home to return to the factories and farmlands. For the career soldiers, the end of the war foretold of a stagnation in their lives. Many budding generals dropped out of the post-war army dissatisfied with the boring everyday existence on dreary army posts throughout the country and the insufficient pay. Promotions were infrequent, duty routine, public ridicule a common occurence. It took a special breed of character to remain in the army.

Like many others of his generation, Patch took a long, hard look at the dreary existence he could expect. Unlike many of his colleagues, however, the army was the only way of life he had ever known, so the choice to remain was easier for him to make. He would stay on in the military until he was eligible for retirement as a Lt. Colonel or full Colonel if he was lucky.

Resigned to his fate, Patch spent the post-war years in a series of humdrm assignments so typical of the army of that period. Fortunately, the endless months of training and routine exercises were broken up by intervals of attendance at the various military schools, infantry school, staff college, and war college. By the time the date he had previously selected for retirement began to approach, events had taken a dramatic turn.

Adolf Hitler had come to power in Germany in 1933 and, as the end of the decade drew near, war clouds were again gathering over the continent of Europe. Speculation about the possibility of another war caused many officers to delay and finally postpone their plans for retirement.

1939 saw two events which influenced Patch's decision to remain on active duty. George Marshall was appointed Chief of Staff and Hitler precipitated World War II by marching into Poland. Patch had impressed Marshall with his performance in World War I and, like Eisenhower, Patton, and Bradley, had been marked by the new Chief of Staff for higher command. Although once again America vehemently denied the possibility of once more becoming involved in a major war, those on the inside, particularly in the army, felt differently.

Therefore, in 1940, Patch received his first star and was sent to Fort Bragg, North Carolina to train recruits. America's peace time army complement was relatively small and totally inadequate to face the challenge of another war, so the Selective Service Act was revived and recruits began to stream into army training centers. Patch was selected as one of the men responsible for turning these civilians into soldiers capable of meeting any crisis.

1940-41 were years of foreboding for the free nations of the world. France stood defeated, Russia was reeling from a massive German onslaught, and the North African shores were dominated by Axis formations. In the Pacific, Japan had conquered Manchuria and huge slices of Chinese territory and were making overtures in Southeast Asia. Suddenly, on December

7, 1941, America was plunged into the war with the Japanese attack on Pearl Harbor. In her hour of need, the country turned to those men who had doggedly resisted the temptation to abandon their weary, drab, and much-maligned profession.

The Japanese advance in the Pacific resembled a tidal wave sweeping everything before it. The Philippines, Dutch East Indies, and Indo-China fell in swift succession. Australia was threatened along with the French possession of New Caledonia.

After France's fall, General Charles de Gaulle formed a government in exile, the Free French movement. Overseas possessions either elected to remain loayl to the Vichy government of Marshal Petain or joined Degaulle's movement. As the various factions jockeyed for position on New Caledonia, de Gaulle reacted by dispatching one of his followers, Henri Sautot, to the island with orders to establish a Free French government. Later, the island was offered to the United States for use as an advanced Naval base in return for protection. After months of negotiation, the attack on Hawaii convinced the American government to accept the Fench offer.

By this time, Patch was commanding the Infantry Placement Center at Camp Croft, South Carolina. Early in January 1942, a high priority telegram arrived at his office ordering him to report to Washington immediately. Wasting little time, the General arrived in the Capitol the next day and was informed that he was to take command of the forces being gathered for the defense of New Caledonia.

Those units hastily being assembled were a multinational hodgepodge of Army Reserve formations from Alabama, Georgia, Massachusetts, Kentucky, New York, Arkansas, Virginia, Texas, Missouri, Tennessee, South Carolina, and Mississippi. This group was designated Task Force 6814. Assembling these units quickly would require considerable organizational skill and administrative talent. Patch was up to the task. By January 23, all units were aboard transports in New York harbor ready to set sail for the South Pacific. Patch placed the task force in the hands of one of his subordinates and remained behind in Washington to monitor the progress of the war in the Pacific. He planned to fly to Australia at a later date and join the force there.

The French in New Caledonia, however, were impatient. They threatened to withdraw permission to build an airfield on the island unless American troops arrived immediately. The War Department did not wish to compromise the security of the task force by informing the French of its sailing, so Patch was ordered to leave at once and stop off at Noumea, the capital of New Caledonia, en route to Australia and bring the French up to date on America's intention. The General had worn himself out through overwork and, when his plane landed to refuel in Trinidad, it was discovered that he had contracted pneumonia. He was quickly returned to the United States and hospitalized.

For a general impatiently anticipating his first command, confinement to a hospital bed was an agonizing experience. Therefore, before the doctors agreed that he was ready to leave, Patch discharged himself from the hospital and set off for the Pacific via San Francisco.

On March 7, the General arrived in Noumea where he met with the island's governor, Admiral d'Argenlieu. Patch briefed the Admiral about American plans and in turn was offered the complete cooperation of the population and the government. Meanwhile, the day before, Task Force 6814 had left

Australia on the final leg of its journey to the island.

Just prior to the arrival of the task force, advance members of Patch's staff arrived by plane and brought him up to date on the latest war information and current developments in the Pacific. His official orders simply stated:

In cooperation with the military forces of the United Nations hold New Caledonia against attack.[1]

New Caledonia is an elongated island approximately two hundred and fifty miles in length and thirty miles wide. It is strategically located off the west coast of Australia where its presence acts as a buffer between the latter and island chains of the Pacific. When Patch arrived, he found the island defended by a handful of French and Australian forces, hardly enough to forestall a Japanese invasion. Fortunately, the Japanese were busy elsewhere, in the Solomons, on New Guinea, at Hong Kong, and in the Philippines. Since there were not enough forces to go around, they elected to ignore New Caledonia and thus, missed the boat.

On March 12, Task Force 6814 steamed into Noumea harbor after an uneventful voyage through the Coral Sea. If the Japanese decided to attack now, they would face stiff opposition.

Patch immediately began preparing the defenses of the island. Construction of a second airfield was begun and the force split three ways. One group was sent to the northern part of the island, another to the opposite end, and the third was dispatched to the New Hebrides Islands, two hundred and fifty miles further east. This area had also been placed under Patch's command.

As defensive positions were prepared, additional reinforcements kept arriving until eventually Patch's conglomeration of units reached divisional proportions. However, the command situation as it existed was too unwieldy. Since no numerical designation for a division was forthcoming from Washington, the commanding general decided that since he had structured the chain of command along these lines, the force needed a name for morale purposes.

Suggestions were solicited from the troops and one soldier's recommendation stood out. Since the formation was comprised of units from a number of states and had been formed into a division on New Caledonia, why not call it the Americal Division.

Patch liked the idea and forwarded it to Washington for approval. Amazingly, the War Department concurred. Thus was born one of the few units in World War II not denoted on the rolls numerically, The Americal Division.

While Patch busied himself with defensive preparations on New Caledonia, significant events were occurring throughout the Pacific. The Battle of the Coral Sea halted the Japanese drive on Port Moresby, New Guinea in May. A month later, the United States scored a resounding triumph at Midway by sending four enemy fleet aircraft carriers to the bottom and sustaining the loss of only the carrier Yorktown.

Also in May, the Japanese landed at Tulagi in the Solomon Islands. After establishing themselves there, they crossed to the neighboring island of Guadalcanal and began construction of an airfield. The American command in the Pacific was quick to recognize the threat posed by this action and made plans to invade the island.

On August 8, elements of the 1st Marine Division under General Alexander Vandergrift landed simultaneously on the Solomon islands of Tulagi, Florida, Gavutu, Tanambogo, and Guadalcanal. On the latter, little enemy resistance was encountered and the incomplete airstrip was overrun the following day. Renamed Henderson Field, the airstrip was completed by the Marines who moved rapidly to organize a defensive perimeter and establish control of the island. Despite the apparent lack of opposition, the Japanese were determined to hold onto Guadalcanal. During the succeeding weeks, their navy landed almost three thousand troops to bolster the force already present. Meanwhile, on August 20, Henderson Field received its first contingent of fighter planes.

Then the Japs struck back. During the course of the campaign, no less than seven naval battles were fought near or over Guadalcanal. Two days after the American landings, the enemy caught an Allied fleet napping. At the Battle of Savo Island, they sent the cruisers USS Astoria, Quincy, Vincennes, and HMAS Canberra to the bottom without any loss of their own. On August 24, it was the United States' turn at the Battle of the Eastern Solomons. A U.S. carrier force destroyed the Japanese light carrier Ryujo, the cruiser Jintsu, and a destroyer.

During the next few weeks, while the marines fought and died on this heretofore inconspicuous piece of real estate, the naval struggle continued unabated. On October 11, during an attempt to land reinforcements, the Japanese lost a heavy cruiser and three destroyers at the Battle of Cape Esperance. The American cruisers Salt Lake City and Boise were damaged in this engagement. Three weeks later, the United States lost the valuable carrier Hornet at the Battle of Santa Cruz. The waters off Guadalcanal now took on an ominous name, Ironbottom Sound.

Two separate engagements took place in the second

week of November and are known as the First and Second Battles of Guadalcanal. During the first the Americans lost the cruisers Atlanta, Juneau, and four destroyers. The Japanese battleship Hiei and two destroyers were lost in turn. Two nights later, the Japanese battleship Kirishima joined her sister on the bottom of Ironbottom Sound along with three American destroyers.

But November was not over. Under Rear Admiral Tanaka, (Tenacious Tanaka), a fleet of Japanese destroyers (dubbed the Tokyo Express by the marines) began making nightly trips down The Slot, a body of water between the twin chain of the Solomon Islands. They brought reinforcements and supplies to their garrison. Escorting warships made frequent forays into Ironbottom Sound and bombarded the marine positions and Henderson Field with heavy caliber gunfire.

Thus it was on the night of November 30 when American naval units surprised the Tokyo Express. Tanaka's fleet promptly inflicted heavy damage on the cruisers Pensacola, New Orleans, and Minneapolis, sunk the Northampton, and escaped unscathed with the loss of one lone destroyer.

Meanwhile, on the island itself, the Marines were locked in a life and death struggle for survival. A heavy Japanese attack on August 21 near the Ilu River was driven back with the enemy losing almost eight hundred men. Vandergrift immediately launched a limited counterattack designed to consolidate his position.

On September 13, during the first Battle of Bloody Ridge, the Americans suffered heavily but managed to hold their position. Five days later another four thousand marines landed and drove the enemy away from Henderson Field.

Two weeks later, Vandergrift launched another offensive designed to force the Japanese back, but heavy rain hampered the attack and only a limited success was achieved. However, American patrols discovered that the Japanese were preparing a major offensive of their own.

The Japanese Army commander, General Maruyama, planned a pincer move against both ends of the marine positions on Bloody Ridge. On the night of October 23, after a heavy preliminary artillery barrage, the Japanese assaulted one end of the line but were beaten back with the loss of six hundred men. Unfortunately, the marines had suffered heavily also. Luckily, the other wing of the Japanese pincer failed to coordinate its attack and did not join the others on the first night. But the next night, thousands of shouting Japanese rushed out of the jungle. The marines held, but the attack continued for three nights. Both sides incurred heavy losses, but at the end of the three days, the marines still clung to their position while the enemy called off the fight and slunk off into the jungle. Repeated efforts by the Americans to exploit their success during the balance of the month merely resulted in limited gains and heavy casualties. Finally, as December approached, the marines were worn out and their ranks were dangerously thin.

Early in October, Admiral Ghormley, commanding that portion of the South Pacific encompassing Guadalcanal, had ordered Patch to send one of his regiments from the Americal Division to the beleaguered island. Ghormley knew that the marine strength was gradually dwindling away and wished to reinforce them before it was too late. Patch responded by sending the 164th Regiment, a North Dakota National Guard unit. A week later, the American Chief of Naval Operations, Admiral King, replaced

Ghormley with Admiral William Halsey.

Halsey immediately formed the conclusion that the marines were battle-weary and required immediate replacement. Disease had taken as heavy a toll as the Japanese.

The island of Guadalcanal was hardly a battlefield anyone would choose to fight on. It was certainly not the tropical paradise of travel brochures. The air was heavy with humidity and the average daily temperature was in the eighties. Tangled jungle growth covered most of the island and the few open spots were overgrown with high grass whose sharp edges could slice into flesh as easily as a knife. Malaria-carrying mosquitos abounded and showed little preference for friend or foe. Dengue, dysentery, and jungle rot were everyday occurrences and took a heavy toll. Deadly snakes thrived in the jungle, and in the numerous streams and rivers crocodiles feared no man.

After drawing his conclusions, Halsey decided to replace the balance of the Americal Division. General Patch had taken command of this jumble of diversified units, molded it into a division, and created a fighting force to be reckoned with. On Guadalcanal the division would receive its baptism of fire.

During the first week in December, Army units began arriving on the island and started to relieve the gallant 1st Marine Division. On the ninth, Patch officially took command of all units on Guadalcanal. This meant that he had to relinquish direct command of the Americal since Halsey was not content with the commitment of one division. The 2nd Marine Division and General J. Lawton Collins' 25th Army Division, en route to Hawaii were diverted to Guadalcanal. A corps headquarters, the XIV, was eventually established with Patch as corps commander. Wasting little time, Patch began to make immediate plans for launching an all-out offensive in January designed to throw the Japanese out once and for all.

On December 12, Collins preceded his division to the island and was immediately impressed by the tall, thin general whom he considered full of nervous energy and drive.

> As we entered his underground C.P., located in direct prolongation of the runway of Henderson Field an air-raid alert sounded. Sandy said 'Don't let that disturb you. Happens all the time' and nonchalantly proceeded with his briefing.[2]

Halsey's orders were simple and to the point. Eliminate all Japanese forces!

The veteran troops on Guadalcanal had seen their ranks decimated by sickness and enemy action and were now sorely understrength. In some units the malaria rate alone approached seventy-five percent. Patch knew that he could not win victories with battle-weary, sick, and worn-out troops, so he decided to bide his time until all of the 2nd Marine and 25th Army divisions were landed and had moved into position. In the meantime, he decided to launch a small-scale attack against enemy-held positions on Mt. Austin.

Mt. Austin was the highest point in the low mountain range at the center of the island. Defenders of the mountain could observe all movement and report it to their own forces. The Japanese recognized the importance of this position relatively early in the game and had built a strong defensive system of fortified bunkers there. Elimination of this strongpoint was Patch's first objective.

On December 16, Patch ordered the 132nd infantry regiment to capture the enemy positions on Mt.

Austin. The following morning, the regiment began to ascend the slopes. Hampered by the jungle terrain and stiff enemy resistance, they were shortly halted by a withering fire from the main Japanese strongpoint known as Gifu. The Japanese were experts at the construction of defensive positions and the ones on Mt. Austin were a tribute to their ability. Log-covered bunkers were built with dug-in supporting machine gun positions. The entire system was honycombed with trenches through which the enemy communicated with and reinforced his outposts. The positions were impervious to all but a direct hit with heavy artillery. The Americans attacked Gifu without letup for two weeks. At the end of that time, the Japanese positions remained intact and the 132nd had to pause and regroup after having suffered a high rate of casualties.

Meanwhile, on January 1, the Japanese High Command finally yielded to the pleas of their Army and Naval commanders in the Solomons and agreed to evacuate Guadalcanal and withdraw up the slot to New Georgia. Their decision was hastened by the fact that their 28th Division had been virtually wiped out when American aircraft had intercepted the convoy carrying the division to Guadalcanal and sent most of the transports to the bottom. However, the Japanese High Command elected not to inform their forces on Guadalcanal of the decision until the last possible moment a few weeks hence. In the interim, the defenders of the island would fight on feeling that they were there to stay. Reinforcements would still be fed in until the evacuation was ready to proceed.

On the same day that the Japanese were debating the fate of their garrison on Guadalcanal, the Americans renewed their efforts to take Mt. Austin. This latest effort made some initial headway, but the tenacious Japanese defense made it obvious that a quick victory was beyond the ability of the attackers.

By that time, replacement of Vandergrift's 1st Marine Division was almost complete. As American reinforcements continued to pour onto the island, Patch, now elevated to the command of XIV Corps, decided to relieve the 132nd infantry on Mt. Austin with the fresh troops of Collins' 25th Division.

The planned offensive for the rest of the island called for the assaulting units to break out of the defensive perimeter around Henderson Field. They would assemble in a two-pronged drive towards the center of the island and towards Cape Esperance at the northern end. There could be no broad front since the jungle terrain prohibited that type of assault. The attackers would be required to move forward in single columns and outflank and cut off enemy pockets of resistance.

Patch's offensive began promptly on January 10 after an intense artillery barrage. Immediately after the last gun ceased firing, the attack jumped off. Progress was slow and measured in yards as the Americans were forced to hack their way through the heavy jungle growth and the columns were required to halt frequently to deal with enemy rearguard holding up the advance.

Some of the initial objectives fell quickly, but the skilled and determined Japanese resisted every step. Each day's attack was preceded by the usual deadly fire. Then the assault moved forward. The enemy was encountered everywhere along the jungle tracks and gains were slow and short.

On the 14th, the Tokyo Express landed six hundred reinforcements at Cape Esperance, bolstering the Japanese belief that the island was to be held at all cost. Thus, the Americans were forced to fight for each step. Nevertheless, steady progress was made.

After over a week of repeated attacks, however, Patch was forced to sanction a pause to regroup. Meanwhile, the defenders of Mt. Austin continued to cling tenaciously to their positions.

After moving fresh troops to the front, Patch ordered the attack to go forward on the 22nd. At the same time Collins' troops noticed a weakening of the enemy defense. A daily artillery and aerial pounding was beginning to take its toll.

Five days before Patch renewed the offensive, the Japanese formally received word of the intended evacuation. By that time, the Imperial troops were half-starved, disease-riddled, and exhausted from the constant American attacks on land and in the air.

On January 23, relentless American pressure finally yielded results. A large pocket of Japanese was surrounded by American troops driving through the jungle. The pocket was systematically eliminated by rifle and artillery fire. All but a few of the enemy force were destroyed. That same day, the last defenders of Mt. Austin perished as Collins' troops overran their positions. Since the Japanese rarely surrendered, the Americans had to kill each enemy soldier before declaring the position secure.

Now the drive for Cape Esperance gathered steam. But the Tokyo Express continued to make its presence felt. As the bulk of the enemy troops fell back to the Cape, their rearguards continued to impede the American advance and progress remained slow. The Americans were unaware of the Japanese decision to evacuate Guadalcanal and they took advantage of this. Therefore, there was little slackening in the ferocity of the defense. In the meantime, another chapter in the naval battle for Guadalcanal was written.

Unaware that the enemy had written off

Guadalcanal, the Americans continued to reinforce the island. Convoys reaching the area had to be protected from Japanese attacks and naturally required the presence of escorting warships. During the unloading of one of the convoys, the veteran of the Battle of Savo, the USS Chicago, was sunk by Japanese aircraft shortly after the Battle of Rennell Island. They had intended to attack the supply convoy, but were diverted by the presence of the Chicago and decided to destroy that hapless vessel instead.

As Patch's forces approached the coast, the Tokyo Express began to evacuate the Japanese forces. On the 1st of February, three thousand survivors of General Sano's 38th Division once over eight thousand strong, boarded transports and left Guadalcanal behind. Two nights later, the remnants of the once powerful Sendai Division, their ranks now decimated, took their turn. The Sendai would never again be a significant force in battle. Finally, on the night of February 7, the three thousand-man rearguard, having successfully held off all American attacks, boarded ship and sailed away.

After linking up on the 4th, Patch's two columns had driven for the coast but, unaware of Japanese intentions, proceeded cautiously. There had been too many ambushes, too many enemies lurking behind each tree and fallen log. It would have been sheer folly to drive headlong into a force skilled in the defensive use of the jungle who preferred death to surrender. Patch knew that eventually American superiority would prevail and was unwilling to accept a high butcher's bill. In addition, neither he nor the American naval commanders had any idea that the enemy intended to abandon the island. That concept was in direct conflict with prior Japanese strategy.

Although small pockets of abandoned Japanese required mopping up, by the middle of February all organized resistance on Guadalcanal had ceased. Major General Patch's XIV Corps had earned the first American land victory of the war. Enemy losses on the island itself approached twenty-five thousand. Countless more had perished en route. Sixteen thousand American marines, soldiers, and sailors died over the steaming jungles. In addition, another five thousand had been wounded or laid low by disease. It was a costly but significant victory.

On the positive side, the myth of Japanese invincibility was shattered forever. Even more vital, since places like New Georgia and Bougainville lay ahead, invaluable jungle fighting experience was gained.

American marine and army troops had written a glorious chapter in the annals of American arms. One Japanese general felt that his army had 'bled to death in the jungles of Guadalcanal.' He was correct. On February 8, General Patch sent the following message to Halsey.

Organized resistance on Guadalcanal has ceased.[3]

Halsey replied:

When I sent a patch to act as tailor for Guadalcanal, I did not expect him to remove the enemy's pants and sew it on so quickly. Thanks and congratulations.[4]

Unbeknownst to Patch, his performance on Guadalcanal had come under close scrutiny by Marshall. The Chief of Staff was deeply impressed and marked Patch down for future employment in a responsible position. For the present, however, he decided to remove Patch from the Pacific and hold him in reserve until such time as a suitable assignment could be found. Marshall did not care to have Patch's talents squandered under MacArthur. Therefore, in April 1943, Alexander Patch left the Pacific behind and returned home to assume command of the Fourth Army.

Fourth Army was predominantly a training command charged with the defense of the western portion of the United States. As such, it was part of the Western Defense Command. Many officers would have considered this a banishment to the backwaters of the war effort. Fortunately, Patch knew better. By this time, he knew that Marshall had other plans for him so the Fourth Army command simply meant that he was marking time.

In January 1944, the summons came. Patch was ordered to pack his bags and head for Europe to assume command of the Seventh Army.

Under Patton, Seventh Army had played the key role in the conquest of Sicily. Patton himself had relinquished his post on January 1 when he was ordered to England to participate in preparation for the cross-Channel attack. Mark Clark, the Fifth Army commander in Italy, took over temporarily retaining control of his own army. Marshall had earmarked Seventh Army for use in Operation Anvil, the proposed invasion of Southern France.

The fate of Anvil, however, hung in the balance since the British Chiefs of Staff supported by Churchill opposed the operation and would continue to do so right up until the eve of the invasion.

The British, though, failed to reckon with the determination of Marshall and Eisenhower. (See Introduction and Eisenhower, Chapter 5). The American Chief of Staff and the Supreme Commander doggedly resisted every British effort to forestall Anvil. In the meantime, Seventh Army needed a commander and the assignment went to Patch.

On the last day of January 1944, Patch met Patton in London. The two generals were old friends of many years. Although he lacked Patton's expertise in armor, Patch shared his fighting spirit, a fact that Marshall had recognized. Patch, though, was more discreet in his dealings with the press and within the army command itself. Other than that, the two made ideal companions.

They managed to mix business with pleasure by attending shows and taking advantage of the limited social atmosphere of wartime London. During the course of discussions about Seventh Army, Patton managed to persuade his colleague to allow most of his old staff from Sicily to join him in London as part of Third Army. Patch did not consider this an undue hardship. He knew that Patton would be a hard act to follow and did not wish to have his immediate circle constantly comparing his method of command to that of his illustrious predecessor. Anyway, there was ample time to put together a new staff, and Patch had already formed some ideas about the composition of this group.

Satisfied that he had learned all there was to know from Patton, Patch set out for Sicily where he spent the next month familiarizing himself with the new command and observing its various formations. On March 2, Clark formally turned command over to Patch.

Plans for Anvil now went forward full tilt. Originally, the landings were scheduled to coincide with the Normandy invasion, but a number of factors, foremost being the shortage of landing craft, precluded this possibility. Consequently, the operation was rescheduled for mid-August. The delay allowed Patch additional time to train the units involved in the intricacies of amphibious warfare. A side benefit of the postponement was that additional time was allotted for reviewing the final plan and making those modifications necessary to insure success.

Seventh Army's objective was to secure the coast of southern France before driving due north up the Rhône Valley with the purpose of meeting the Allied forces driving eastward from Normandy. Coincidentally, the southern wing of the latter group was George Patton's Third Army.

Defending southern France was the German Army Group G, commanded by General Johannes Blaskowitz. He was an unspectacular but nevertheless highly competent officer who had found himself in Hitler's doghouse early in the war. Of all the generals holding the rank of Colonel General at the beginning of the war, Blaskowitz was the only one who failed to be made a Field Marshal. Army Group G was comprised of General Weise's Nineteenth Army facing the Mediterranean and von der Chevallerie's First Army guarding the Bay of Biscay and the Spanish/French frontier.

Patch could not have known the ramifications that the failure to capture ports early would have on the forces invading France from the west. Therefore, on his own, he came to the conclusion that taking the important ports of Marseilles and Toulon early were key objectives. Possession of the port facilities of these two cities would eliminate supply problems. Or so he thought.

Under command for Anvil, the Seventh Army had the U.S. VI Corps led by one of America's finest corps commanders. Major General Lucian Truscott was the victor at Anzio and the man who had spearheaded Patton's amazing drive across northern Sicily. For political reasons, the II French Corps was added under the command of General Jean-Marie de Lattre de Tassigny, one of France's most capable field commanders.

De Lattre was to Patch what Patton was to Eisenhower. He was impulsive, headstrong, prone to interpret orders to suit his own need, and eager to avenge the humiliation France had suffered at the hands of the Germans. In short, de Lattre was difficult to handle. Fortunately, both he and Patch quickly developed a mutual respect for each other. The task was made easier by Patch's understanding of how anxious the French were to free their homeland. Thus, he allowed de Lattre to take liberties that normally would be denied to other commanders. The Frenchman responded by providing victories in the field.

Patch's critics were quick to point their finger at his relatively slow advance during the latter stages of the Guadalcanal campaign. Seventh Army's spectacular advance up the Rhone would dispel this criticism, thanks to one of the most amazing drives of the entire war.

A week before the invasion was scheduled to begin, Patch was rewarded with a third star, denoting his promotion to the rank of Lt. General. By this time, Anvil had been renamed Dragoon.

In the early morning hours of August 15, 1944, ten thousand men of the First Airborne Task Force dropped from the sky approximately twenty miles inland from the shores of the French Riviera. Their objective was to draw enemy formations away from the coast and sow confusion in the German rear. At dawn, an Allied fleet of American, British, and French warships steaming offshore bombarded enemy positions with heavy-caliber gunfire. Overhead, Allied warplanes strafed and bombed the beaches of Provence.

At precisely 8:00 a.m., American forces began to land, the 30th Division near St. Raphael, the 3rd at St. Tropez, and the 45th in between. French commandos moved ashore of those forces that landed between Toulon and Cannes.

The airborne drop had succeeded magnificently. Resistance was light and, by the end of the day, ninety-four thousand troops were ashore at a cost of less than two hundred casualties. The Americans began a move inland immediately to exploit their success.

The next morning, as the Americans consolidated their bridgehead, de Lattre's forces landed, passed through the U.S. lines, and made off for Toulon and Marseilles. During the planning stages of Anvil, Patch had insisted that the French be allowed the honor of liberating these two cities. Meanwhile, the rest of Seventh Army fanned out and moved inland.

The 3rd and 45th divisions drove northeast on Avignon and the 36th Texas division drove north for Grenoble. In support, the paratroopers moved to capture Cannes and Nice.

Thanks to Ultra intercepts, Patch knew that the Germans had no intention of transferring units from Italy to harass his flank. In addition, by the 17th, Patton and Montgomery were preparing to close the jaws of a gigantic pincer around the German Seventh Army near Falaise. Consequently, the entire German western front was in a state of confusion. Hitler ordered Blaskowitz to begin withdrawing Nineteenth Army northward. As a result, Patch could drive his army in that direction with little to fear except the enemy in his front. (See map 1)

On the 20th, Aix fell to the 3rd Division and, two days later, the same fate awaited Grenoble as the swift

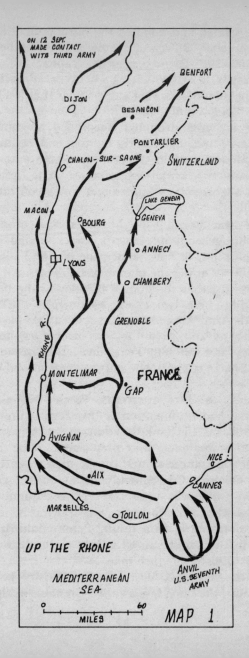

ON 12 SEPT.
MADE CONTACT
WITH THIRD ARMY

BENFORT

DIJON

BESANCON

PONTARLIER

CHALON - SUR - SAONE

SWITZERLAND

MACON

BOURG

LAKE GENEVA

GENEVA

ANNECY

LYONS

CHAMBERY

RHONE R.

GRENOBLE

FRANCE

MONTELIMAR

GAP

AVIGNON

NICE

AIX

CANNES

MARSELLES

TOULON

UP THE RHONE

MEDITERRANEAN
SEA

ANVIL
U.S. SEVENTH
ARMY

0   60
MILES

MAP 1

drive of the Texans kept the enemy reeling and off balance. Grenoble was over one hundred miles from the beachhead.

En route to Grenoble, an armored task force split from the main drive at Gap and made a ninety degree swing westward, capturing Montelimar on the Rhone on the 21st and trapping the retreating enemy between themselves and the pursuing 3rd and 45th divisions. Unfortunately, the roadblock proved too weak and failed to prevent the German escape. Led by the 11th Panzer Division, the enemy blasted their way through the thin American screen, but American artillery exacted a heavy toll. Although brilliant in concept, Patch simply lacked sufficient resources to fortify the thin screen holding the Rhone Valley near Montelimar.

Meanwhile, the French continued their drive along the coast towards the two vital ports. By the 22nd, the outskirts of both towns were in French hands and de Lattre asked Patch to attack both ports simultaneously. Although skeptical at first, Patch granted the Frenchman's request. His faith was rewarded a week later when both German garrisons surrendered on the 28th. Originally, the Allied high command in the Mediterranean had thought that the capture of Toulon and Marseilles would take forty-five days at least and more likely sixty days. The French under Patch had taken less than fifteen days.

While the battle for the two cities raged, the 3rd Division entered Avignon on the 25th and continued up the Rhone Valley.

After the fall of Grenoble and Avignon, the entire VI Corps set out for Lyons without pausing to catch their breath. The 36th pivoted northeast from Grenoble while its two brother divisions pursued the Germans up the east bank of the Rhone. On the west bank, elements of the French II Corps kept pace with the advance. On September 2, the Texans reached the outskirts of Lyons. There they were halted by the orders of Truscott who graciously allowed French troops to enter the city first.

The next major city along the path of advance was Dijon, one hundred miles beyond Lyons. Patch threw the entire might of Seventh Army into the race.

Meanwhile, von der Chevallerie's First German Army had received orders to withdraw before Seventh Army could close the emergency exit at Lyons.

With two entire German armies in headlong retreat, spurred on by the amazing drives of Truscott and de Lattre, Patch decided to take a calculated gamble. Since the German exodus resembled a route more than a retreat, he ordered VI Corps to swing northeast and head for Belfort near the Swiss frontier. Belfort was the traditional gateway to the area that had been fought over for centuries by France and Germany, the Alsace.

On September 3, VI Corps pivoted and set out for Belfort. Weise immediately recognized the significance of the redirected thrust and decided to stand and fight. Loss of Belfort would be tantamount to annihilation of both his and von der Chevallerie's armies.

As VI Corps continued the push, they suddenly noticed a stiffening of the German resistance. The breakneck speed of the previous weeks slowed as Weise struggled to hold open the door at Belfort.

While Seventh Army advanced up the Rhone, French troops continued to stream into the bridgehead through Marseilles and Toulon. As soon as enough units were available, another French corps, the I, was formed and directed up the right-hand flank of the VI Corps advance. Thus, the Americans were flanked on both sides by French forces. The I Corps added their weight to Truscott's drive on Belfort, but the Americans, having outrun their supplies and become exhausted from the breakneck pace of the preceding weeks, were not up to the task.

In an effort to alleviate the supply situation, Patch organized airborne drops, but they were not enough. Patch had been most perceptive in insisting on the early liberation of Toulon and Marseilles, but even possession of these two ports failed to help the matter. The supply columns simply could not maintain the hectic pace of the Seventh Army advance. In addition, the Germans, desperate lest they be completely trapped, struggled valiantly to hold open the gateway to Germany.

On September 9, Dijon fell to the French II Corps. De Lattre paused just long enough to consolidate his formations before pushing additional units beyond the city. That same day, his 1st Division linked up with elements of Patton's Third Army near Sombernon. Ironically, the southernmost unit of Third Army was General LeClerc's 2nd French Armored Division. This unit had marched across the Sahara desert from Lake Chad, fought in North Africa, and landed at Normandy. Now, just as they were moving up to assault the Siegfried Line, they made contact with their fellow countrymen streaking up the historic Rhone Valley from the Mediterranean. In the brief span of four weeks, Patch had driven clear from the Riviera to the German border and made contact with the American armies that had crossed the English Channel and roared across France.

Patch was fortunate in having Truscott and de Lattre as corps commanders. The Frenchman was a hard charger motivated by the prospect of driving the enemy from the soil of his homeland. As for Truscott, few commanders in the entire Allied team could equal his forceful ability to move units forward.

Unfortunately, however, Seventh Army once more failed to swing the trap shut. Hours before the French linkup with Patton's forces, the remnants of the German First Army moved through the gap between the two armies. In addition, now that he was able to fight on an interior line where supply distances were relatively short and his flanks were secure, Weise was able to forestall Truscott's advance. Both German armies had nevertheless lost over half their strength. Large groups of Germans were overtaken during the drive and found themselves with little choice but to throw down their arms. Furthermore, since the swiftness of the advance kept the Germans constantly off balance, Allied casualties had been relatively light.

Along with the rout of the German First and Nineteenth Armies, the capture of Toulon and Marseilles was equally vital. With the Allies in western France experiencing critical shortages due to the lack of adequate port facilities, the seizure of the two Mediterranean cities took on added importance. Tons of supplies came ashore through those two ports and were rushed up the Rhone where they became the life's blood of Seventh, Third, and the newly established First French Army. Patton's advance had been slowed to a crawl by the supply priorities of other armies further north. Now he could resume the attack.

On September 15, the two French Corps were united to form the First French Army under de Lattre and removed from Patch's control. Seventh Army was left with one corps. At the same time, the Sixth Army Group was officially activated under the American general, Jacob Devers. Devers' command included Patch's Seventh and de Lattre's First French armies.

A general reshuffling of positions now took place.

The French were shifted to the extreme right flank and took over responsibility for Belfort. Seventh Army found itself between de Lattre and Patton. To bring Seventh Army back up to strength, on September 29 the XV Corps of Third Army was transferred to Seventh Army. This corps was commanded by the man responsible for precipitating the trap at Falaise, Wade Hampton Haislip. Patch gained another offensive-mined general.

Now that the Allies possessed a continuous front running from Belgium to the Mediterranean, they began to move forward to the Rhine. A major offensive was planned for November.

On November 20, the 36th division spearheaded the VI Corps crossing of the Moselle near Eloyes and headed for St. Die. XV Corps crossed the following day. Seventh Army's objective was to cross the Vosges Mountains on the west bank of the Rhine and capture Strasbourg. This city was the capital of the Alsace region and was situated on the German border where it controlled the upper Rhine.

A new German commander, General Hermann Balck, had meanwhile replaced the unfortunate Blaskowitz. The latter had been a steady and competent commander, but he was no Balck. A veteran armored commander from the Russian front, Balck was one of Germany's finest field commanders.

One of the first things Balck had done upon assuming command was to order a counterattack against the French spearheads nearing Belfort. On November 13, the French had launched a strong attack towards the Belfort Gap. Three days later they broke through the enemy defenses and moved forward. Balck's counterattack failed to achieve success, but it did hand Patch an opportunity.

Fleshed out by the addition of the 100 and 103rd infantry divisions and the 14th Armored, Patch set Seventh Army in motion. They were to take advantage of the weakening of the German positions on his front due to the attack against the French. Truscott had left VI Corps to command a Fifth Army in Italy, but his replacement, General Edward H. Brooks, filled the void admirably. As already seen, VI Corps had crossed the Moselle on the 20th, broke through the disintegrating German defenses and, by the 22nd, the 'Rock of the Marne,' the veteran 3rd Division, captured St. Die.

Meanwhile to the north, Haislip mounted a strong attack of his own. It was a typical pell-mell Haislip advance through the Saverne Gap in the Vosges. Spearheaded by LeClerc's 2nd French Armored Division, XV Corps drove headlong on Strasbourg and reached the outskirts of the city on November 25. The following morning, LeClerc liberated the capital of Alsace. Patch had been quick to exploit the weakening of the German defenses on his front to support the counterattack on the French. His quick exploitation was rewarded by the fall of Strasbourg to LeClerc on November 23. This coup was followed three days later by 3rd Division's breakout from the Vosges into the Alsace Plain. Instead of allowing XV Corps to cross the Rhine on the run, however, Eisenhower ordered Patch to swing up the west bank of the river and support Patton's drive on the Saar.

As Patch and de Lattre drove forward to their respective objectives, it became accepted practice to bypass small pockets of enemy resistance, leaving them to be mopped up by units following up the main advance. One such pocket now existed in the area of Colmar. A large portion of Weise's Nineteenth Army had managed to form a strong defensive perimeter with its base anchored on the Rhine. This pocket was bypassed in turn by both Allied armies. Devers ordered the French to eliminate the pocket, but none of the Allied generals knew just how strong the enemy forces were. All French attempts were repulsed. With Patch now driving north, the Colmar Pocket posed a dangerous threat to his rear. (See Map 2)

Late autumn of 1944 witnessed a general slowdown all along the line of the heretofore rapid Allied advance. On the extreme left, Montgomery's drive on the Ruhr was delayed by the necessity of clearing the Scheldt Estuary in order to open the port of Antwerp. South of the British, Courtney Hodges' First American Army was locked in a life-and-death struggle around Aachen. On the extreme southern flank, the Germans continued to resist all French efforts to eliminate the Colmar Pocket. In the center, Patton's drive was delayed by a determined German defense around the forts of Metz. Patch's drive on the upper Rhine was slowed by a spirited enemy defense and Seventh Army's support of Patton.

Eisenhower's redirection of Patch's forces robbed Seventh Army of its momentum. With their backs to the wall, the Germans demonstrated that they were far from licked. By the end of the month, Patch's advance had slowed to a crawl, thanks to a stiffening of enemy resistance all along the front.

On December 2, Devers ordered Patch to pause and regroup for a major attack northward three days later. At the same time, the magnificent 2nd French Armored Division of LeClerc was transferred to de Lattre. Although LeClerc was relatively new to Seventh Army, having joined when XV Corps was placed under Patch's command, the latter had come to admire the indomitable fighting spirit of the gallant little Frenchman and his troops. Patch deeply regretted seeing them go.

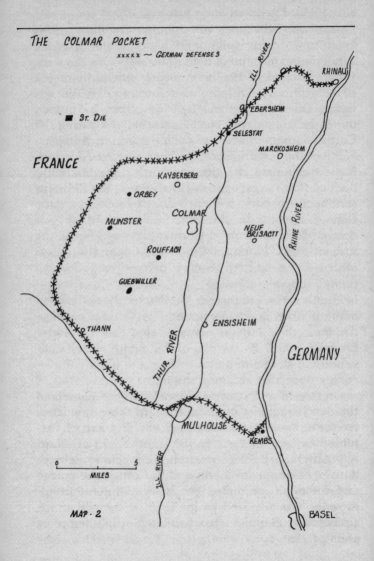

THE COLMAR POCKET

xxxxx ~ GERMAN DEFENSES

ILL RIVER

RHINAU

EBERSHEIM

■ ST. DIE

SELESTAT

MARCKOSHEIM

FRANCE

KAYSERBERG

● ORBEY

COLMAR

NEUF
BRISACTT

MUNSTER

RHINE RIVER

ROUFFACH

GUEBWILLER

THANN

ENSISHEIM

THUR RIVER

GERMANY

MULHOUSE

KEMBS

0   5
MILES

ILL RIVER

MAP · 2

BASEL

Early in the morning of December 5, both corps of Seventh Army began to attack northwards toward where the Germans were defending the antiquated French Maginot Line. Beyond that lay the vaunted West Wall, more commonly known as the Siegfried Line, the main German defensive position in the west. Progress was slow, but both corps continued to move steadily forward behind a strong attack. Haislip was halted briefly at the Maginot Line, but he quickly overcame the enemy roadblock. Both XV and VI Corps continued their push to the German frontier.

Meanwhile, the French had begun a concerted effort to eliminate the Colmar Pocket. On the 17th, both of Patch's corps brushed up against the Siegfried Line where their attack stalled in front of the deep German fortifications. Patch was not unduly concerned since he knew that the Siegfried Line was a strong defensive position constructed over the course of many months. Breaching this bulwark would therefore require a strong and dedicated effort. What he didn't anticipate was the launching of a major German offensive against First Army in the vicinity of the Ardennes. But Patch was not alone. Of all the Allied generals, only Patton suspected that the Germans had something nasty up their sleeves.

On December 16, two German Panzer Armies roared out of the Ardennes forest and quickly overran the American units on their front. As the Americans fell back, Eisenhower was forced to call a halt to Patton's attack in the Saar and divert portions of Third Army northward to deal with the crisis. However, portions of Third Army were grappling with the enemy and could not be pulled out of line. Since Patton's presence was required to lead Third Army's attack against the German spearheads, the southernmost units of that army were placed under Patch's command. All offensive action in Seventh Army's sector was halted and Patch was directed to conduct a holding operation until such time as the crisis had passed.

Once the German's Ardennes offensive ground to a halt, First and Third Armies still found themselves attempting to push the enemy back and reduce the salient. Since they were now on the defensive in the Ardennes, the Germans were forced to look elsewhere for a spot to create mischief. That elsewhere was on Seventh Army's front.

On January 1, Balck launched 'Operation Nordwind,' a heavy attack against XV Corps. Eisenhower immediately ordered Patch to withdraw from the Alsace and consolidate his position. This meant abandoning Strasbourg. DeGaulle refused to hear of it. In the face of the French leader's vehement protests, Eisenhower modified his orders and turned responsibility for the defense of Strasbourg over to the First French Army. His orders to Patch stood.

Patch found himself with little option but to obey. On the 2nd, the hard-pressed VI Corps fell back to the Maginot Line. By the 5th, Balck had succeeded in establishing a bridgehead over the Rhine and was feeding in additional units. Seventh Army counterattacks failed to slow the German advance as all along the line the Americans were pushed back. Meanwhile, the French had relieved the U.S. units in Strasbourg.

For a full week, Seventh Army was forced back as Balck maintained the pressure. The French found themselves locked in a bitter struggle to retain their hold on Strasbourg. Neither XV or VI Corps seemed able to halt the German offensive.

On January 13, Eisenhower moved the XXI Corps with three fresh divisions into line on the left of Seventh Army in an effort to stem the tide. Two days later, VI Corps turned on their tormentors and attacked the German bridgehead, albeit with little success.

After another week of pulling back, Patch ordered Seventh Army to dig in. It worked. Although they had managed to drive the 45th division out of its defensive positions, the German offensive was spent. On the last day of the month, Patch swung over to the offensive and began a systematic reduction of the enemy salients all along Seventh Army's front. The attack was a limited one since Patch's troops had received a bloody nose and it would take time for the wounds to heal.

Meanwhile, the French intensified the effort to clean up the Colmar Pocket once and for all. Aided by a few American units, de Lattre's forces cut the pocket in half on the 5th and managed to subdue the balance of the salient during the next four days as Weise pulled his remaining forces back across the Rhine.

In the middle of February, Patch moved XV Corps forward to clear out the remaining German strongpoints and capture Saarbrucken. Then he drew the rest of the army up to positions on the Saar River.

At the beginning of March, Patch and Patton received orders to cooperate with each other in clearing up the Saar-Palatinate triangle between the Rhine, Moselle, and Saar rivers. On the 14th, Third Army jumped the Moselle and headed east. Two days later, Patch launched all three of his corps against the defenses of the Siegfried Line. After forty-eight hours of intense attacks, Seventh Army breeched the line and Patch pushed them through and began to exploit the break.

The fact that VI Corps was struggling to enlarge their bridgehead failed to deter Patch's enthusiasm for the offensive. He had well over half the army through the West Wall (the exception was VI Corps whose advance was held up by a determined enemy stand). Third Army was also driving at breakneck speed. Both army leaders continued to prod their corps commanders lest the momentum slip away. Patton's well-deserved reputation for hard-driving, far-ranging attacks was already legend. However, in the drive across southern Germany, Patch proved he was the equal of his renowned colleague.

By March 24, most of the enemy had retreated across the Rhine where they felt a sense of security. The Rhine was Germany's formidable natural barrier and had kept potential invaders at bay for centuries. Patch and Patton soon dispelled that vision. Unwilling to allow the Germans time to regroup, Patton crossed the Rhine near Oppenheim on March 25. Not to be outdone, Patch sent Haislip's XV Corps across at two points near Hamm and Wurms the following day.

Both armies then continued to stream east. Huge formations of the enemy found themselves suddenly cut off and bypassed as the American steamroller rolled inexorably east. The ignored Germans simply threw down their arms and melted away or surrendered to the first American units they met.

Two days after crossing the Rhine, Patton had sent an armored strike force into the German rear in an attempt to liberate a POW camp near Hammelburg. It had been reported that American troops were being held at the camp. Patton had supposedly received information that the Germans were preparing to evacuate the American prisoners deeper into Germany. Since his son-in-law was reported to be among the captives, Patton acted. The attempt ended in a bloody repulse of the armored force.

Third Army's reversal failed to deter Patch. XV

Corps was driving towards Nuremberg, so Patch merely ordered it to detour in a wide arc northward. On April 5, Hammelburg fell. Reversing his course, Haislip captured Neustadt forty-eight hours later and continued the drive on Nuremberg with a move through the north of the Black Forest. Two days later, XV Corps pulled up in front of the Nazi party's hallowed city and began to probe its defenses. The fanatical SS troops defending Nuremberg remained faithful to the Nazi dogma and vowed to prevent the city's fall. XXI Corps, after crossing the Main River on April 5, was maintaining pace on Haislip's right flank and captured Furth, a few miles west of where XV Corps was battling the zealous SS troops. General Milburn added the weight of his corps to Haislip's attack and on the 20th, Nuremberg, symbol of Nazi greatness, was in American hands.

Both corps paused only long enough to refuel before pressing south. Meanwhile, VI Corps had finally broken through the Siegfried Line, assisted the First French Army in their capture of Stuttgart, and headed for the Danube. On the 24th, this corps and the XXI established bridgeheads over the fabled river near Ulm and Dillingen respectively.

On XV Corps front, during its drive towards Munich, elements of the corps found itself near the town of Dachau on April 29.

The vanguard of the Rainbow Division had to overpower some 300 of the SS before seeing the Freight Cars full of piled cadavers . . . bloody heaps at the rail car doors when weakened prisoners trying to get out, were machine-gunned to death . . .
. . . rooms stacked high with tangled human bodies . . .[5]

After recovering their senses from the appalling scene, XV Corps pushed on towards Austria.

On the final day of the month, all three of Patch's corps crossed the border into Austria. Salzburg and Innsbruck fell in quick succession. Patch then ordered Haislip to head for Berchtesgaden, Hitler's mountain retreat. XV Corps crossed back into Germany and made for the madman's lair.

Shortly after crossing the Danube, VI Corps received orders from Patch's headquarters to secure the Alpine passes leading to Italy. Brushing aside a dispirited German effort to resist the drive, a patrol of the corps penetrated into the Brenner Pass where it linked up with a patrol from II Corps, Fifth Army advancing from the Italian side. Ironically, the commander of the Fifth Army was the same man who had led VI Corps ashore in the Mediterranean and pushed it up the Rhone, Lucian Truscott.

On May 5, at Haislip's XV Corps headquarters, the commander of the German Army Group G surrendered all forces in southern Germany to Devers. Two days later, General Alfred Jodl signed a document at Eisenhower's headquarters at Rheims, ending the war in Europe.

Patch never had placed much credence in the myth of a German Alpine fortress, the so called National Redoubt. When ordered by Eisenhower to pivot and drive into southern Germany and Austria to deal with this threat, Patch viewed the order as simply an opportunity to defeat the enemy with a rapid armored drive. If indeed the Germans were preparing a last ditch stand in the Alps, then he would deal with it when the time came. In the interim, he certainly was not about to allow an unconfirmed rumor to dictate strategy or cause him to be overcautious.

Nowhere was the sympathetic and sensitive nature of the Seventh Army commander more in evidence than during the drive through lower Germany. The scenes of horror at places like Dachau unnerved him as only he knew. He was saddened by the necessary destruction of historic cities like Nuremberg, Stuttgart, Munich, and others.

Patch's soldierly bearing and devotion to duty received a stern test when Seventh Army began to overrun the remnants of General Andreii Vlasov's Army of Liberation. Vlasov was a much decorated Russian general who had distinguished himself during the defense of Moscow. After being captured by the Germans, he agreed to form an army comprised of Russian prisoners-of-war to fight for Germany against the tyranny of Stalin.

> (Patch) was approached by representatives of Vlasov's army seeking asylum. He said he lacked authority to grant it but would ask Ike. The next day a message from Eisenhower said the case would be referred to Washington. Patch requested the Russians to lay down their arms. In turn he would treat them like German POWs.[6]

It was obvious that Patch sympathized with the unfortunate Russians, but he was powerless to act. Just the thought of turning these men over to the Russians appalled him and offended his sense of justice since he knew what fate lay in store for them.

Unlike Patton, Montgomery and even Eisenhower, Patch did not go out of his way to seek the limelight. Neither was he as reticent as Simpson or Hodges. He was open with the press, but refused to court their favor. Jealousy was alien to his nature, so if the world knew of his exploits all well and good. If they didn't, so be it.

The criticism of the pace of his advance on Guadalcanal seemed to haunt him. In France and Germany, it seemed as if he was going to dispel these critics (although he would never admit it), if only to satisfy whatever doubts that might have lingered in his own mind. Patch was above, however, wasting troops to prove his own ability to others.

He was a man completely at home with the offensive-minded generals. Patton was a close friend, he and Truscott proved a magnificent team, Haislip was a man after his heart. So infectious was the offensive spirit surrounding Seventh Army, when Brooks replaced Truscott at the head of VI Corps there was no noticeable dropoff in quality. Later, when Milburn joined up with XXI Corps he too became caught up in the enthusiasm and proved equally adept at driving his units full speed ahead.

Despite what a few critics may say, Patch's drive up the Rhone was a masterpiece of military attack. Not once was the enemy allowed time to pause and regain his balance until he reached the relative safety of the West Wall. During the initial battles for the Siegfried Line, when Patch's only son was killed (he was an artillery officer with Seventh Army), he refused to allow his grief to interfere with the completion of the job at hand. Then he found himself facing the talents of Generals Hermann Balck and Paul Hausser (see Volume I, *The Germans*,) two of the very finest field commanders the Germans had to offer. Sandy Patch proved more than a match for both of them.

Was the invasion of southern France justified? Absolutely. By war's end nearly a million Allied troops had landed in France through the ports of Marseilles and Toulon, not to mention the countless tons of supplies. Patch had been quick to recognize the vital importance of these ports and gave their early capture a high priority. Consequently, unlike the channel ports which the Germans had time to turn into fortresses that defied capture for months at a time, Marseilles and Toulon fell quickly and were rapidly put to use sustaining the armies ashore. Although Patch eventually outran his supplies during the drive up the Rhone, it was not due to lack of port facilities. Instead, the logistical system was simply not equipped to support such a fast moving offensive.

Patch also demonstrated a rare talent for dealing with various subordinates and superiors. On Guadalcanal, he commanded U.S. Marines, traditional rivals of the Army, while reporting to the Navy in the personage of Halsey. The memory of his administration on New Caledonia is recalled to this day with respect. During the drive up the Rhone, one of his key commanders was the admittedly difficult de Lattre. In his own memoirs, the French general pays tribute to Patch's personality. During a strategy conference shortly after the invasion, a disagreement arose about the tactics to be used against Toulon and Marseilles. De Lattre presented his arguments and

suddenly those clear and serious eyes of the American Commander seemed to soften. With a gesture of hesitation that was full of modesty, he pulled from his pocket his wallet, and from it withdrew a little flower, whose petals were beginning to fade. 'Take this' he said, breaking off one of the petals. 'It was given to me by a young girl on the slopes of Vesuvius on the eve of embarking. She told me it would bring good luck. Let us each keep a part of this charm, and it may lead our two armies, side by side, to victory.'[7]

Eisenhower considered Patch one of the finest field commanders in Europe and repeatedly stated the same in post-war interviews. The noted historian Charles MacDonald considered Patch

"steady, workmanlike, accomplished."[8]

These words are probably the most apt description of Alexander Patch.

Late in August, he returned home to resume command of Fourth Army since Seventh Army was being broken up. After a brief stopover in Washington where he was cheered by a crowd attending a Washington Senators baseball game at Griffith Stadium, Patch continued on to Texas to take up his command. Shortly thereafter, his lung condition, the result of influenza during World War I and the pneumonia at the outbreak of the recently concluded conflict, deteriorated even further. He was immediately hospitalized at Fort Sam Houston where he died on November 21, 1945.

Patch was truly one of the most underrated generals of the war. Respected by his peers and admired by his allies, Sandy Patch was without doubt an American military hero. Unfortunately, his untimely death caused attention and acclaim to be directed towards those who survived and his great achievements have been relatively ignored.

Chapter 2

"I served with Patton." How often one hears that remark from a veteran of the Third Army. When interviewing actual participants in World War II, most responded to the question about their experiences with the fact that they had served in a particular Army, i.e., First Army, Ninth Army, etc. However, when we spoke with veterans of Third Army, all we heard was that short sentence said with distinct pride and often emotion, "I served with Patton." Such was the reputation of this illustrious man that, in retrospect, men were proud to have served under him.

George Patton! America's answer to the German Blitzkrieg, her lone knight in quest of the Holy Grail, a man whose very life harkens to days of old. A romantic hero who courageously went into the fray believing in eternal glory to be found on the battlefield, a man convinced that he was present in the great battles of the past, fighting with Alexander the Great, Caesar, and Napoleon. This gallant and dashing cavalryman was truly America's greatest fighting machine.

Despite the notoriety achieved by the flamboyant MacArthur and the popular Eisenhower as Commanders in Chief of their respective theaters, it is the name of Patton that conjures up images of assaults against the forces of evil. Indeed, it is the rare individual that successfully bridges the gap between great leader and great general. Patton was one of these few.

Unlike many of his contemporaries, Patton was born into affluence. His maternal grandfather was a wealthy landowner and farmer in southern California. He died before George was born and his grandmother remarried a former Confederate cavalry officer whose influence on young George would go a long way towards shaping the character and determining the destiny of the future general.

John Mosby, a former Confederate guerilla leader and cavalryman renowned for his daring exploits, was a frequent visitor at the Patton household during George's formative years. George, himself an accomplished rider and lover of horses, spent many hours avidly digesting Mosby's tales of his remarkable accomplishments during the Civil War. Visions of military glory danced before the young, impressionable George as he imagined himself in the role of a military adventurer.

It was a Patton family tradition to attend the Virginia Military Institute. After one year at V.M.I., he passed the entrance exams for the United States Military Academy and, in 1904, headed north to West Point.

As a member of the Long Gray Line, Patton stood first in his class for conduct, distinguishing himself as an outstanding athlete. Before graduating in 1909, he rose to the position of Adjutant of the Corps of Cadets.

Having been born into wealth, Patton traveled in select circles. It was here that Patton met Beatrice Ayer, daughter of a Boston textile tycoon. Having known each other as children, George renewed the acquaintance while still a cadet at West Point and, upon graduation, he and Bea were promptly married.

For an aristocrat, equestrian, and sportsman, there

was but one branch of the service deemed suitable. This brash young 2nd Lieutenant went into the cavalry. His first command was an obscure post in Illinois. It was not long before he infuriated most of his subsequent commanding officers with his ostentatious style of living. Wherever the Pattons went, they tried to live in the style to which they were accustomed. They dressed for dinner, had private vehicles, and traveled with a bevy of polo ponies.

In 1916, Patton was attached to General Pershing's staff at Fort Bliss in El Paso, Texas during the latter's punitive expedition into Mexico against the bandit, Pancho Villa. Patton's personal bravery and flair for recklessness made a lasting impression on Pershing. "A disciple of the action school in the Army, young Patton appealed to Pershing."[1] Patton himself went into Mexico searching for Villa. He failed to find the bandit leader, but did manage to track down his bodyguard, Colonel Julio Cardenas. Patton, in a quick-triggered attack like that of a western gunfighter, shot down the bandit, tied the body on a vehicle, and rode into Pershing's headquarters. This fighter, who made this lasting impression on 'Black Jack' Pershing, would not be forgotten when his commander was selected to lead the American Expeditionary Force in Europe. After America's entry into the First World War, Patton was one of the first to be selected for the Commanding General's staff.

As a prodigy of Pershing's, Patton had little difficulty obtaining a command in the newly-created tank corps which actually consisted of only a few brigades with a handful of British and French hand-me-down tanks.

Nevertheless, Patton assumed his command with relish, training his men and working them in a style that would come to typify him. Night and day he drilled them, familiarizing them with this new weapon of war.

In the summer of 1918, during the Meuse-Argonne offensive, Patton saw action for the first time. Although he aquitted himself credibly, the tank performance left much to be desired. His maverick tendencies and his boldness were both observed by his superiors. The hard-to-handle personality that would cause his superiors in the Second World War endless grief was easily recognizable as Patton stretched his orders to suit his own convenience. Despite receiving a serious wound which ended his participation in the First World War, his appetite for battlefield action had been whetted. Furthermore, he became firmly convinced that tanks would be the future queen of the battlefield. With that, he elected to remain with that branch of the service.

After the war, America, which was sheltered by its oceans and sickened by its foray into the labyrinth of European politics, isolated itself from the Old World and all thought of fighting. Accordingly, government allocations for war expansion were drastically reduced and so, despite Patton's enthusiasm for the tank, funds were drastically reduced for this arm.

For Patton, the army was all important. His European peers were fighting for the future of the tank; soldiers such as Liddell-Hart, Fuller, and Guderian, were placing their cause above their career. Patton did the very opposite, abandoning the tanks and returning to the cavalry.

After the excitement and rapid promotion of the battlefield (Patton had reached the temporary rank of Lt. Colonel during the war before reverting to his permanent rank of Captain at war's end), peace time duty with its subsequent return to permanent rank must have been sheer boredom for the headstrong and action-loving Patton. Nevertheless, he managed to make the best of a bad situation by devoting his energies to playing polo, flying his own private plane, traveling in a style that befitted his wealth, but above all, antagonizing his superiors.

The peace time years, however, were not totally wasted for during this period he managed to cultivate many important friendships. Among them were Dwight Eisenhower, George C. Marshall, and Douglas MacArthur. One of the most important friendships that he pursued was that of Henry Stimson, Secretary of War during the First World War and destined to hold that position again during the Second World War.

By the time Marshall became Army Chief of Staff, he had already ticketed Patton for future service. Reviewing the German successes against Poland and France, Marshall authorized the creation of America's first Armored Corps and promoted the one man with enough dash and knowledge to train and command a division within it, George S. Patton. The latter was given command of the 2nd Armored Division.

Once more, Patton found himself training and organizing an armored force, but this time on a much larger scale. Already having earned a reputation as somewhat of a martinet who insisted on hard work, spit and polish, and conformity to regulations, he drove his men mercilessly. For Patton there could be no such thing as second best. Besides, he was fifty-four, making him one of the older general officers holding an active field command. He had a reputation to uphold and was determined to succeed.

1941 was a year of training and maneuvers. During these maneuvers, Patton demonstrated for Marshall the value of tanks being used independently. He sent them on large sweeping and flanking movements which completely confused and outmaneuvered his bewildered opponents, causing some very embarrasing moments for the anti-tank strategists.

With Pearl Harbor and the declaration of war, Patton more than ever was chomping at the bit for action. He did not have long to wait before being ordered to Washington in August 1942. Marshall had assigned him a key command in the first American operation against the European Axis forces, "Operation Torch," the invasion of North Africa.

On October 24, 1942, Patton, at the head of the invasion forces, set sail across the Atlantic for French-held Morocco. The Americans were expecting to be welcomed as allies by the French forces occupying that country, but an entangling web of political intrigue caused the French to put up a spirited resistance led by the Vichy Resident General, Auguste Nogues. Within three days, however, Patton's forces managed to secure the country and the Americans occupied Casablanca. (See Map 3)

George Patton will forever be known as America's greatest combat general. However, World War II demanded more from this conqueror than blood and guts; he was also required to play a political role. He became military governor of Morocco and, in this capacity, Patton made his first blunders. Being politically naive and a Francophile at heart, he allowed Nogues and other Vichyites to retain control in Morocco. The safer choice would have been General Marie-Emile Bethouart, an avowed ally, who was allowed to languish in prison at Nogues' discretion until political pressure eventually demanded his release.

Patton was reveling in the pomp of the role of military governor. He attended parties, reviewed lavish parades staged by the Sultan of Morocco, and entertained distinguished guests such as Roosevelt and

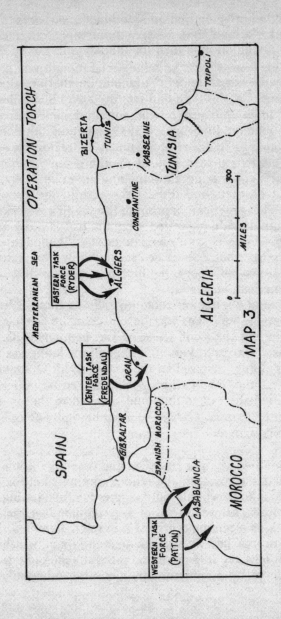

OPERATION TORCH

MEDITERRANEAN SEA

SPAIN

GIBRALTAR

SPANISH MOROCCO

MOROCCO

CASABLANCA

WESTERN TASK FORCE (PATTON)

CENTER TASK FORCE (FREDENDALL)

ORAN

EASTERN TASK FORCE (RYDER)

ALGIERS

ALGERIA

CONSTANTINE

BIZERTA

TUNIS

KASSERINE

TUNISIA

TRIPOLI

0   300
MILES

MAP 3

Churchill who arrived in Casablanca in January of 1943 for a high level military conference. Yet, events were taking an ugly turn for the Allies in the muddy hills of Tunisia.

The Germans, under the famed 'Desert Fox,' Erwin Rommel, by this time had retreated over fifteen hundred miles, pursued by the equally famed Bernard Montgomery. In February 1943, Rommel felt confident enough to ignore Montgomery's threat to his rear and elected to turn instead on the green American troops at Kasserine Pass, hoping to inflict a grave defeat on them and disrupt the entire American effort. This American baptism of fire, its first American encounter with organized German troops, had far-reaching effects on American morale. Although the individual troops performed satisfactorily, the tactical dispositions were poor, resulting in a loss of confidence in American leadership.

General Eisenhower promptly relieved those officers responsible and sent for the one man he felt could restore the lost confidence to the bedraggled G.I., General Geroge S. Patton. Although the latter was already deeply involved in the planning of 'Operation Husky,' the invasion of Sicily, he enthusiastically answered the call to duty and traveled to the dreary desert of Tunisia. Charles Whiting has aptly described Patton's arrival:

> Standing upright in the lead car like some Roman charioteer, the officer wore his most formidable scowl, his hard aggressive jaw jutting against the web strap of his lacquered helmet with its gleaming oversized twin stars. These stars were matched by two others even larger, which adorned the stiff red metal plate attached to one side of his command car, while the other side

bore another plate bearing the initials "WTF" meaning Western Task Force.[2]

On March 7, 1943, Patton arrived to restore the American position. Although firmly directed by Eisenhower to cooperate fully with the British, Patton refused to sit idly by and allow Montgomery's Eighth Army to plod methodically on while the American forces took a back seat.

Patton held command for only one month, but in that month he created more than a minor miracle as he disciplined his troops, making fighting soldiers out of undisciplined moraleless forces. Although he did not direct the II Corps to ultimate victory in Tunisia in May (that would be left to General Omar Bradley), he could rightfully be considered the directing force which had inspired the American troops. Even the Allied Ground Forces commander, Sir Harold Alexander, who himself had little confidence in either the quality of the American troops or their leadership, had only praise about the abilities of Patton.

Patton left Tunisia in April to resume preparations for the invasion of Sicily, having accomplished his primary job, not to win any great campaign, but to reorganize a badly-mauled and discredited corps of green soldiers, to instill in them ironclad discipline and fighting spirit, to make them battle-worthy. This he so eminently accomplished.

Patton was now about to direct what was his most sought-after dream, the command of an army.

The lodestar of Patton's life in particular had always been the dream that he would one day command a great army which, winning spectacular victory after victory by surprise and speed, would enshrine forever the glory of

American arms and his own name. Now, in the longest combined operation in history, it seemed to be on the verge of realisation and in the romantic setting of Sicily, the stepping stone between Africa and Europe where Hannibal, Scipio, and Belisarius had trod.[3]

Now Patton was about to fulfill his dream. After three months of intensive planning, 'Operation Husky,' the invastion of Sicily, was finally presented to Eisenhower in April 1943. Ike's satisfaction with the plan was echoed by both Admiral Andrew Cunningham and Air Marshal Arthur Tedder, Naval Commander and Air Force Commander for 'Husky,' respectively. This plan called for Montgomery's Eighth Army to land at the east cost port of Syracuse while Patton's Seventh Army was assigned to the northwest port of Palermo. On the whole, the plan appeared sound with only one major fault, Montgomery did not like it.

To the British, war-weary and disheartened, General, later Field Marshal, Sir Bernard Law Montgomery, embodied the new Wellington. He gave the British people hope and was the war hero they so desperately needed. But deep down within the areas where battles are lost and won, Montgomery's effect was not as glamorous as it appeared to the British people. In the words of that great historian, Martin Blumenson, Montgomery was "the most overrated general of the war." Montgomery's primary goal throughout the war seemed to be a burning determination to insure that, come what may, it would be Monty and no one else who would receive the accolades, all other considerations be damned. The tragedy of this behavior is that it was condoned throughout the war by Montgomery's superiors at the expense of the total war effort. This sop to Montgomery's vanity was evident in Sicily, at Caen, Falaise, Antwerp, and Arnhem, to name the most prominent.

The original 'Husky' plan was not acceptable to Montgomery because it divided the effort equally between he and Patton. Instead, Montgomery, always the superb salesman, managed to convince the Allied leadership that they were overly ambitious in considering a broad front. As an alternative, he directed his staff to draw up a plan calling for a landing by Eighth Army over the beaches of southeastern Sicily, near Pachino, while Patton's forces would land further east near Gela and secure Montgomery's flank. This would allow the latter to "drive swiftly on Syracuse," thus capturing a major port through which the Allied forces could be supplied.

Unfortunately, Montgomery's plan was adopted in its entirety. When Alexander told Patton of his new task, the American saluted, obeyed, and stated to the surprise of Alexander that he always believed in following orders. Inwardly, however, Patton was furious and in reference to Eisenhower he said, "This is what happens when your commander-in-chief ceases to be an American and becomes an ally."[4] Patton accepted the orders, but knew that the United States forces were relegated to a secondary role. Even more significant was that the assigned beaches were open and exposed which would make it difficult to supply Seventh Army. Undaunted, but a bit ruffled, Patton obeyed and proceeded with training his troops furiously. (See Map 4)

The invasion was preceded during the evening of July 9 and 10 by a combined American and British airborne attack, the objectives being the capture of key airfields and bridge and road junctions a few miles inland from the beaches. The attack failed to achieve

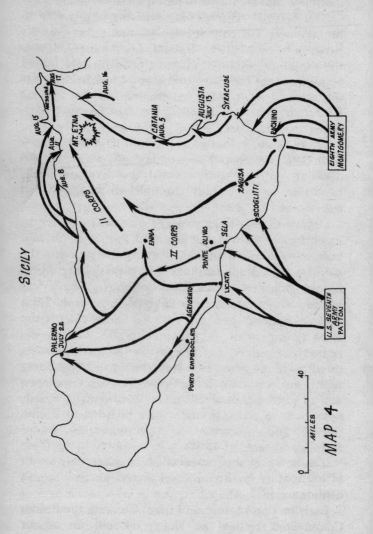

SICILY

MAP 4

the desired results as some units were dropped short or missed their landing zones completely.

Despite these difficultues, the landings on the Eighth Army front proceeded virtually unhindered in the face of little opposition. Resistance on Patton's front was somewhat stronger. A fierce German counterattack against the 45th Division was halted only by the effective gunfire of cruisers and destroyers offshore which managed to take its toll of the leading Panzers of General Conrath's Herman Goering Division.

Despite Eighth Army's achievements which netted them Syracuse by the end of the first day, Patton's situation was somewhat different. And yet the problem could have been even more critical if the German and Italian forces had not been deceived into thinking that Sardinia and Greece were both viable targets for an Allied invasion after North Africa. Thanks to such bogus plans as 'Operation Mincemeat' which saw the use of a dead body to plant information pointing to Greece and Sardinia as Allied objectives, Sicily was not as heavily reinforced as it could have been. Even at that, the Seventh Army position at evening of the first day left a lot to be desired.

The American 1st Division, the other American group which landed on the first day, was led by Terry Allen, an independent-minded commander who was not a favorite of Patton's. Patton considered the division to be rather cocky and marked Allen as a man who was hard to handle. Nevertheless, Patton had insisted on having the 1st Division included in his command for the Sicilian invasion for he was keenly aware of its fighting quality. D + 1 would justify Patton's confidence in the 'Big Red One.'

Early on that morning, General Guzzoni, the Italian Commander-in-Chief in Sicily, ordered an all-out assault by Conrath's division. The attack jumped off with full fury against Allen's troops at Gela. Although decimated because of their lack of anti-tank weapons, Allen refused to authorize the yielding of ground. This determination to hold fast saved the day and managed to blunt the German spearheads. The one enemy column that managed to break through to the coast fell prey to the guns of the USS Boise, steaming offshore.

Patton, meanwhile, had come ashore and, in the style most typical of him, was dashing from one command post to another, getting a feel of this situation. The only command decision taken by Patton at this early juncture of the campaign was to order the tanks of the 2nd Armored Division ashore to close the gap between the 3rd Division which landed at Licata on the right and Allen's 1st Division near Gela. It had been a close call for the 1st Division. At one point, it appeared that the division would be thrown back into the sea, leaving the flanks of Lucian Truscott's 3rd Division at Licata and Troy Middleton's 45th Division exposed. Omar Bradley attributed the narrow victory to Patton's perception in insisting on the 1st Division's inclusion in his command.

The specter of Montgomery now began to rear its ugly head. For sometime now, the British general had been clamoring for one overall ground commander, namely himself. Alexander agreed, but Eisenhower sharply rejected the proposal.

The strategic plum of the entire Sicilian campaign was the port of Messina in the northeastern section of the island. Possession of this city would serve to trap all existing Axis forces on the island. Montgomery's master plan called for the rapid capture of this all-important port. Indeed, it was for this purpose that Patton's position was changed from Palermo to the southern beaches in order to give aid to the 'rapid'

British drive. Despite the fact that Montgomery possessed two ports through which supplies could be brought ashore, while Patton was being supplied over open beaches, the British attack bogged down. It seemed that Montgomery was simply incapable of rapid movement. His plodding advance gave the Axis formations time to man positions that effectively delayed the British drive towards Messina.

Halted by stiff Axis resistance before the highly defended Mt. Etna line, Montgomery decided to shift his emphasis inland around the western end of the mountain. However, only one decent road was available for this maneuver, that being Highway 117 which had been designated for the use of Bradley's II Corps. This corps was moving along the highway in their drive northwards. Montgomery therefore appealed to Alexander with another 'master plan' designed to throw the enemy off balance and allow for a swift thrust to Messina. Alexander acceded to Montgomery's wishes and duly ordered Patton to relinquish Highway 117.

Summoning Bradley to his headquarters, Patton summarized the new directive from Alexander and ordered the II Corps commander to comply. The usually placid Bradley exploded with anger and protested bitterly but in vain. Patton, however, with tongue in cheek simply stated, "Sorry Brad, orders are orders," and left it at that. There appeared to be an ominous reason for the usually quick-tempered and volatile Patton to give in so readily. Patton was about to strike a deal with Alexander and decided to grease the pan.

Meanwhile, on July 13, Field Marshal Albert Kesselring, overall German Commander-in-chief South, (See Volume 1, Chapter 5) telephoned a report to General Alfred Jodl describing the situation on the island as critical. Because of Allied strength, he went on to say, and the failure of the Italian coastal units coupled with the lack of mobility of the German units, there was no chance to mount another concerted counterattack against the Allied beachheads. To fight for time was the best he could hope for. Kesselring recommended continuing the defense of Sicily, but Hitler redefined the task of the German troops on the island, " . . . to delay the enemy advance as much as possible and to bring it to a halt in front of Mt. Etna."

This is precisely what was happening to Eighth Army. They were effectively stalled before Mt. Etna, even with the swing to the west. The Axis defenders had stopped Montgomery cold.

Patton, being assigned a relatively static role, one not suited to him, visited 3rd Division on July 14 and told General Truscott something of his future plans. He wanted Palermo, but before he could get to it, he needed Porto Empedocle and Agrigento. He thus ordered Truscott to conduct a reconnaissance in force towards Agrigento. Then, with a new proposal in hand, he went off to see Alexander.

General Sir Harold Alexander was probably the only British general under whom the Americans would agree to serve. A soft-spoken, distinguished diplomat, he appealed to the divergent personalities of both the British and American commanders. By now, although too much of a gentleman to admit it, this brilliant and perceptive leader was also becoming disenchanted with Montgomery's failure to deliver the promised bold strokes and rapid drives. He was therefore in an agreeable mood when Patton approached him with a request for a drive on Palermo. Alexander readily gave his approval.

On July 18, Patton ordered Truscott to be in Palermo in three days. He then constructed a provisional corps which included Truscott's 3rd Division, the 82nd Airborne, and 2nd Armored Divisions. This corps was placed under the leadership of General Geoffrey Keyes, Patton's Chief-of-Staff.

Patton had directed Keyes to begin operations immediately and to take Palermo by July 24. After a mad dash over two hundred miles, over roads barely passable and rugged terrain, Keyes accepted the surrender of Palermo on July 22, two days earlier than Patton's forecast. It was a remarkable feat, but proved to be a hollow victory because it served to put Patton and Montgomery on a divergent axis. They should have been combining to close the enemy escape door at Messina.

With Palermo secured and with supplies being built up through the port, Patton could now turn his full attention to getting Seventh Army on the move east again, towards Messina, the ultimate prize of the entire campaign. By now, Alexander considered the port fair game for either army. Accordingly, collaborating with both Patton and Montgomery, he drafted a plan for capturing Messina, setting August 1 as the date for the resumption of the offensive. Messina was up for grabs.

The race for Messina actually began on July 30, when XXX British Corps, reinforced with fresh units, managed to shake off their German shackles near Catania.

Seventh Army, meanwhile, set off in a series of leapfrog attacks designed to insure that fresh units were constantly available for attacking strongpoints. Contrary to popular belief, Patton was not reduced to fighting dispirited second-rate Italian troops while Montgomery encountered the cream of the German army. The Seventh Army was facing difficult terrain and a most tenacious foe, highly skilled in the conduct of defensive operations.

Field Marshal Kesselring, in an effort to insure a strong defense in order to delay Allied overtures towards the only escape port, shored up the sagging defenses by dispatching reinforcements. These were under the command of General Hans Hube, a one-armed Panzer veteran, saved for this campaign because he had been flown out of Stalingrad at Hitler's orders just before the city fell. General von Senger, another talented general, was also dispatched to Sicily by Kesselring. Consequently, there were enough first-rate German troops under talented leadership to go around.

Patton, in his desire to reach Messina, utilized all his ability to reduce German strongpoints. Seventh Army came up against its stiffest fighting of the entire campaign to date. Patton, however, had no intention of allowing German strongpoints to hinder his advance. During the drive along the coastal road, he ordered a series of amphibious landings behind enemy lines. It was the first time in World War II that this type of action was used to reduce pockets of resistance. So intent was Patton on reaching Messina before Montgomery that he differed with Bradley over tactics, threatened to sack his favorite commander, Truscott, when the latter questioned the wisdom of using amphibious operations at Brolo, and was finally forced to fire Terry Allen of the 1st Division along with the assistant divisional commander, Theodore Roosevelt, Jr. Allen, though a rebel in his own right, just never could get along with Patton.

It was against this background of delay with heavy casualties and open subordination, as Patton saw it, that the Seventh Army commander involved himself in the incidents that nearly cost him his commission and contributed materially to the fact that he never received the top command in the campaign in north-west Europe. This will be analyzed later.

While Eighth Army was finally breaking its chains and resuming the advance towards Messina, Seventh Army was driving relentlessly forward.

By August 8, General Hube was ready to retreat towards Messina, concluding that human beings could endure just so much of a pounding. He, therefore, ordered the evacuation of all German troops to the Italian mainland without permission from Hitler. The Fuhrer, however, concurred immediately. The German withdrawal was conducted in a highly efficient manner. Although, by necessity, much of the equipment was left behind, the bulk of the German units arrived safely on the mainland of Italy, ready to stand and fight again.

With the virtual collapse of resistance, both Patton and Montgomery intensified their drives on Messina. Early in the morning of August 17, Truscott's 3rd Division managed to secure the center of the city and, while Truscott was formally accepting the surrender, a delegation from Montgomery arrived with the same purpose in mind. Patton had won the race by a very narrow margin.

A great deal of criticism had been leveled at the Allied command for allowing the bulk of the German forces to escape from Sicily. It has been stated that Patton's drive on Palermo was an unnecessary action by a headstrong and glory-seeking commander which served little purpose. In order to gauge this charge accurately, one must examine the evidence. Montgomery's insistence on hogging the show in order to maintain his own reputation relegated Seventh Army to a secondary role. His confiscation of II Corps' route merely magnified the situation, effectively thwarting Bradley's drive to the north coast. In effect, by subordinating Patton, Montgomery was compromising victory in pursuit of his own ambition. Patton, therefore, frustrated and impatient with his lack of activity, decided that some sort of action was infinitely better than none at all. As a result, he had little choice but to seek new fields to conquer and Palermo was his choice. He was confident that success there would gain Alexander's approval for a push to Messina.

Granted, Patton's capture of Palermo was of little strategic importance for it could in no way stop the successful German evacuation. However, Patton's action, instead of merely becoming a holding operation against Montgomery's drive from the south, forced the Axis troops to face opposition from two points. Furthermore, Patton's inactivity on Montgomery's flank did not significantly add to Eighth Army's swift capture of Messina. Thus, if Monty's master plain failed to achieve its goal, why not allow Patton to push off on his own? Thanks to Alexander's willingness to allow Patton this opportunity, a potential stagnation of the entire front at the foot of Mt. Etna was avoided.

Probably the most striking results of Patton's Sicilian victory were not measured in terms of territory conquered or enemy soldiers killed. Rather, it was in the birth of the reputation that the American leadership could indeed conduct both brilliant and imaginative operations independently. It also earned for the American G.I. the healthy respect of his Allied peers. The American standing had suffered from the poor initial impression given at Kasserine Pass. As the Official History of the Sicilian campaign states:

On this Italian island, the American infantryman was a first class fighter, in top physical condition, aggressive, always pushing ahead. The tenacious defense by the 1st Division at Gela; the aggressive hard-moving actions by the 157th and 179th combat teams at Cosimo, Scoglitti, and Vittoria; the 3rd Divisions capture of Agrigento; the 505th Parachute Infantry at Brazza Bridge; the sweep across western Sicily where daily thirty and forty foot mile marches were common; the fighting at Bloody Ridge and San Fratello; Troina; Randazzao, Brolo, all stand in testimony to this man's fighting ability.[5]

For these reasons, Sicily must rank as one of the decisive battles of World War II. For Patton, it was but a taste of things to come. Unfortunately, instead of wearing the laurels of the conquering hero, Patton found himself faced with the possible conclusion of his military career.

During the advance from Palermo to Messina, Patton, visibly feeling the fatigue and strain of the difficult battlefield conditions, stopped to visit wounded troops at a field hospital on August 4. When he happened upon an unfortunate soldier with no visible wounds who admitted to not being emotionally equipped for battle, Patton slapped his face and ordered him back up to the front. Although Patton saw fit to comment on this incident in his diary, no one else deemed it worthy of mention. However, on August 10, a repetition of the incident took place at yet another field hospital. As he went from one man to the next,

The next patient was sitting huddled up and shivering. When asked what his trouble was, the man replied, 'It's my nerves,' and began to sob. The general then screamed at him, 'What did you say?' He replied, 'It's my nerves, I can't take the shelling any more.' He was still sobbing. The general then yelled at him, 'Your nerves, Hell, you are just a goddam coward, you yellow son of a bitch.' He then slapped the man and said, 'Shut up that goddam crying. I won't have these brave men here who have been shot seeing a yellow bastard sitting there crying.'[6]

Patton struck him, knocking off the soldier's helmet. Then he threatened to shoot him personally. This time Patton had gone too far. The surgeon in charge saw fit to forward a report to his superiors. This memo ultimately found its way to the desk of Omar Bradley, commander of II Corps.

Bradley was not one whom history can accuse of participating in intrigue to undermine his commanding officer. He, therefore, read the report and ordered it locked in his safe after insisting his Chief-of-Staff, General Kean, forget the incident. Although Bradley personally did not approve of Patton's flamboyant conduct; his twin revolvers, the staff car with oversize stars, his insistence on spit and polish at all times, his fining of troops for not wearing ties or not being properly shaved, above all he despised Patton's profanity. And yet, Bradley was steadfastly loyal to his commanding officer and refused to forward the report.

Alexander also refused to become embroiled. When reports of Patton's conduct reached his headquarters, he simply ignored them, electing instead to treat it as a strictly American affair. He washed his hands of the entire matter.

Unfortunately for Patton, the offended head surgeon was not satisfied. He, therefore, forwarded a copy of his report to the Theater Surgeon General, who personally saw to it that a copy reached Eisenhower. Ike's first instinct was to quash the report, but he felt that an investigation was warranted. He could not foresee the reaction of the press, from whom he attempted to conceal the incriminating evidence.

A leak to the press corps attached to Eisenhower's headquarters caused such a clamor that it forced the Supreme Commander's hand. Eisenhower already had decided to order Patton to apologize to the entire Seventh Army and in particular those medical units and patients present during the slapping incident. At a hastily convened news conference, Eisenhower managed to obtain from the members of the press corps a gentleman's agreement not to reveal the incident in the papers. He effectively used the argument that Patton's brilliance in the field was urgently required for the difficult task ahead.

One correspondent, however, refused to be bound by the gentleman's agreement. On November 21, 1943, the scandal burst into the public eye. Drew Pearson, always eager to enhance his own reputation, while hiding behind the much-abused excuse of the 'public's right to know,' broke the news on his regular Sunday radio program on the American Broadcasting Company network. His airing of this rather stale story, since the incident had occurred over three months before, hit the nation with the force of a blockbuster, with much criticism being leveled at Eisenhower's apparent attempt to hush up the incident. The resultant public outcry was more than Generals Marshall and Eisenhower could diplomatically handle.

Although Eisenhower and Marshall tried valiantly to avoid recalling Patton, only the intercession of an old friend, Secretary of War Henry Stimson, coupled with President Roosevelt's endorsement, saved Patton's career.

Marshall and Eisenhower were now faced with a painful predicament, what to do with Patton. Patton was originally considered to command the up and coming cross-channel attack, but that option was now lost due to the public outrage against him. Instead, the command went to Bradley and George Patton was left to languish in sunny Sicily.

Eisenhower still intended to utilize Patton's amazing command ability but, during the initial planning stages for Overlord (code name for the Allied invasion of Europe), he allowed his impulsive subordinate to stew and fret. Finally, in January 1944, Patton was summoned to England as part of the Allied team. He arrived in England hopeful, but willing to accept any role in the forthcoming invasion, painfully aware that his actions had forfeited any claim he may have had to primary command.

After a severe warning to hold his emotions in check, Eisenhower informed Patton that he was to command the Third Army. This army, however, would be held back until the proper moment. Till then, Patton was required to play another highly critical role.

Through Ultra (the British codebreaking system), the Allies learned that of all their generals, Patton was the one most feared by the Germans. The Allies were determined to use Patton's reputation to their fullest advantage.

Although technically Patton was to command Third Army, a phantom army group, supposedly under Patton's command, was established in southern England directly opposite the Pas de Calais. The Allied intention was to convince the Germans that the invasion would be directed at that area of France instead of the actual area of Normandy. In reality, this phantom army group, which was designated the First United States Army Group, consisted of little more than dummy installations which were put together in the style of a Hollywood set with vehicles and various wireless stations. By use of frequent radio transmissions, it gave the semblance of an active army group containing a million men.

To dwell at length on this operation would require altogether too much space. Suffice it to say that the entire concept proved a smashing success. (Ultra intercepts referring to Army Group Patton convinced the Allied planners that their plan was working to perfection.) Even after the Normandy invasion became a definite reality, Hitler refused for weeks to strip the Pas de Calais of troops urgently needed at the Normandy front for fear that Patton would storm ashore at Calais.

Patton, meanwhile, was not idle. Although his command was not included in the original invasion of France, he kept himself occupied by training new forces recently arrived from the United States, educating his staff, and finally, to the great dismay of his bosses, getting himself in the doghouse again.

Once more, Patton's habit of allowing his mouth to run at higher speeds than his brain, resulted in a furor. During a seemingly innocent ladies reception in the town of Knutsford, Patton was asked to speak. Being assured that the press was not present, he innocently informed the women that he was proud to be on a team with their fellow British citizens because it was America's and Britain's destiny to rule the world.

The Russians were furious and menacing. Messages flew back and forth between embassies causing the State Department a great degree of embarassment. The politically amateurish Patton failed to grasp the significance of his remarks. Once more, Eisenhower had to convince Marshall that Patton's presence was absolutely vital for victory in Europe. Marshall, however, left Eisenhower to handle the matter. In a letter to his wife, Beatrice, on May 3, 1944, Patton said:

Everything is again OK because Divine Destiny came through in a big way. I am sorry that in some of my recent letters I sounded whiney. I don't often indulge. I guess my trouble is that I don't realize that I am always news, but you can bet I know it now.[7]

The incident was smoothed over, but it had been a close shave for Patton. The question remained, how much would his superiors be able to weather before being forced to relieve him?

On June 6, troops under Montgomery and Bradley stormed the beaches at Normandy. D-Day had finally arrived. Europe was now facing liberation at last. After heavy fighting, particularly on Bradley's First Army front, the Allies managed to secure a bridgehead.

One month of heavy fighting later found Bradley's First Army still involved in a slugging match amid the hedgerows of Normandy. Progress was slow, but it was progress, nevertheless. Meanwhile, Montgomery found himself involved in heavy fighting around Caen, his D + 1 objective.

On July 6, Patton landed in France. It had been difficult for him, languishing in England during the initial stages of Overlord. Upon arriving in France, Patton presented his scheme for the breaking out of the Cotentin peninsula by directing a narrow but powerful attack led by armor against the area of Avranches. From there, Brittany and the entire area west of the Seine would be exposed and, even more important, it would allow the Allies room for maneuvers after the terrible weeks in northern France. His report was pigeonholed, but an idea had been born.

After spending two weeks touring the front in the role of advisor while waiting for transhipment of his command, Patton found Bradley thinking along the same lines as those contained within Patton's original plan.

The Germans were utilizing the hedgerows brilliantly, forming impenetrable barriers which had effectively slowed the Allied forces to a snail's pace. Clearly, some type of an offensive was called for. Thus was born 'Operation Cobra.'

Cobra was designed to break the German front with a strong, but narrow attack towards Coutances by units of Troy Middleton's VIII Corps and 'Lightning Joe' Collins' VII Corps. Once the breakthrough was achieved, Patton's Third Army would be activated. For 'Operation Cobra,' however, Patton would have to content himself with acting as Deputy Army Commander with no official command status.

Patton was by now chomping at the bit. He recognized that Cobra was but a modification of his own plan and the changes included seeking a limited objective, Coutances, and leading the attack with infantry as opposed to armor.

On July 25, Bradley unleashed Cobra after a massive shower of bombs was dropped on the Germans within the corridor where Bradley intended to send Collins' Corps. Collins hit the stunned Germans and was quickly able to break through their defensive positions, followed shortly thereafter by Middleton to the west. By the 27th, the entire offensive appeared to be progressing beyond original estimates because Patton exceeded his authority by ordering Middleton to throw his armor into the offensive. As a result, VIII Corps captured Coutances and pushed beyond, toward Avranches at the base of the Cotentin peninsula.

Patton's Third Army was due to become operational on August 1. Two days before that date, Bradley had informed Patton that the reins were finally going to be removed. Knowing this, Patton decided to pave the way for Third Army's baptism by continuing the attack towards Avranches, although nominally under the direction of Middleton. Avranches fell to Wood's 4th Armored Division on July 31, thus justifying Patton's decision to use armor as the spearhead. The gateway from Normandy into greater France was now blown open. Furthermore, the Brittany peninsula, containing the great port of Brest, now lay open to the nearly operational Third Army.

Meanwhile, Montgomery's Second Army, under the very capable command of General Sir Miles Dempsey, was struggling gallantly to wrest control of Caen from the Germans. From July 18 through July 21 in 'Operation Goodwood,' General Crocker's I Corps advanced to a position southeast of Caen. In the same time, Dempsey's VIII Corps, commanded by the desert hero General Sir Richard O'Connor, was exerting pressure on the opposite side of the city. Although little penetration was made, the entire operation succeeded in making one very important contribution; it drew the bulk of the German armored reinforcements into the Caen area in an effort to stop Montgomery's offensive. This effectively prevented them from interfering on Bradley's front, contributing greatly to the American success.

The threat from Patton, now at Avranches, began to cause the Germans concern. Hitler was acutely aware of the consequences should Third Army be allowed to proceed unhindered into metropolitan France. He therefore ordered the newly appointed Commander-in-Chief West, Field Marshal Gunther von Kluge, to prepare a counterattack aimed at severing Third Army's line which stretched from Coutances to Avranches. Thus he cut them off from the remainder of the Allied armies.

Kluge, Hausser (commander of Seventh Army), and Eberbach (Commander of Panzer Group West) protested this decision. Hausser and Eberbach both realized the futility of attacking over open roads dominated by Allied fighter bombers. Both concluded that the operation could only result in failure with dire consequences for the Germans.

Kluge, however, was even more perceptive. He realized too that the operation held little hope of success. From his position, it appeared obvious that by committing Seventh Army to a futile attack and by concentrating that in the area of Mortain, their own flanks and rear would be dangerously exposed. The Allies, in turn, were assured of relative security thanks to aerial supremacy and the weakness of the German front. Kluge was absolutely certain that without the assistance of reinforcements from Fifteenth Army, still tied down in the Pas de Calais awaiting the 'actual invasion' of Army Group Patton, the offensive was doomed to failure with potentially catastrophic results.

Kluge staked his whole career on trying to stop this attack. In his last signal he pulled no punches and boldly stated that it could only end in disaster. It was not hard to imagine the feelings of this courageous man; one could get a glimmer of his utter hopelessness from his signals. He must have known it was the end for him anyway. Back now, without even a comment, came the order from the Fuhrer to proceed. Kluge had now no alternative.[8]

On August 1, when Headquarters Third Army was finally activated, Patton was handed command of three corps, Troy Middleton's VIII Corps, Wade Haislip's XV Corps, and Walton Walker's XX Corps. Breaking out from Avranches with all three, Third Army exploded in a shellburst pattern. (See Map 5)

With the need to capture another major port in order to relieve the supply problem, Patton split VIII Corps in two. He sent one force across the base of the Brittany Peninsula towards Vannes and Lorient on the bay of Biscay, spearheaded by General Wood's 4th Armored Division. Patton ordered the other force, 6th Armored Division under General Robert Grow, down the center of the peninsula with the port of Brest as its objective.

The area of the breakout from Avranches was pitifully narrow. Through this tight corridor, Patton was obliged to move three corps, creating the potential for the world's worst traffic jam. The Third Army commander was constantly at the front, threatening, prodding, pushing, and ordering the units onward. At one point, Patton himself actually stood at one intersection directing traffic. He was a man on the move and speed was essential for he was determined to take advantage of the opportunity finally offered him. Besides, Patton too was aware of the very same consequence that Kluge had vainly attempted to press on his superiors at the German High Command, the exposure of the rear of the German Seventh Army.

It was a Tuesday, shortly after activation, when Patton informed General Grow that he had wagered Montgomery that Third Army would be in Brest on the western tip of the Brittany Peninsula by Saturday. 6th Armored Division was ordered to proceed at full speed towards that objective. It was a tall order, indeed, for the division would have to traverse over two

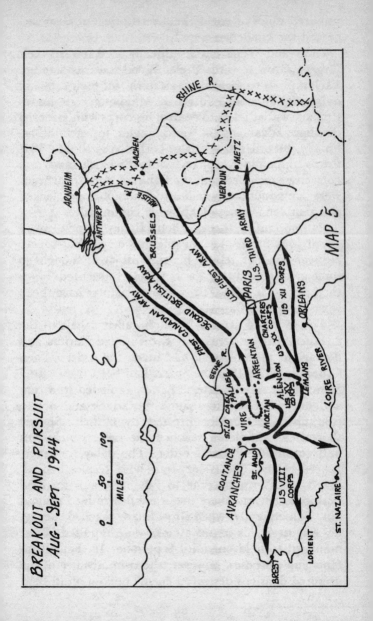

BREAKOUT AND PURSUIT
AUG - SEPT 1944

MAP 5

MILES
0   50   100

hundred miles of enemy-held territory, but Grow accepted the challenge eagerly.

Grow and Wood enthusiastically sped toward their targets, Grow towards Brest, Wood towards Vannes. Each one, in true cavalryman spirit, set their sights in only one direction, forward. Middleton, an infantryman, was at a loss to control his corps with armored divisions advancing at right angles to each other. Finally, he ordered a halt to both divisions. The VIII Corps commander kept reviewing the battle maps and correctly concluded that the flanks of both spearheads were dangerously exposed. Middleton obviously lacked the gambler instinct of his army commander.

Patton had a theory about flanks. 'Don't worry about your flanks. Let the enemy worry about them.' He was fond of telling his subordinates. 'Long ago some general said that flanks should be secured. Since then, poor bastards throughout history have been worrying about flanks.'

The morning after Middleton called a halt to the advance, Patton arrived at Grow's headquarters and demanded to know who had made the order. When Grow explained that the orders had been transmitted from Corps Headquarters, Patton exploded in a fury and ordered Grow to resume the attack and not to stop unless personally directed by himself. Shortly thereafter, Middleton reached the same conclusions and confirmed Patton's order. The delay, however, proved costly. The twenty-four hour respite had allowed the Germans time to fall back into fortified positions at Brest where they were determined to hold out. Consequently, when Grow finally reached the city on August 7, his initial attacks were repulsed. Brest managed to hold out until September 18. For all intents and purposes, however, the twin advance of the armored divisions destroyed enemy opposition in Brittany and it ceased to be a battlefront.

Patton was in his element during the Brittany campaign.

Patton was bombed, strafed, shelled — but he thrived on it. At the summit of a badly littered road over a hill he stopped to survey the scarred and scorched landscape of war — rubbish that used to be farm fields in which the grass was burning, hundreds of stiff-legged dead cattle. He threw out his arms as if trying to embrace the scene and shouted to the sky, 'Could anything be more magnificent?' That split second an invisible battery opened up with a salvo. Patton had to raise his voice to a still higher pitch as he exclaimed, 'Compared to war, all other forms of human endeavor shrink to insignificance. God, how I love it.'

While VIII Corps was occupying itself in the Brittany Peninsula, the other two corps of Third Army were also making huge gains. Advancing due south, General Walker's XX Corps cut directly across the base of the Brittany Peninsula and, by August 6, found itself in Nantes at the mouth of the Loire River.

By far the most significant gains, however, were made by Wade Haislip's XV Corps striking southeastward from Avranches. Bypassing pockets of resistance, XV Corps crossed the Mayenne River and by August 8 had captured Lemans. There it paused to regroup.

On August 7, the Mortain offensive was finally launched by Kluge. First Army's VII Corps under Collins and XIX Corps under Corlett managed to prevent the Germans from cutting the base of Third Army. Kluge had played right into Patton's hands. With XV

Corps now sitting at LeMans, the entire rear of the German Seventh Army lay exposed to Patton who was already preparing to spring a trap. Shortly after Third Army had been completed activated, the idea of cutting off the German army in France began to intrigue Patton. Now, with the enemy attacking due west with XV Corps on its southern flank, Patton seized the opportunity with relish.

However, Patton was not the only one to recognize the opportunity. So obvious was the situation that Eisenhower, Bradley, and Montgomery were all keenly aware of the potential afforded to the Allies, a huge encirclement of the German Seventh Army. With great satisfaction, the higher commanders listened to the Ultra messages that commanded Kluge to continue the offensive for the further west he traveled, the deeper into the jaws of an Allied pincer the Seventh Army moved. (See Map 6)

Montgomery, as usual, dominated the stage, suggesting a drive toward Falaise coupled with a drive by First Army. Bradley went him one better, proposing that a drive from the south should close up to the British, thus dooming the German forces facing them. Orders were therefore issued for Patton to turn Haislip's corps around at LeMans and order it to attack northeast towards Argentan where he would link up with First Canadian Army driving south from Falaise.

On August 8, Montgomery's forces set off for Falaise to meet Haislip coming up from the south. Unfortunately, they met heavy opposition from German troops sitting astride the Caen-Falaise road and the attack was halted in its tracks.

At this point, Haislip was driving on Argentan. Included in his command was the 2nd French Armored Division under General Jacques LeClerc. It was a

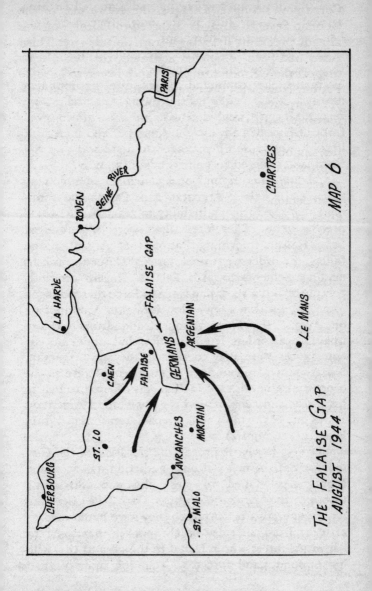

THE FALAISE GAP
AUGUST 1944

MAP 6

PARIS

SEINE RIVER

ROUEN

LA HARVE

CHARTRES

FALAISE GAP

CAEN

FALAISE

GERMANS

ARGENTAN

LE MANS

ST. LO

AVRANCHES

MORTAIN

CHERBOURG

ST. MALO

great day for France when the 2nd Armored Division arrived there on July 30 for now Frenchmen were helping to free their homeland.

The Germans meanwhile recognized the catastrophe about to befall them. Despite the failure of the German higher command to recognize the imminent disaster, they began withdrawing on their own recognizance. A weak defensive line was thrown up in front of Haislip's advance at Argentan and incredibly it held. The reason it managed to do so was that XV Corps was ordered to halt its advance. Why?

Although the original plan called for Montgomery to close the Falaise-Argentan gap, Patton was confident that the former's inability to react swiftly would preclude this. Therefore, when word was received from Haislip informing Patton that Argentan had fallen, the order went back for XV Corps to push its leading elements towards Falaise. Haislip promptly complied with a reconnaissance in force that managed to probe to within a few miles of Falaise. Around noon on August 13, Third Army Headquarters received unequivocal orders from Bradley that under no circumstances were they to proceed beyond Argentan. No amount of pleading by Patton could reverse the order and a bewildered Haislip was ordered to halt in his tracks and consolidate his gains around Argentan. It was one of the most controversial decisions of World War II.(See Map 7)

Needless to say, it proved the salvation of the German Seventh Army. Patton's prediction was accurate; Montgomery failed to close the gap. Streaming through the Argentan-Falaise Gap, the Germans retreated eastward. Although they were hammered by artillery from all sides of the pocket, harrassed by Allied air forces who referred to the area as the 'Killing Ground.' and forced to abandon most of their

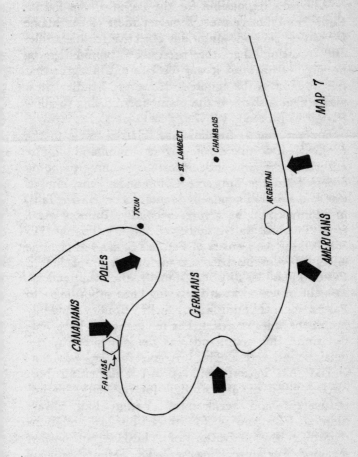

MAP 7

equipment and arms, a large portion of Seventh Army was allowed to escape in order to stand and fight another day. By the time the Canadians finally reached Argentan, Third Army was sweeping forward with elements of XX Corps southeast of Paris.

Who was responsible for the fiasco of the Falaise Gap? Montgomery must shoulder most of the blame for setting such an ambitious objective for his armies and insisting that the prescribed boundaries be honored. Only after it was too late did he agree that the boundaries be ignored. However, Bradley must also accept a share of the blame for refusing to allow Patton to proceed. Why?

For one thing, Bradley was relatively new to the rarefied atmosphere of higher command. Quite naturally, he was uncomfortable countermanding orders from the Supreme Commander who himself was sold a 'bill of goods' by Montgomery. Having faith in Monty could be trying. Secondly, Bradley came from the conservative school of military thought. His concern for the security of Patton's flanks was genuine and steeped in the strictest tradition. He simply lacked Patton's gambler's instinct. Finally, the command arrangement was awkward. Having been subordinate to Patton in both Tunisia and Sicily, Bradley suddenly found the roles reversed. His reluctance to have Patton under his command was demonstrated by the delay in activating Third Army. Bradley was convinced that Patton would prove a difficult subordinate, given the latter's flair for publicity, his impulsiveness and recklessness. Patton had always blamed Montgomery for thwarting his ambitions regarding the activation of Third Army out of jealousy. For once, however, poor Monty appears innocent.

A great chance had been missed. In the words of Essame:

All in all, posterity may justifiably conclude that the complete annihilation of the Germans could have been achieved and a decision reached which might well have enabled the war to be ended in 1944.[10]

Patton fumed and raved about this missed opportunity. Essame concludes:

They failed to exploit his talents and in the process took the first steps which would ensure the unnecessary prolongation of the war to 1945.[11]

These words, from a British writer and retired Major General who served under Montgomery in the Northwest European Campaign, represent a very significant and damning evaluation. Yet, life is always full of missed opportunities, it is regrettable some are more costly than others. Luckily, Patton was a man of resilience who refused to allow the crisis to affect his performance. The amazing advances that Third Army would yet perform offer testimony to this.

The advance east for Third Army was on a three corps front. By August 20, Paris was open to attack from three points. Haislip and Walker had secured bridgeheads over the Seine at Nantes, north of Paris, and Melun, south of the city, all within forty miles of the French capital. General Manton Eddy of XII Corps, now assigned to Third Army, had captured Orleans on August 17 and was making preparations for a drive on Troyes, sixty-five miles from that city.

It was most appropriate that a Francophile and the most newsworthy of American commanders was about to liberate the first city of Europe. Personalities, however, played a dramatic part in denying Patton the share of the glory and credit for driving the Germans out, a reward he richly deserved. Eisenhower, for motives known only to himself, ordered Bradley to break the news to Third Army, which he attempted as diplomatically as possible. The assignment of liberating Paris went to General Leonard Gerow's V Corps of First Army. Gerow's corps had relieved Haislip in front of Falaise and were awaiting further orders. In addition, LeClerc's 2nd French Armored Division was transferred from XV Corps to V Corps in order to allow French troops to enter the city first, a concession made to General Charles DeGaulle.

For Patton it proved a bitter pill to swallow. Didn't his Third Army deserve the privilege? Hadn't they driven to all points of the compass after the breakout from Avranches, capturing Brittany, destroying an entire German Army, and exposing the French capital to liberation? Patton, however, merely shrugged, no doubt remembering that day in Tunisia when he had informed Alexander that, as a soldier, he was prepared to accept orders.

Third Army, however, had the last laugh. For when LeClerc entered the city he promptly announced to the cheering Parisians that his division was part of the Third Army. "The BBC said this morning that Patton's Third Army had taken Paris. Poetic justice. It will be refuted, but no one will pay any attention."[12] The dashing and proud little Frenchman not only possessed loyalty, he had class.

Patton's headlong dash across France continued at breakneck speed. By the second week in September, Third Army was preparing to cross the Moselle River and attack the Saar region. Events, however, were taking an ominous turn. Montgomery had always advocated advancing on a single front as opposed to Eisenhower's safer, broad front strategy. Flanks would be secure on a wider front by armies advancing abreast. Now, however, in the air of optimism engendered by the mad dash pursuit and seeming collapse of the Germans, Eisenhower once more caved in to Montgomery's arguments. This time he listened to the one about a strong and rapid thrust towards Antwerp and the Ruhr. To accomplish this, the bulk of supplies flowing onto the continent would be required for Montgomery's 21st Army Group. After agreeing with Monty's proposal during a face-to-face confrontation, Ike changed his mind the next day during a meeting with Bradley and Patton. Within a week he reversed his position again and promised Montgomery that the Saar offensive would be halted. Patton would once more receive the short end of the stick. One could reasonably question Eisenhower's handling of Montgomery after Tunisia, Sicily, Caen, and Falaise.

Needless to say, the rapid thrust that sounded so promising when detailed by the British field marshal failed to achieve the desired results. Its death throes ended with the bloody fiasco of 'Operation Market Garden' in the Dutch city of Arnhem.

Out of gas, short of every essential supply necessary for sustaining an army in the field, the advance of Patton's Third Army slowed to a crawl. Only by draining the tanks of captured vehicles and diverting supplies destined for other commands was Third Army able to make any headway at all. Consequently, through the remaining weeks of September and for most of October, Third Army sat virtually inactive.

To his credit, Bradley objected violently to the strategy dictated by Montgomery's needs. Everyone was quite aware that Monty was a notorious hoarder, always insuring that there were more than enough supplies on hand before precipitating a battle. Unfortunately, Montgomery had consistently failed to deliver on his promises of rapid advances and bold strokes. Bradley became increasingly disenchanted with the British Commander and dismayed by Eisenhower's apparent willingness to accede to every one of his demands. Some historians blame Bradley for Patton's shortages, but it must be remembered that Bradley was a man who was also required to follow orders. He was directed to protect Montgomery's flank as the British drove into Holland. This necessitated the 12th Army Group fuel allocation to go to First Army which was saddled with the assignment of protecting the British flank. Patton, further to the south, had to suffer.

But fuel was not the only obstacle to Patton's advance. Recognizing Patton's threat to the Saar and fearing him above all other Allied generals, the Germans reinforced Third Army front with the best troops available and gave ground grudgingly in their determination to hold onto the vital Saar and man the Siegfried Line.

Other factors also influenced Patton's Moselle campaign. The weather in October turned terrible. Combined with the weariness of the American soldiers after their headlong surge across France, the lack of replacements from the United States, and a determined and threatened foe, this killed the initiative. Hard fighting seemed inevitable. The September shutdown of Patton's supplies had robbed the Third Army of its momentum and allowed the Germans time to consolidate their defenses. When the offensive was resumed, it was hampered by lack of supplies and heavy autumn rains.

In November, Patton found himself battling at the fortress of Metz. It was not until early December that he began probing the Siegfried Line, seeking a suitable area to exploit a breakthrough.

Meanwhile, Patton's staff had reached some alarming conclusions. From carefully sifted intelligence reports, it was deduced that the Germans were pulling a number of first-rate divisions out of the line. In addition, these sources indicated a buildup of strong armored concentrations north of the Saar, opposite First Army. Obviously, the Germans were planning a nasty surprise for someone. For once, Ultra was alarmingly quiet. So secret were Hitler's plans that the Germans who were aware of them were ordered not to transmit messages using their code. Secrecy was the order of the day for the Germans and the Allies were left completely in the dark.

That nasty surprise was about to fall on Troy Middleton's command. His VIII Corps headquarters, after the Brittany campaign were transferred to Belgium, opposite the Ardennes Forest, the traditional route of invading German armies. Despite the evidence of the intelligence gatherers, both Army Group and Supreme Headquarters failed to take the German buildup seriously. VIII Corps was comprised of two green divisions fresh from the States and two others recuperating after having been mauled during the bitter fall battles in the Huertgen Forest. The Ardennes was, in effect, a rest and relaxation front with only Patton and his staff casting a wary eye in that direction.

Third Army's Saar campaign was in full swing when, on December 16, two complete German armies roared out of the Ardennes and hit VIII Corps head on. Third Army, further south, moved forward to protect its flanks from the attacking panzers.

Before jumping off against the Saar, Patton had directed Third Army staff to draw up a plan allowing for the possibility of swinging the army around ninety degrees and attacking north. Although the men wondered about developing a plan that would obviously be a theoretical exercise only, a suitable one was devised and made available. Patton's perception now paid huge dividends.

Bradley phoned Patton and ordered him to transfer 10 Armored Division to First Army. This call from Bradley was the first indication that there was a true crisis. Patton, however, was furious. With his Siegfried Line campaign in full gear and the coveted breakthrough in sight, losing an armored division would naturally be the last thing Patton could afford. Bradley refused to discuss the situation over the phone, but reiterated his orders and informed Patton that there was no choice. Magnanimously, Patton the soldier agreed without further dissent for he sensed that something dramatic was afoot. Why else would Bradley order one of his divisions away at the height of a major offensive?

On December 18, Patton was summoned to Bradley's headquarters in Luxembourg. After reviewing the rapidly deteriorating situation, Bradley asked Patton which units he could make available. The latter offered the 4th Armored along with the 80th and 26th Infantry Divisions. Bradley, anticipating an explosive response, was instead relieved by Patton's graciousness.

Upon arrival back at Third Army headquarters, Patton found himself summoned to yet another conference, this time with the Supreme Commander himself the following morning. Before leaving, he and his staff decided upon three courses of action which could possibly be enacted and issued code names to each. Depending on what would be revealed at Eisenhower's headquarters, Patton would then simply call his Chief-of-Staff, issue the appropriate code word and the attack would commence.

When he arrived at Eisenhower's hastily convened conference in Verdun, Patton was bursting with enthusiasm. Eisenhower quickly reviewed the situation and informed Patton that he was to attack the German salient with six divisions. Patton, being the type of commander he was, saw the possibilities that were now open to the Allies. He realized that this was the last bolt of a dying giant and the deeper the giant went, the harder it would be for him to extradite himself. Patton suggested that the Germans be allowed to continue farther before cutting them off. "Hell, let's have the guts to let the sons of bitches go all the way to Paris. Then we'll really cut them off and show them up!"[13]

After reviewing the situation, Eisenhower asked Patton, "When can you start?" "As soon as you are through with me," Patton answered confidently. Eisenhower frowned, "What do you mean?" he asked. Most of the attendants at the conference looked on in disbelief, some British officers even chuckled. Eisenhower was dismayed by Patton's apparently cavalier attitude towards the seriousness of the situation. The Supreme Commander's feelings were soothed only after Patton explained that his staff had already worked out the possible moves. Eisenhower asked again, "When can you start?" Patton replied, "The morning of 22 December."

Patton's optimism knew no bounds for he sensed that a golden opportunity for additional fame and glory had been flung at his feet. He told Bradley, "This time the Kraut's stuck his head in a meat grinder and I've got hold of the handle." He further promised to be in the beseiged town of Bastogne by Christmas. Then he dashed off to set his plans in motion.

In *A Soldier's Story,* General Bradley relates:

* * *

Until the Battle of the Bulge I did not share George's enthusiasm for his Third Army Staff which, unlike those of both the First and Ninth Armies, lacked outstanding individual performers. However, five months in Europe had seasoned that staff and the greatly matured Patton succeeded in coaxing from it the brilliant effort that characterized Third Army's turnabout in the Bulge.[14]

In *Lucky Forward,* however, Colonel Robert S. Allen, a member of Patton's staff takes exception:

Third Army Headquarters was in a class by itself, it had no competitor on its level. It was outstandingly the ablest, smoothest, fastest functioning and most soldierly staff in the ETO. Also the cockiest.[15]

Whichever version is accurate, Third Army's staff had unquestionably turned in a brilliant piece of work. Third Army was presented with a challenge not unlike the cavalry to the rescue fantasy created in the studios of Hollywood; it was ready to move. Patton was in his glory, using such superlatives as glorious, magnificent, and superb as he encouraged his troops onward. (See Map 8).

One of the key points in the Ardennes was the town of Bastogne. Many of the better roads in eastern Belgium converged at this strategic town. Consequently, Bastogne was a critical objective for General Hasso von Maunteuffel's Fifth Panzer Army.

Early in the battle, when it appeared to the Americans that the German attack was for real, elements of the United States 101st Airborne Division

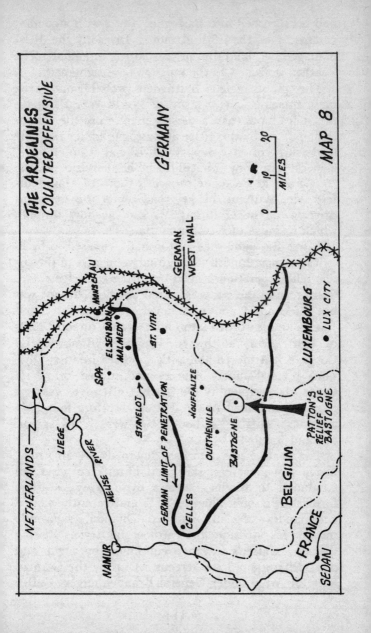

THE ARDENNES
COUNTER OFFENSIVE

NETHERLANDS

GERMANY

GERMAN
WEST WALL

MONSCHAU

ELSENBORN

MALMEDY

SPA

ST. VITH

STAVELOT

GERMAN LIMIT OF PENETRATION

LIEGE

MEUSE RIVER

HOUFFALIZE

OURTHEVILLE

CELLES

NAMUR

BASTOGNE

LUXEMBOURG

LUX CITY

PATTON'S
RELIEF OF
BASTOGNE

BELGIUM

FRANCE

SEDAN

0 10 20
MILES

MAP 8

had been rushed into Bastogne. Along with a combat command of the 10th Armored Division, the 101st managed to hold on as casualties mounted. The weather worsened as the enemy noose tightened.

The epic struggle at Bastogne is probably one of the most amazing feats of arms of World War II. Space precludes more than a passing mention of the valiant fight put on by the 101st at Bastogne under the able leadership of its deputy Divisional Commander, General Anthony McAuliffe. The heroism of the Americans at Bastogne proved a thorn in Maunteuffel's side. Without this key road center, his westward drive would suffer through lack of avenues through which to move men and material.

It was Bastogne that Patton had promised to be in by Christmas. Indeed, the primary objective of the entire relief operation hinged on lifting the seige there. Compressing the pocket created by the Germans was but a secondary consideration.

True to his word, Patton immediately directed units of Third Army northward. Under Headquarters III Corps, 4th Armored and 26th and 80th Infantry Divisions pivoted ninety degrees and moved off. VIII Corps, the recipient of the German offensive, was now returned to Third Army. Patton therefore found six divisions available, although two were badly spread out and mauled.

The weather was notorious. Icy roads, freezing rain, heavy snow, overcast skies and bitter cold wind, all combined to hinder Patton's drive. Hugh Gaffey, formerly Patton's Chief-of-Staff and recently named commander of 4th Armored Division, vigorously moved his division in Pattonesque style. Risking disaster, Gaffey's advance continued by night and day, driving amid the screens set up by the German Seventh Army under General Brandenberger. Gaffey was intent on letting nothing deter him from his ultimate goal, Bastogne.

The Germans resisted ferociously. Although 4th Armored on its drive was accompanied by a combat command of 10 Armored on its left and 26th Division on its right, progress was slow but steady. Christmas came and still Bastogne was surrounded. Patton had set too ambitious an objective. He should have allowed himself another twenty-four hours for, on the evening of December 26, elements of 4th Armored Division made contact with the defenders of Bastogne. The siege was finally lifted and the back of Manteuffel's offensive broken.

Meanwhile, further north, the disposition instituted by General Courtney Hodges, commander of the First Army, had successfully blunted the drive of Sepp Dietrich's Sixth SS Panzer Army. Low on fuel, unable to capture Allied dumps, harrassed by pockets of resistance, his momentum lost, Dietrich's attack eventually stalled.

Early in the battle, Eisenhower divided responsibility for both sides of the Bulge between Bradley and Montgomery. For Bradley, this was the nadir of his role as commander. First Army was placed under Montgomery, leaving him only Patton's Third Army to command. Bradley was content to allow Patton to have his own way on the southern front, refusing to interfere and offering only minimal advice. The entire concept of strategy and tactics on the southern side of the Bulge was entirely Patton's.

Montgomery also made few changes in the dispositions set by Hodges. Apart from offering the services of his own XXX Corps, the United States First Army bore the brunt of the battle with minimal assistance from the British. But, whereas Bradley was content to allow Patton the spotlight, Montgomery announced to the world that his assumption of command had been the determining factor in turning the tide. The British press heralded Montgomery as the savior of the entire United States Army. Although Patton, Bradley, and Hodges were furious, Montgomery's attitude had one positive effect; Eisenhower finally saw Montgomery for what he really was.

Third Army continued to apply pressure. Patton with his two corps attacked all along the front, forcing the Germans onto the defensive. To avoid being cut off, the Germans streamed back across the Siegfried Line; the similarity between the Bulge and the Falaise Gap was not lost on them. By the end of January, with the entire Third Army applying the leverage, the whole front was restored to its original position. Thousands of Germans had been captured or killed by Patton's fierce drive from the south.

Although Patton had been compelled to pull III Corps out of line and swing it around ninety degrees, XII Corps and XX Corps were still maintaining pressure in the Saar. (XV Corps had been reassigned to Patch's Seventh Army as compensation for the loss of DeLattre's French Corps. See Patch, Chapter 1.)

With the Germans so obviously beaten, the last three months of the war were relatively anticlimatic. The highlight was the speed of Patton's advance over the Rhine, across Germany into Austria, and beyond.

The Rhine crossing was exceptionally satisfying for Patton. Although Hodges' First Army had managed to capture an intact bridge at Remagen, that was more an accident than a planned assault. Although Montgomery was preparing a highly publicized offensive over the Rhine opposite the Ruhr, Patton was anxious to cross and cross quickly. In the blare of publicity, Montgomery, in his traditional way, prepared to launch the assault on March 24. Two days before, however, the 5th Division of the Third Army crossed the Rhine near Koblenz. The next day, Patton urged Bradley to make an official announcement and the latter responded immediately. Just as Churchill was publicly announcing the first assault crossing of a major river by Montgomery's Army Group, the American press was heralding the fact that Third Army had crossed thirty-six hours earlier. Patton finally had the best of Montgomery, a suitable reward for the many frustrations suffered by Third Army at the hands of the British field marshal.

The final great offensive of this magnificent warrior was the Palatenate campaign. Bursting out of their Rhine bridgeheads, Third Army struck out northeast through Thuringia in a huge arc through Gotha, Ohrdruf, and Weimar before swinging due south on Seventh Army's flank into Bohemia and lower Bavaria.

It seemed that Patton had an affinity for trouble. Shortly after leaving the Rhine behind, Patton ordered the creation of a small armored combat command. This unit was issued orders to slice through the German lines and head east to liberate a prisoner-of-war camp near the town of Hammelberg over 40 miles behind the front. According to Patton, his information indicated that the Germans were preparing to evacuate the American prisoners at the camp deeper into Germany. Was the fact that his son-in-law, Colonel John Waters, was confined to this camp mere coincidence or was it the determining factor behind Patton's decision? Whatever the reasoning, it was only after suffering heavy casualties that the would-be liberators managed to reach Hammelberg. Few of the rescuers or prisoners managed to make it back to friendly lines without having been either recaptured or wounded. Among the latter was Colonel Waters who received a leg wound during the abortive escape. XV Corps of Patch's Seventh Army overran Hammelberg a week later.

As the Third Army steamroller moved irresistibly deeper into Germany, enemy opposition melted before its firepower. The pace of the advance rivaled that of the previous year's dash across France following the breakout from Normandy.

On April 4, Third Army had its first taste of the horrors of Nazi Germany. XX Corps under General Walton Walker, a Pattonesque commander and a particular favorite of the Third Army leader's, liberated a concentration camp near Ohrdruf.

When the XX Corps took over the area, General Walker compelled the Ohrdruf burgomaster and his wife to view the camp; they went home and hanged themselves.[16]

As April receded, Third Army was racing down the Danube into Austria. Eisenhower ordered Patton to divert units into Czechoslovakia but to halt short of Prague and link up with the Russians on the Elbe River. Under no circumstances was he to cross the river. Once more Patton was wont to interpret orders liberally. With minimal connivance from Bradley, he prepared to liberate the Czech capitol despite the fact that it was an objective of the Russians. Eisenhower would not hear of it and let it be known in no uncertain terms that Third Army was to remain where it was or Patton would have to suffer the consequences. In effect, for Third Army, the war was over.

With the war in Europe over, Patton hoped for a reassignment to the Pacific where the war continued to rage. Courtney Hodges and his First Army staff had already been ordered there and Patton was eager to remain involved in fighting the enemy. MacArthur spurned the opportunity to have Patton under his command, citing the fact that in the Pacific theater, there was little or no opportunity for Patton's broad-ranging, hard-charging, armored thrusts and that his talents failed to fit into the tactics of island fighting. In reality, MacArthur was unwilling to share the glory with anyone else. This was the second time that an egotistical commander rejected an opportunity to avail himself of Patton's ability. In January of 1944, when portions of Fifth Army found itself bogged down at Anzio in Italy, Mark Clark refused Eisenhower's offer to send Patton in to take over the beachhead. Clark was not about to share the headlines and he told Ike that there was no room in his theater for Patton.

After a brief trip home to the United States during which his exploits were hailed and applauded, Patton returned to Germany and settled down to days of dreary occupation duty. Amazingly, during the round of speeches accompanying the honors bestowed on him during his brief visit home, Patton had not allowed his mouth to get him into trouble. That was reserved for his return to Europe.

Appointed military governor of Bavaria and responsible for carrying out a denazification program, Patton hesitated. His contempt for the Russians surfaced publicly and he advocated rearming the Germans and using them as Allies against the Russians. In this he was supported by Montgomery who was more discreet. When pressed by Eisenhower to get on with the denazification program, Patton saw to it that all former German army units were disarmed totally and confined. Unfortunately, he hesitated when it came to disarming former SS units. Many of these were allowed to retain their weapons under the guise of acting as civilian police forces. In addition, former high-ranking SS members were installed as key political figures in the local government. Finally, as a last straw, he equated membership in the Nazi Party with that of membership in American political parties.

The first indiscretion, i.e., his reluctance to disarm the SS, cost him command of his beloved Third Army which was handed to his old friend from Sicily, Lucian Truscott. The last misguided utterance was more than Eisenhower could reasonably accept. With Roosevelt, his ardent admirer, dead and with the need for a peaceful reconstruction period, Patton was deemed expendable.

Patton was transferred to command of the Fifteenth Army. This army was but a paper force with responsibility for analyzing the tactics and strategy used during the war. Headlines announcing that Patton had been 'fired' reverberated across the United States, but he accepted his punishment magnanimously.

As December approached, Patton's job was winding down and he was preparing to return permanently to the United States. On the 9th of the month, he set out for a day of pheasant hunting with his chief-of-staff, General Hobart Gay. Enroute, his vehicle became involved in a relatively minor auto accident. Patton, however, had taken a severe jolt, breaking his neck. Rushed to a nearby army hospital, it was diagnosed that the man of action was paralyzed from the neck down. He accepted his fate and soon his spirits began to rise. Unfortunately, the paralysis and related inactivity soon resulted in pneumonia. Patton sensed that he was doomed.

Despite all efforts to save him, General George Patton died peacefully on December 21, 1945. He was buried in the American military cemetery at Hamm, Luxembourg, where he joined six thousand dead comrades of the Third Army.

* * *

At the cemetery in Hamm, standing at solemn attention beside contingents from the British, French, and Belgian armies, a composite battalion of infantry and cavalry soldiers represented the Third Army, under the personal command of General Lucian K. Truscott. Patton was seen to his final rest by a distinguished group of honorary pallbearers, remarkable for a last-minute change in its composition. The original list of thirteen included high-ranking officers in the Theater and three members of his staff. At the request of Mrs. Patton, however, one man was dropped and one man substituted. Dropped was the name of Lt. General Walter Bedell Smith, of whom Patton had told General Eisenhower during a friendly dinner on the evening of October 12, to which Smith had been invited. 'In light of what happened, I cannot hereafter eat at the same table with Beetle Smith.' He did not care to see him at his bedside, and obviously he would not have wanted him at his funeral either.[17]

Patton always blamed Smith for the breakdown in his relationship with Eisenhower.

In recent years, there has been much speculation that perhaps Patton was assassinated, probably by the Russians who feared his hostility towards them. Advocates of this theory have been unable to present anything but the flimsiest of circumstantial evidence, however. On the other hand, Mr. Ladislas Farago in his recent book, *The Last Days of Patton*, offers what the authors of this book feel is irrefutable evidence that Patton's death was the result of nothing other than what the official record indicates, an accident.

George Patton was unequivocally the most dashing and boldest commander of any army in Europe, also the most controversial. His flair for showmanship and the dramatic made him the darling of the press corps. While alive, his exploits became legend and have been magnified since. Nicknamed 'Old Blood and Guts,' his driving methods certainly gave indication that he was determined to live up to that name. As he was so fond of saying, "My job is to kill Krauts." He was spectacular, swaggering, pistol-packing, deeply religious, violently profane, attired in high boots, riding breeches, and highly polished helmet. He was a correspondent's delight. Never one to shun the limelight, his feelings towards another glory-seeker, Montgomery, were certainly no secret and bordered on open hostility.

It was his work on the battlefield, however, which stamped him with greatness. Sicily marked a dramatic turning point in the war. With American morale and prestige greatly reduced after the disastrous set back at Kasserine Pass in Tunisia, it was Patton's lightning speed and cleverly conducted campaign that proved without a doubt that the American GI was indeed the equal of his British counterpart, capable of holding his own in any battle.

The Normandy breakout with its shellburst effect was a unique masterpiece. It sealed the fate of the German Seventh Army even before the latter's abortive offensive which then provided Patton with the opportunity for complete annihilation of his foe at Falaise. Though the gap failed to close in time to destroy the complete Seventh Army, it was not Patton's conduct which was criticized for this failure. The fault lay in other quarters.

Finally, his anticipation of the disaster in the Ardennes and his predetermined preparation to foil the German intentions resulted in the American army suffering less embarrassment that it should reasonably have expected. His inspirational leadership and exhortations during the drive to Bastogne were truly magnificent. To pull attacking formations out of line, change the axis of attack ninety degrees, then swing this axis around parallel to its original one was an unheard-of feat which Patton made to appear routine.

Of all the Allied field commanders in Europe after D-Day, Patton definitely exercised the most dramatic influence and was without question its star performer.

Chapter 3

Though not as flamboyant as Patton nor prone to the theatrics of MacArthur, General Omar Nelson Bradley gained the respect and admiration of his subordinates and colleagues and was held in high regard by his superiors.

Dubbed the 'Soldier's General' by Ernie Pyle, he was considered a commander who placed the welfare of his troops above individual glory. Yet, his concern did not make him a cautious commander. He was certainly not as conservative as, for example, his British counterpart, Field Marshal Montgomery, but decidedly more so than Patton.

One of the foremost historians on World War II, Mr. Martin Blumenson, aptly summed up Bradley's ability when he named him the "the most brilliant practitioner of grand tactics in the European theater."[1] It was Bradley's steady hand, his concern for logistics, that paved the way for Patton's spectacular breakout.

Probably the most descriptive words to sum up Bradley quickly are 'sure but steady.' Although his influence was enormous, his endeavors were not as newsworthy as those of Patton. Bradley focused his attention on the details of war and his true value lay in the field of logistics; food for the troops, gasoline for the engines, replacements for casualties, spare parts for worn-out machines. This was his true field of conquest. The masterful way he handled detail paved the way for ultimate American victory.

One must not allow Bradley's bespectacled and fatherly appearance to give the impression of a weakling. His quiet, unassuming manner should not be misinterpreted as timidity. Forrest Pogue, the noted biographer of Generals George Marshall and Dwight Eisenhower had this to say of Bradley,

> Seen in the field or at a conference table, Bradley often puzzled his colleagues by his quietness and soft voice. Permitting full discussion and disagreement, he sometimes seemed to be lax in control. Then suddenly he would cut through verbiage and desultory quibbling to seize the central point of a conference and announce a decision.[2]

Here was a commander, unassuming and reserved, yet totally in control of the situation.

At the end of the Second World War, this quiet warrior would find himself in command of the largest number of American troops in the country's history, encompassing no less than four field armies totaling over a million and a half men. What background prepared him for America's greatest field command in the largest conflict in world history?

Omar Nelson Bradley was born in Clark, Missouri on February 12, 1893. The name Omar was in honor of an editor friend of his parents and Nelson was the name of the local doctor who delivered the child. With the death of his father in 1908, young Omar and his mother moved to Moberly, Missouri. Two years later, upon completing high school, the future general found employment in the workshops of the Wabash

Railroad. His financial situation necessitated delaying his entrance to the state university until he could save enough money to help his mother and finance his future education. In 1911, the industrious young man found himself still struggling to save enough money for college when the superintendent of his church suggested that he apply to the United States Military Academy. At first, he hesitated, unaware that if he were accepted his education would be free. However, when he found out that the Army paid cadets while providing an education at the same time, he became enthusiastic with the prospect. After passing the necessary entrance examinations, he received an appointment and was told to report to the academy on August 1, 1911.

Four years later, Omar Bradley graduated with the class of 1915, finishing 44th. Another member of that same class was a young, fair-haired man from Kansas named Dwight D. Eisenhower. Little did the two realize how destiny would later link them together.

As a commissioned Second Lt., Bradley was assigned to the infantry.

A soldier's mind is filled with visions of great deeds on the battlefield; Bradley was no exception. By the time he graduated, war had been raging in Europe for almost a year. Though America was not then a participant in the conflict, it appeared to be only a matter of time before her eager youth would clamor to join the fight. Bradley prepared himself. When America finally did enter the struggle, to his immense disappointment he was appointed to a guard company of the 14th Infantry Regiment at the Butte Copper mines. At war's end, the honors went to the brave who had fought in the trenches of Europe. Bradley was disconsolate, feeling that his career was over. He fell into a state of deep depression.

Peacetime armies present the soldier with endless humdrum assignments that allow little opportunity for advancement. Bradley's career between the wars was typical in that respect. He passed through a number of various duties, but one quality consistently stood out above all the rest, his dedication to duty no matter how boring and commonplace it was.

In 1924, he attended the Advanced Students Infantry Course where he did exceedingly well in the stiff competition, placing second out of all the participants. Many of those same men were former front line soldiers who had experienced the brutality of war first hand. Bradley's confidence was restored.

During these peacetime years, Bradley had the opportunity to forge a closer relationship with his former classmate, Eisenhower, and the then Lt. Colonel George C. Marshall when the latter was the assistant commandant of the Infantry School. Both of these friendships would greatly influence Bradley's later career.

In 1940, George Marshall, by now a general and Chief of Staff of the Army, ordered Bradley to join him as Assistant Secretary of the General Staff. A year later, he was transferred to Fort Benning as the commandant of the Infantry School, a very prestigious position. Bradley held that post when the fatal blow was struck by the Japanese at Pearl Harbor.

With the advent of war for the second time in his career, Bradley fervently hoped that this time he would not be passed over for a combat command. In this, he was not disappointed. Marshall assigned him to the command of his very first divisional responsibility, the 82nd, later to gain fame as one of America's elite airborne divisions. Within a few months' time, he was transferred to the 28th Infantry Division, another unit destined to achieve fame on the battlefields of Europe. Marshall was highly impressed by Bradley's methods. The 28th excelled in maneuvers and Bradley's star was on the rise. Through 1942 and into 1943, he gained command experience, waiting for the day when he could exchange drilling for the real thing. However, Marshall was not quite sure in what capacity to use Bradley.

For the second time in this century, the United States went to war unprepared to take an immediate active role in the fight. American strategy was based on the pragmatic concept that the destruction of the enemy could best be accomplished by an immediate cross-Channel attack. Although the nation's military leaders felt that way, its ally, Great Britain, did not. England had been fighting the Axis alone since the defeat of France in 1940. By 1942, the toll on her resources was enormous and the strain noticeable. True, a ray of hope developed when Hitler invaded Russia, but by the end of 1941 it appeared certain that Russia too would follow the same route as France. Now, a new ally had arrived to help, but where were the American troops? Only a few divisions were combat worthy and there was much talk about using these against the Japanese. General Marshall, however, was committed to the prewar staff studies which concluded that, in the event America found herself embroiled in a two-ocean war, the European enemy was potentially the most dangerous and must therefore be defeated first.

The British were happy with Marshall's support of a Europe-first strategy. However, they were not happy with his insistence on a cross-Channel attack in 1942. Any invasion that early would have to be a predominantly British effort since there were not yet enough combat-trained American divisions available. The sacrifice would be too much for Britain to bear. Instead, Churchill insisted, Mediterranean operations appeared to present an opportunity to hasten the Axis defeat without having to invade Fortress Europe at its strongest point. There in North Africa, Italy, and the Balkans was the Axis' 'soft underbelly.' The British Prime Minister was so persuasive that he convinced President Roosevelt to delay the cross-Channel operation and instead conduct an invasion of northwest Africa, aimed at hitting the enemy from behind while the already committed British Eighth Army struck frontally in Egypt.

Operation Torch, the Anglo-American invasion hit the African beaches on November 8, 1942. Vichy French resistance was eliminated in a few days and the 'Torch' forces moved towards Tunisia. However, Hitler was not willing to relinquish his hold on North African soil without a struggle, so he immediately sent German troops to Tunis and Bizerta. The Axis beat the Allies into Tunisia by a few days, eliminating the prospect of a quick victory. Meanwhile, Rommel was in retreat from Egypt but had not been destroyed. Consequently, he was able to systematically withdraw towards Tunisia. Then the North African winter struck with all its fury. Incessant rains turned every road into a river of mud and bogged down the opposing forces, resulting in a stalemate.

During this time, in January of 1943, as Rommel retreated across Libya and the fighting in Tunisia was locked in a tie, a high level conference was held in Casablanca with both the President of the United States and the Prime Minister of Great Britain in attendance. They were joined there by the combined

Chiefs of Staff.

After this conference was over, General Marshall traveled to Algiers where he visited Eisenhower's headquarters. Seeing for himself just how overwhelming Eisenhower's responsibility was, he suggested to Ike that perhaps he could use a little help.

> You ought to have a man to be your eyes and ears. Naturally he'd have to be a man who has ability and someone you can trust.[3]

Eisenhower was open to the prospect of having such a man, but the question was whom whereupon Marshall casually mentioned Bradley. Eisenhower eagerly responded in the affirmative. Omar Bradley finally had his overseas assignment.

Bradley's arrival in Algiers on February 24 could not have occurred at a less auspicious time for the United States. The II Corps had just suffered a humiliating defeat at the hands of the wily 'Desert Fox' at a place known as Kasserine Pass. This was America's first encounter with the veteran Germans and the defeat proved embarrassing. Eisenhower demanded answers.

Major General Lloyd Fredendall had been placed in command of the II Corps on January 1 and was given orders to concentrate his forces on the southern Tunisian front in preparation for an attack towards Sfax on the coast. The Allied line stretched over two-hundred-fifty miles from the Mediterranean coast southward into the desert. In January, the elimination of the narrow neck of the Axis' Tunisian bridgehead seemed a far distant objective to the Allies as the enemy continued to reinforce the area with troops and equipment. By the following month, the Allied line was held by a much weakened force while the Axis had been reinforced by Rommel's veterans. The Germans had successfully managed to elude Montgomery after the latter's breakthrough at El Alamein. Then, recognizing the Allied intent, Rommel saw an opportunity to gain a victory before the arrival of Eighth Army in Tunisia. Attacking from the Mareth Line, he sent the Afrika Korps in conjunction with the 10th Panzer Division from von Arnim's command surging towards the Americans. The fabled Afrika Korps pushed the Americans out of Gafsa and by February 18 were squeezing the terrified troops between them at the Kasserine Pass. Thanks to disunity in the Axis camp, the offensive was halted only ten miles from Thala and victory.

Just as the crisis was ending, Bradley arrived in Algiers. Eisenhower was distraught over the American conduct in the battle and needed immediate answers. Therefore, he quickly pressed the newly arrived Bradley into service.

Just as quickly as you can, I want you to get up to the front and look for the things I would want to see myself if I only had the time. Bedell [General Walter Bedell Smith, Eisenhower's Chief of Staff] will give you a letter telling Fredendall and the others that you are to act as my eyes and ears.[4]

Leaving Algiers, Bradley traveled to Constantine, then to the front where he conversed with the divisional and regimental commanders. It appeared to him that the corps commander, Fredendall, had lost the confidence of his divisional commanders thanks to his faulty disposition of units. Eisenhower himself came to the front on March 5 and bluntly asked

Bradley what he thought of the command situation. Bradley responded that it was pretty bad. Eisenhower agreed and said:

> Thanks, Brad, you've confirmed what I thought was wrong. As a matter of fact, I've already ordered Patton up from Rabat. He'll report in tomorrow to take command of II Corps.[5]

George Patton had already established a reputation for being an aggressive commander. It was hoped that his presence would restore confidence to the G.I. and repair the damaged situation. For the first time the names of Bradley, Eisenhower, and Patton were linked together.

What Patton did to the II Corps is examined in detail in the chapter devoted to him. In short, he instilled a sense of rigid discipline on the men who, before his arrival, had lapsed into a state of nonmilitary informality. Patton changed all that immediately. He pushed the men to the brink, causing them to hate him even more than the enemy. That hatred, Patton felt, could easily be transferred to the enemy when the time came. When the hour finally did come, Patton's efforts paid huge dividends.

Bradley was still present at II Corps after Patton assumed command. His presence made Patton uneasy since it appeared that Bradley was spying on him. As Bradley himself said:

> If I was to be in his headquarters, he felt, then I should logically be part of his direct chain of command.[6]

Patton called Bedell Smith and told him that he

needed a number two man and that Bradley would be perfect for the job.

By the middle of March, the strain on the Axis was beginning to tell. Rommel had left on permanent sick leave, leaving General von Arnim in command. Little by little, the initiative swung to the Allies as supplies became more readily available and the amount of forces increased. The North African campaign moved towards its inevitable climax.

With Montgomery ready to assault the Mareth Line, the Army Group commander, General Sir Harold Alexander (see Volume II in this series, *The British*), ordered II Corps to attack on the southern Tunisian front. He planned to lure as much of the enemy strength as possible out of their defensive positions. Hopefully, by striking on the enemy's flank, it would cause them to divert their strength.

For the offensive, II Corps was to apply pressure at three points on the Tunisian front. The main attack was to be from Gafsa through El Guettar towards the coast. Subsidiary drives against enemy communications were farther north beyond Maknassy and still farther north where the remainder of the corps was to provide flank cover. To Patton's dismay, II Corps' thrust was not intended to be an all-out drive to the coast but rather a diversion in order to facilitate Montgomery's main advance into the Mareth Line. It would not be the last time Patton found himself ordered to play second fiddle to Montgomery.

Meanwhile, plans for the forthcoming Sicilian invasion proceeded at Eisenhower's headquarters. Patton was an integral part of that planning and his presence was required in Algiers, but he could not be spared until after the El Guettar attack. This attack proved a huge success. Patton's rigid discipline paid off. Both his and Montgomery's moves caused the enemy to retreat northward into a pocket centered on the port cities of Bizerta and Tunis with the Mediterranean Sea at their backs.

After the success at El Guettar, Patton was ordered to Algiers and Omar Bradley was named to replace him. Finally, a field command was his.

Allied plans for the elimination of the Axis in Tunisia called for the Americans to play a, as they saw it, disappointing role. Alexander's original plan called for Anderson's First British Army to attack in the north central Tunisian plain while Eighth Army attacked from the south. The United States II Corps was slated to play only a minor supporting role with the American forces pinched out before Tunis was reached.

Bradley told this to Patton while the latter was still in command of II Corps. Patton reacted as expected. When Bradley went to Alexander's headquarters, he was informed that the slight was unintentional. In reality, however, Alexander had developed a low opinion of the ability of the American soldier after the fiasco at Kasserine. In time, that opinion would be modified but thus far American feats had simply failed to provide him with a reason for feeling otherwise.

Bradley presented Alexander with three reasons why the whole of II Corps should be employed. First of all, the original plan would deny Alexander the weight of three full divisions if he allowed them to be pinched out by First and Eighth Armies. That, Bradley felt, was a foolish waste of manpower. Second, under the current plan only the 9th U.S. Division would be deployed in the north as a protective screen for Anderson's forces. This, Bradley complained, would splinter the American forces and violate the principle that American troops were to fight together under American command. Finally, Bradley insisted, American troops had earned the right to share the victory.

Alexander was unsympathetic so Bradley went over his head to the Supreme Commander himself and presented the case to his former classmate. He emphasized that it was important for the American forces to fight as a unit for a determined goal. Eisenhower then asked for specifics. Bradley suggested that the entire II Corps, not just the 9th Division, proceed to the north, and that Bizerta be designated as its objective.

Eisenhower threw the ball back into Alexander's court who then agreed to allow the entire II Corps, four divisions, to man the hilly northern section with the port city of Bizerta as its goal. Bradley's persistence paid off.

By April 10, the II Corps had begun its move to the northern front, two hundred miles across the British line of supply. At this point, Bradley officially took command of the corps. Before leaving, however, Patton informed Bradley that he would like to have II Corps as part of the Seventh Army, now in formation, for the Sicilian campaign. Before that could take place, however, Bradley had an important objective: Bizerta.

Though cornered, the Axis were determined to stall the Allies as long as possible. The Axis Commander in Chief South, Field Marshal Albert Kesselring (See Volume I in this series, *The Germans*) intended to delay an Allied assault on Europe. The longer they managed to hold on in Africa, the longer Europe was safe from attack.

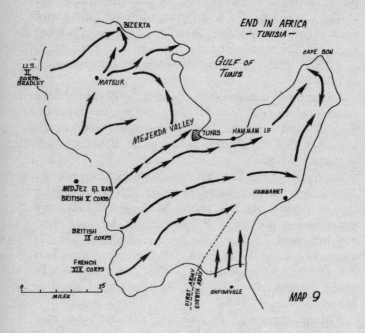

END IN AFRICA
~ TUNISIA ~

CAPE BON

GULF OF
TUNIS

U.S.
II
CORPS·
BRADLEY

BIZERTA

MATEUR

MEJERDA VALLEY

TUNIS

HAMMAM LIF

MEDJEZ EL BAB
BRITISH V CORPS

HAMMAMET

BRITISH
IX CORPS

FRENCH
XIX CORPS

0   25
MILES

FIRST ARMY
EIGHTH ARMY

ENFIDAVILLE

MAP 9

II Corps positioned itself for the offensive. The terrain facing the Americans was difficult, to say the least. Before the one armored and three infantry divisions could descend into the plain in front of Bizerta, they would have to struggle across an extremely rugged belt of spiny mountains and almost impassable thickets in the Sedjenane Valley.

The British First Army was given the starring role in this final offensive. Its goal was Tunis. II Corps in the north and Eighth Army in the south were to draw the enemy's strength from Anderson's front. Even though Bradley was given a subsidiary role, he approached his task with all the dedication and enthusiasm of a rookie commander, determined to show the British and the world what American arms could accomplish.

On April 23, in conjunction with First Army, Bradley began his first offensive as Corps Commander. His conduct during the campaign was outstanding. He exhorted, encouraged, and advised his divisional commanders. His advice to General Ryder, commander of the 34th Division, about using tanks to assault the staunch Axis defenses on the tightly held Hill 609 was inspirational. The Germans were confident that the terrain was unsuitable for tanks. Even Ryder was amazed.

> When Ryder spoke to me of the possibility of flanking the hill from the rear, I offered him a company of tanks for mobile artillery support. He looked at me with mild surprise but readily accepted the help.[7]

A captured German defender of Hill 609 remarked:

> We could have held out against your infantry for another week, but we didn't expect to see tanks.

As a matter of fact you had no right to use them. We had been told that was not tank country and as a result we had few defenses.[8]

In addition to conducting a hotly contested operation, Bradley had to be constantly on guard against British encroachments. One time, Anderson attempted to conscript one American combat team for use in his own army. This was quickly thwarted by Bradley who appealed to Eisenhower.

On May 7, Bizerta was reached and two days later, the Germans on II Corps front surrendered. Thus did the American Army secure its first unconditional surrender of Axis forces.

With the campaign at an end, Bradley now traveled westward to prepare for Operation Husky, the invasion of Sicily.

Though not committed to the extension of Mediterranean operations, the American Chiefs of Staff yielded during the Casablanca Conference to the logic of an invasion of Sicily. This operation, it was argued, would provide the Allies with an unsinkable base from which an air offensive could be launched against the Axis from the south. It would also give the Allies control of the Mediterranean sea lanes. It would also serve to tie down extensive Axis forces and apply pressure on Italy. They thought perhaps they might even drive that country from the war, thereby diverting German strength from the Russian front.

Though General Marshall reluctantly agreed, he extracted from the British promises that the cross-Channel attack would take place in the spring of 1944 and that this Mediterranean operation was in no way an alternative to the all-important invasion of France.

The plan eventually adopted placed the United States Seventh Army to the left of Montgomery's

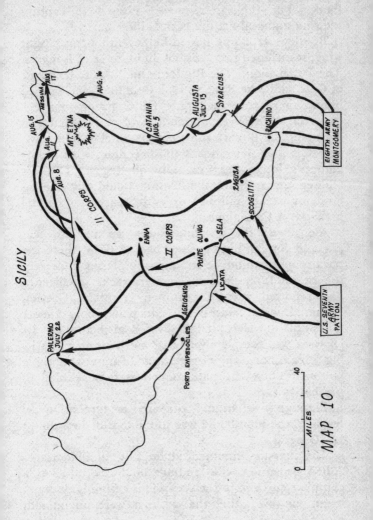

SICILY

PALERMO JULY 22

PORTO EMPEDOCLES

AGRIGENTO

LICATA

II CORPS

ENNA

PONTE OLIVO

SELA

II CORPS

AUG. 8

AUG. 11

AUG. 15

AUG. 17

MESSINA

AUG. 16

MT. ETNA

CATANIA AUG. 5

AUGUSTA JULY 13

SYRACUSE

PACHINO

RAGUSA

SCOGLITTI

EIGHTH ARMY MONTGOMERY

U.S. SEVENTH ARMY (PATTON)

MILES

0   40

MAP 10

Eighth Army. To the dismay of the Americans, especially Patton, the U.S. was slated to play a simple supporting role to the English, protecting the British flank while the latter moved rapidly to capture Messina and seal off the island. (See map 10)

Bradley's II Corps was to be Seventh Army's right wing; it included two divisions and a force of Rangers. The 1st Division, 'The Big Red One,' was to land east of Gela while the Rangers took Gela itself and pushed inland to capture the Ponte Olivo airport. Further east, the 45th Division would land at Scoglitti and make for the Biscari and Comiso airfields. This division was also slated to establish contact with Montgomery's forces near the city of Regusa. Once it secured the airfields, the division would advance inland for twenty miles in order to reach the arterial highway at Caltagione.

Along with the invading forces, an air drop was planned for the high ground behind Gela; there the paratroopers would be strategically placed to protect the beach from possible counterattack. Intelligence had reported that the vaunted Hermann Goering Panzer Division was near Caltagione, only twenty miles north of Gela. If this division hit before the 1st Division was completely landed and able to bring its big guns ashore, the Germans could upset the whole landing. Thus, the paratroopers were scheduled to prevent this.

Through June, Bradley prepared his forces. On the tenth of the month, he was promoted to the rank of Lt. General.

The invasion commenced on July 10. Thanks to Allied deception, the landings on Sicily came as a complete surprise to the Axis. This certainly does not mean, however, that the landings were unopposed.

Patton's Seventh Army bore the brunt of the Axis reaction.

While the invasion was in progress, Bradley had to remain aboard the command ship, *Ancon*, waiting for the divisional commanders to land and establish their communications. The 1st Division landed right on schedule, but the 45th was delayed by heavy swells. Resistance was light as the Germans had not recovered from their initial surprise.

The critical point was not expected to be during the actual landings, but during the counterattack. To the rear of the II Corps beachhead, the Hermann Goering Division waited for the opportunity to pounce.

Bradley was eager to participate in operations before the counterattack occurred. He left the flag ship on D+1 and headed for the beach at Scoglitti where the II Corps had set up its temporary command post. He then moved on to Gela to meet with the commander of the 1st Division, the flamboyant Terry Allen. While there, Bradley witnessed the division's fight against the German panzer attack. Allen's staunch soldiers held on despite severe enemy pressure, but even the paratroop drop of the previous evening was not enough to halt the German attack. Bradley had nothing but praise for the 'Big Red One' and for its maverick commander, Terry Allen.

Only the perverse Big Red One with its no less perverse commander was both hard and experienced enough to take that assault in stride.[9]

Allen quickly brought his corps commander up to date on operations. Bradley asked Allen if he felt that the situation was in hand and the latter responded in the affirmative. Allen had certainly performed a magnificent feat of arms and deserved a great deal of credit, for it was his quick action and iron nerve which actually organized the defense. A lesser commander lacking Allen's guts and ability might have folded in the face of a determined panzer onslaught.

Messina was the primary objective of the entire Sicilian campaign. II Corps' main task was to support the Eighth Army in reaching that objective. After establishing itself firmly on the beach, II Corps moved inland to capture the strategic airfields which lay in its sector. From there, it was to proceed further inland to the Vizzini-Caltagione road. Once this was reached, the corps would swing northward to Enna.

On July 14, as the Corps was pressing toward the critical road, Patton summoned Bradley to Seventh Army headquarters. There, Patton informed his subordinate of the bad news.

We've received a directive from Army Group, Brad. Monty's to get the Vizzini-Caltagione road in his drive to flank Catania and Mount Etna by going through Enna. This means you'll have to sideslip west with your 45th Division.[10]

The normally reticent Bradley exploded. He was counting on the use of that road. Without it, II Corps advance would be significantly slowed since shifting from this main road would require the corps to traverse minor paths through extremely rough terrain. Bradley asked if he could at least use that road to move his 45th Division over to the left of the 1st. It would be much simpler, he emphasized, to push this division to the left rather than sending both divisions over. This way, the 1st's attack could go on as scheduled. Patton replied that Montgomery needed the road immediately and that Bradley would have to abandon it forthwith.

Again Bradley vehemently protested that this effort would delay his corps for two days. The enemy was on the run and this delay would provide them with breathing space and allow them to regain their balance. Yet, all his protesting was to no avail.

The reasoning behind the dramatic change in plans was the stiff opposition encountered by Eighth Army along the route to Catania. It was therefore decided to move portions of Montgomery's army along the Caltagione-Vizzini road in an attempt to outflank the marshes and other natural obstacles along the coast. This would allow it to the greatest natural barrier in Sicily and one heavily defended by the enemy, Mount Etna.

Bradley had no way of knowing that Patton's resistance to the proposal was lukewarm at best. Before acceding to Alexander's request, Patton saw how he could use the situation to his benefit. Before making any agreement he struck a bargain with Alexander at II Corps' expense. All Bradley could see was that it condemned his corps to fight in some of the most difficult terrain yet encountered. His anger was justified. Denied the Vizzini road, he had little option but to shift the 45th by sending the division all the way back to the beaches, then forward again on the left of the 'Big Red One.' Essential time was lost and a great deal of effort expended.

The great prize of Messina had been assigned to Montgomery. Not to be outdone, Patton organized a provisional corps under General Keyes and ordered it to sweep the western part of the island. Keyes fulfilled his assignment and entered Palermo on July 22. This was the culmination of the deal Patton had struck with Alexander. Palermo was taken by Seventh Army and Bradley was without a road.

The Germans recognized early on that an Allied

conquest of Sicily was but a matter of time. Kesselring's only hope was to delay the conquest as long as possible and because of the difficult terrain around Mt. Etna, this was not difficult to do. The field marshal ordered that this area be defended as long as possible while the remaining forces in Sicily conducted an orderly retreat across the narrow Straits of Messina.

Thus, Montgomery, denied easy access to Messina and bogged down before Mt. Etna, had come to a standstill. The Army Group Commander, Alexander, disenchanted with Eighth Army's snail's pace and frustrated that Patton was idle at Palermo, declared Messina fair game. He gave his consent for the Americans to proceed along the northern coastal road toward the town.

While the balance of Patton's forces were involved in clearing the western end of the island, II Corps was struggling across the center of Sicily in a series of fierce nonstop battles. To their right was the British XXX Corps of Oliver Leese. He too was having a difficult time fighting against a most determined enemy. The foe before Enna presented XXX Corps with a defense that was proving impossible to crack. Because of the strength of that defense, Leese drove to the right of Enna. By doing so, he exposed the flank of Bradley's corps. The principal roads from Enna ran back towards the rear area dumps of II Corps. Bradley wrote to Leese about the situation and told him that he was going to let II take Enna which they promptly did. The BBC quickly announced to the world that Enna had been captured by British forces.

On July 23, General Troy Middleton radioed the corps headquarters that his 45th Division had reached the Mediterranean on the north shore of Sicily. The island had been severed from the mainland. Bradley was now directed up the road towards Troina and along the coast. The 45th moved along the shore while the 1st Division pivoted and moved inland along the Troina road.

Now the Americans ran into the heaviest fighting of the campaign. Patton set about racing Montgomery to Messina with a vengeance. No delays were sanctioned. He had no patience for arguments or lagging. There were many who came to detest him for his attitude during the Sicilian campaign. One individual who came to judge harshly his superior's methods was the seemingly shy but competent corps commander, Bradley.

The advance towards Troina was slowed to a trickle as the 1st Division found itself up against a seemingly impenetrable obstacle. Along the coast, the defenders at the seaside village of San Stefano halted all efforts to move ahead.

During this period in late July, at the height of the fighting, the famous war correspondent Ernie Pyle spent some time with Bradley. For three days, the reporter and the general were inseparable. From that encounter, the image of Bradley as the 'G.I.'s General' emerged.

On August 1, the veterans of North Africa, the 3rd Division under Lucian Truscott, assumed responsibility for the coastal road and the worn out 45th Division was sent into reserve to rest and refit for the forthcoming Italian campaign.

Troina was the key to the Axis defenses. If it could be taken, the center of the enemy's line would collapse, necessitating a hasty withdrawal. The town was situated on a mountain top overlooking a bowl-shaped valley. Behind Troina lay the yawning crater of Mt. Etna.

As the 3rd Division moved into line, the 1st Division

went into the bowl. They were quickly hit by a fierce enemy counterattack which threw the Americans back to their starting line. Allen refused to yield and was determined to make another effort. After looking at his maps, he could see that the enemy at Troina was supplied by two roads, one running south and the other off to the northwest. If these roads could be cut by a flanking movement, the Axis defenders would be forced to retire. Thus, he split his forces in a pincer maneuver designed to circumvent the main positions in the town and trap the enemy. For three days, Allen's every effort was thrown back. Each time the division attacked, the Germans counterattacked. Finally, after enduring almost a week's severe pounding from artillery and ground assaults, the Germans abandoned Troina on August 6.

After Troina, the division moved forward to Randazzo where another long, drawn-out battle ensued. At this juncture, Bradley was forced to perform a task which he came to consider one of the most unpleasant of his entire career, the replacement of Terry Allen and his assistant divisional commander, Theodore Roosevelt Jr. Bradley assumed full responsibility for this unpopular action. Both generals were idolized by their troops. Everyone agreed that it was Terry Allen's skill which had saved the original landing from being mauled by the Hermann Goering counterattack. Why then should these two commanders be sacked? It was felt that Allen's excessive devotion to his division blinded him to the overall needs of the rest of the corps, and his maverick tendencies had gotten out of hand. The same could be said for Roosevelt. Bradley simply did what he thought was best for the total effort. Both generals later played a vital part in the northwest European campaign, Roosevelt at Utah Beach in Normandy and Allen as commander of the

104th Division.

But Allen and Roosevelt weren't the only two feeling the strain. Patton himself had worn his nerves to a frazzle and was approaching the breaking point. Twice in early August, he struck enlisted men at mobile hospitals who he thought were goldbrickers. These events had a great effect on his subsequent career. When Bradley received word of these incidents, he loyally pigeonholed the reports, refusing to demean the accomplishments of his superior. He could have ingratiated himself by exposing Patton's actions, but this was not the nature of the man. Eventually, the unfortunate events were exposed without any assistance from Bradley.

On the northern coast, Patton and Bradley utilized a sea envelopment to bypass stiff German defenses at San Fratello. The amphibious landing took place on August 8 at St. Agata, six miles to the rear of the enemy. The Germans, finding themselves pressured from both land and sea, evacuated the position and retreated eastward. 3rd Division was now twelve miles closer to Messina.

Pleased by the success of the San Fratello envelopment, Patton decided to utilize the same tactic again on August 11 to bypass resistance near Brolo. Bradley checked to see if Truscott would be ready to advance by that date. The 3rd Division commander said this was impossible and he could not be ready to link up with seaborne forces until at least the following day. Bradley sought Patton's permission to delay the operation for that time. He reasoned that if the ground forces were unable to link up with the seaborne units the project could fail, if not completely, at least with heavy loss of life. Patton was too impatient and blinded by visions of Messina, so he refused to sanction the delay. Bradley was exasperated with his stubbornness.

On the morning of August 11, the 2nd Battalion of the 30th Infantry Regiment landed near Brolo, twelve miles to the rear of the German position. As anticipated by Bradley, Truscott had difficulty linking up with the 2nd Battalion. Not until the morning of the twelfth was the battalion relieved. By that time, it had incurred heavy losses, but luckily the II Corps was now only forty miles from Messina. George Patton impatiently anticipated his next move.

In the interim, while Seventh and Eighth Armies converged on Messina, the very able German commander, Albert Kesselring, systematically evacuated the island via a crossing of the narrow Straits of Messina.

Nevertheless, Patton was determined to beat Montgomery to the prize. He ordered a third amphibious envelopment on August 16 and by that evening, the 3rd Division found itself a mere twelve miles from their goal. On the following morning, a platoon from the division entered the town. Patton had beaten Montgomery, and Bradley's corps had paved the path for Patton's day of glory.

Throughout the entire Sicilian campaign, Bradley conducted a very professional operation. His concern for his men and his logistical know-how impressed his superiors. While North Africa had been his debut and proving ground, in Sicily he was the cool, experienced professional. His talent was certain to be tapped for the most important Allied campaign, the invasion of northwest Europe.

Shortly after the conclusion of the Sicilian campaign, Bradley was summoned to England to help plan for the largest amphibious operation of the war, the Normandy invasion. Patton had lost his chance at the prestigious command thanks to the slapping incident. Thus, while he remained behind in sunny Sicily, his former subordinate, Bradley, moved on to London.

During the planning stages for Operation Overlord, code name for the cross-Channel attack, Bradley had to wear two hats. He took command of the United States First Army and also was ordered to establish a headquarters for an American Army Group. Was it simply luck and chance which netted Bradley this high position? Yes, it was to a degree, but his ability cannot be overlooked. The luck aspect can be derived from Marshall's decision back in January of 1943 that Eisenhower needed 'eyes and ears.' It was lucky too that Patton refused to tolerate what he considered a spy and thus made Bradley his assistant. It was bad luck for Patton that he slapped a soldier in Sicily, but for Bradley, this was decisive. His career advanced while Patton would remain an Army commander. Yes, Bradley was indeed lucky to know the right people and be at the right place at the right time, but his superb handling of the II Corps in Tunisia and Sicily warranted his consideration for the top field command.

Joining SHAEF (Supreme Headquarters Allied Expeditionary Force), Bradley worked with the Supreme Commander, Eisenhower, his deputy Arthur Tedder, and the British ground commander General Montgomery, to formulate the plans for Overlord. Bradley was to command First Army during the assault. His immediate superior during the course of the actual invasion was to be Montgomery. This, however, would be a temporary situation until the beachhead was expanded enough to allow the establishment of a second U.S. Army. Then, Bradley would move from Army Commander to Army Group command, making him the equal of Montgomery.

In the assault, First Army was to land on two of the

five designated beaches on the Normandy coast, Omaha and Utah. Its immediate objective was to knit the two beaches together and make contact with the British on the left. Then, First Army would cut off the Cotentin Peninsula to forestall any enemy attempt to reinforce the port city of Cherbourg. The British Second Army, landing on the three other beaches, Sword, Juno, and Gold, before proceeding north to capture Cherbourg, would seize the important road center at Caen on D-Day and expand its own beach-head towards the flat lands beyond the city. Then, the American forces were to pivot on the British position and move in the direction of Paris to isolate the Brittany Peninsula. After that, Third Army would advance into Brittany, clean up the peninsula, and capture its all-important ports while the balance of the American forces drove towards the Seine with their right flank on the Loire.

This was the plan SHAEF discussed through the spring of 1944. Everyone realized that deception would play a crucial part. Thanks to Ultra, the Allies were aware that the Germans anticipated an assault sometime in 1944. The most likely target, the Germans felt, was at the point where the English Channel was the narrowest, the Pas de Calais. There, Hitler positioned his Fifteenth Army and most of his armor. It was left to the Allied deception agencies to feed those beliefs and keep German reinforcements away from Normandy. Codenamed Operation Bodyguard, many different suboperations were created to deceive the Germans about the actual landing point. Operation Fortitude was by far the most elaborate of these deceptions. This involved the creation of an entire bogus U.S. Army Group commanded by none other than General George Patton. Since he was the Allied general the Germans most expected to head the invasion, Patton was placed in command of this First United States Army Group whose objective was supposedly an invasion of Europe via the Pas de Calais.

While this detailed subterfuge was being fabricated, the real invasion plans took shape. Weather permitting, June 5 was the date designated for the start of the invasion. However, a storm forced Eisenhower to postpone the operation for another day. Group Captain Stagg, Eisenhower's meterologist, predicted a period of clear weather just long enough to land the troops on shore. Even nature seemed to be on the side of the Allies, for no German weather reports detected this clearing trend. So, with relaxed security, the Germans peacefully passed the night of June 5. Rommel, the commander of Army Group B, was not present at his headquarters but instead was home in Germany enjoying his wife's birthday celebration.

Shortly after midnight on June 6, 1944, the invasion commenced with an Allied airborne attack. The penetration of Hitler's Festung Europa had begun. (See Map 11)

At daylight, the U.S. 4th Division hit Utah Beach while the 'Big Red One,' veterans of North Africa and Sicily, landed on Omaha. Less than three hours later, the 4th had full control of their beach and began to push inland to link up with the paratroopers who had landed during the night. Though some initial progress was made, the flooded terrain slowed the advance and the meeting was not accomplished on the first day as anticipated.

At Omaha, the story was quite different. There the 'Atlantic Wall' was strong and Rommel's 'devil's garden' was at its best. Hedgehogs, tetrahedra, concrete cones, slanting poles topped with mines, barbed wire, thousands of anti-personnel mines, and huge anti-tank guns situated on the bluffs overlooking the

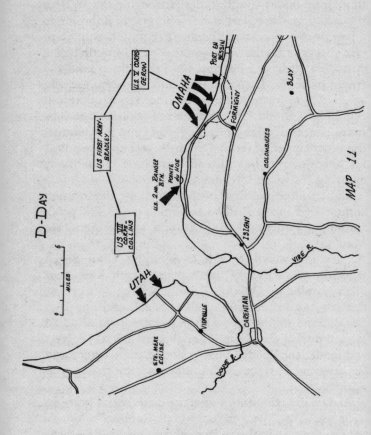

D-DAY

MAP 11

beach were trained on the landing areas waiting to usher any invader to his eternal reward. In addition to that, the German 352nd Infantry Division, one of the best, had just recently been transferred from St. Lo to the area of Omaha for a defense exercise. By the time Allied intelligence discovered the shift, it was too late to warn the troops.

Bradley's first command decision of the invasion took place on this bloody beach. From his flagship, the USS *Augusta*, he began planning for the evacuation of the beachhead and the diversion of subsequent waves to either Utah or the British beaches. The 1st Division, however, did not disappoint the army commander. They fought bravely, held on tenaciously, and gradually established a beachhead, but at a heavy cost. Though the situation remained critical on the morning of D + 1, it was obvious that the Americans were there to stay. Bradley had weathered his first crisis.

By dawn of June 7, Overlord had achieved its first crucial goal; it was lodged ashore. However, nowhere had the D-Day objectives been met. (It makes one wonder what might have happened if the Germans had anticipated the invasion at Normany and were there waiting in full force.) That, of course, gave rise to a crucial question, what would the Germans do now? Rommel's Army Group B and Field Marshal Gerd von Rundstedt's other forces greatly outnumbered the Allies on the continent. If they attacked with everything available and rushed reinforcements into Normandy, they could easily overwhelm the Allies and throw them back into the sea.

The continuation of Fortitude was mandatory in order to convince the Germans that Normandy was simply a feint. The Allied deception agencies did a superb job along that score. By July 24, with the Allies having landed thirty divisions in Normandy, they continued to intercept German messages stating that, even though the Allies had landed in force in Normandy, there were still more divisions waiting in Dover to land at the Pas de Calais. The enemy continued to believe this piece of fiction and kept the Fifteenth Army idle, awaiting an invasion that would never come. When they finally realized that Normandy was indeed the real thing, it was too late. Hundreds of their finest tanks and thousands of the best fighting men had been kept out of the crucial battle in order to meet a purely imaginary threat. Even at that, the Normandy fighting was far from a picnic.

After securing the beachhead, which was finally united on June 12, the battle of the exploitation inland commenced. Two goals were the target of the Americans, the port of Cherbourg and the provincial capital and road hub, St. Lo.

The terrain in Normandy, however, precluded rapid movement. It was hedgerow country. These were hedges several feet thick and five or more feet high, surrounding the tens of thousands of tiny fields dotting the countryside. For centuries, the farmers of Normandy have used these hedgerows to fence their cattle and protect their crops from the ocean winds. The French call this region the *bocage* because of the dense growth. Between some of the fields are trails surrounded on two sides by the hedgerows. Over the years, the trails have sunk so low, due to erosion of the soil, that they now resemble trenches. Over the years the hedges have grown over these sunken trails, making damp and gloomy tunnels. These sunken lanes provided the Germans with a built-in trench system while the hedgerows furnished defensive walls. Through this forbidden terrain, Bradley would have to move First Army.

Slowly, ever slowly, bloody hedgerow by bloody hedgerow, the American forces advanced. First Army contained two corps, the V under General Leonard T. Gerow and the VII under General 'Lightning Joe' Collins. The latter had the objective of cutting the Cotentin Peninsula at its neck and proceeding northward to Cherbourg. By late evening of June 17, Collins reported that the peninsula had been cut and Cherbourg was sealed off. With his three divisions, Collins then wheeled VII Corps northward on June 19 while Bradley took the opportunity to introduce General Troy Middleton's VIII Corps to combat by placing it across the neck of the Cotentin in order to protect Collins' flank. VII Corps moved towards Cherbourg.

The commander of the port garrison, General Karl von Schlieben, was under strict orders from Hitler not to surrender the city. Though von Schlieben had fortified the area, armed the garrison to the teeth, and built up the morale of the forces to a fever pitch, Collins broke the defenses and captured the port by June 26, although a few fanatical pockets continued to hold out until the following day. Bradley refused to observe the cordialities of war by receiving von Schlieben, arguing that he did not care to meet anyone who had caused so many unnecessary American casualties.

When VII Corps entered Cherbourg, they found the port installations destroyed. Piers, cranes, bridges, power stations, had been dynamited and burned. Salvage crews began working immediately to clear the harbor. For the next five months, Cherbourg would remain the only port supplying the invasion armies.

On July 1, Bradley took stock of his situation. His First Army was firmly established in Normandy, Cherbourg had fallen and its port was already being prepared to begin supplying the armies. But the terrain and the hedgerows were a thorn in his side.

Suitable ground for maneuver was required for his armored forces who were yearning to exert their decisive influence. It was mandatory, therefore, to gain possession of land advantageous for offensive operations.

Only a breakout would enable us to crash into the enemy's rear where we could fight a war of movement on our own best terms.[11]

The burning question, however, was where should the breakout occur?

After conferring with his corps commander and with Montgomery, Bradley considered the options available to him. At what point could he amass enough strength to enable him to punch a path through the German defenses? Looking over the map of Normandy, he chose a spot adjacent to the west coast from La Haye du Puits through to Coutance. The terrain there, however, was the horrible marshy *bocage*, ringed by hedgerows. Each one of these was in itself a barrier that could readily hinder the progress of armor and be easily defended by a mere handful of determined enemies.

On July 3, Middleton's VIII Corps proceeded down the west coast road full of enthusiasm, convinced that the Germans would collapse under the weight of their advance. After six days of slogging in the *bocage*, with their progress measuring only a few miles, the enthusiasm waned. In one slug fest lasting three days, VIII Corps managed a mere six hundred yards, the length of six football fields. Though exhausted and frustrated, Middleton coerced his forces onward. To his right, VII Corps managed little more and casualties continued to mount. The murderous terrain was proving a most difficult handicap. Finally, on July 14, Bradley ordered Middleton to halt, twelve miles from his objective, Coutance. In his own book, Bradley wrote:

> It was obvious that the Coutance-St. Lo Line had become too costly an objective to warrant our insisting upon it as a starting point for the breakout. We would settle, I said, for a less desirable springboard somewhere short of that cross-shoulder line.[12]

The new starting lines for a breakout were found in the St. Lo-Periers road.

Why did Bradley fail in his first attempt to break out of Normandy? Charles Whiting, in his book on Bradley, says that he underestimated the terrain. The hedgerow country was not properly traversed because Bradley lacked the mechanical means of overcoming the *bocage*. Secondly, he also says that Bradley underestimated the ability of the Germans facing him and that he dispersed his forces too widely. In looking for a soft spot to exploit, he fought too broadly from the coast eastward to St. Lo. These important factors contributed to his inability to find a clear path for a breakthrough. In the third week of July, Bradley prepared new plans. The results would show that he had learned his lessons well.

Among the many ideas presented to him at this time, one of inestimable value was the 'Rhino,' a Sherman tank fitted with iron cutters. With these cutters, a tank could dig into the earth, allowing it to slice through the hedgerows rather than turn its soft underbelly upward, exposing its most vulnerable spot to the enemy. This special tank was a welcomed addition.

On July 6, General Patton, fresh from his role as a decoy, arrived in Normandy. His Third Army was scheduled to become operational once the breakthrough was achieved. To say the least, Patton was champing at the bit for action. Soon after his arrival in France, German officers attempted to assassinate Hitler. Patton was afraid the war might end before he had a chance to deploy Third Army.

Patton wondered if he would be able to redeem his somewhat tarnished reputation. Though he arrived on the continent on the sixth, he did not meet Bradley until three days later. At that meeting Patton stated:

> For God's sake, Brad, you've got to get me into this fight before the war is over. I'mm in the doghouse now and I' apt to die there, unless I pull something spectacular to get me out.[13]

The addition of the 'Rhino' and Patton's added expertise allowed Bradley to plan a breakout, codenamed 'Cobra.'

As Bradley devised this offensive, his immediate superior, Montgomery, formulated plans for a British attack from Caen designated 'Operation Goodwood.' Eisenhower looked on Montgomery's plan with optimism for the Britisher promised 'bold strokes' and 'massive moves.' He amassed a vast array of power for this offensive. Unfortunately for him, the bold strokes of this ill-fated move netted no gain. It began on July 17 and was abandoned three days later on the twentieth. Though Eisenhower was disappointed, Montgomery's enigmatic strategy proved a boon to Bradley. In fact, Montgomery would later claim that his strategy all along was to tie down the German armor, thus allowing the Americans to break through in their sector more easily. There was some merit in the field marshal's claim. The British faced the combined might of seven panzer divisions while only one was present in the American sector. By drawing the enemy to his front, Montgomery paved the way for the success of 'Cobra.'

Bradley had truly learned his lessons from the previous unsuccessful attempt at a breakthrough. This time he planned to concentrate his forces on a narrow, six thousand-yard wide front, five miles west of St. Lo. He ordered the air force to lay a carpet of bombs along the highway in front of Collins' VII Corps. After saturating the corridor with bombs, it was planned to crash through with two infantry divisions. Then the armor could charge through the hole leading to Coutance and Avranches. (See Map 12)

Bradley was somewhat apprehensive about the air bombardment. Bombs dropped short are always a distinct possibility and he wanted to be sure this would not occur. He felt somewhat comfortable using the Periers Road as the bombing line because it would be, he reasoned, easily recognizable from the air.

> The bombers, I reasoned, could fly parallel to it without danger of mistaking our front line.[14]

To be doubly sure the bombs would not fall short, Bradley went back to London to discuss the operation with the chief airmen. He returned from England with a bombing plan even greater than he had anticipated. The airmen were most helpful and anxious to be of assistance. Bradley was still, however, fearful of bombs falling short, but he extracted a promise that the bombers would fly parallel to the road, thus insuring against mistaken targets.

Cobra was originally scheduled for July 21, but bad weather forced its postponement until the twenty-fourth and finally the twenty-fifth. On the first of those two days some of the bombers failed to hear the abort order and flew to the carpet area where they

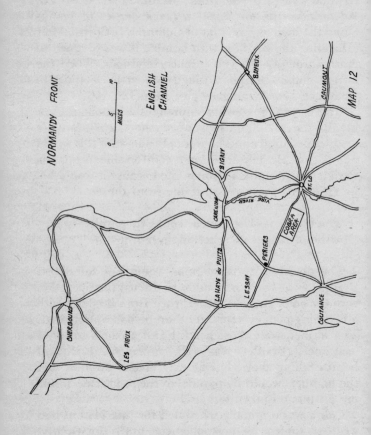

NORMANDY FRONT

ENGLISH CHANNEL

MAP 12

CHERBOURG

LES PIEUX

LA HAYE du PUITS

LESSAY

COUTANCE

PERIERS

COBRA AREA

VIRE RIVER

CARENTAN

ISIGNY

BAYEUX

ST LO

CAUMONT

MILES
0   5   10

dropped their load. Tragedy struck as some of the bombs fell short, the very thing Bradley was afraid of. How was that possible if the planes were flying parallel to the road? Very easy, the bombers did not make a parallel approach, but instead, came in perpendicular to the target. Why? Since it would take better than two and one half hours to funnel fifteen hundred heavy bombers down a narrow path parallel to the Periers Road, the air chiefs changed the approach. Bradley was deeply angered for a number of Americans lay dead and wounded from the 'friendly fire.' He transmitted his displeasure to the air chiefs who swore that it would not happen again.

On the morning of July 25, the sky dawned clear, a necessary prerequisite for the bombardment. 'Cobra' was on. For two hours and twenty minutes, the bombers dropped their lethal loads and pounded the ground in front of VII Corps. Miles away, the earth shook as if the area was being visited by a massive earthquake. Unfortunately, during the attack, as each successive wave of bombers dropped their loads shorter than the ones previous, some of the bombs landed on American units, causing more casualties, among them General Lesley McNair who was present as a forward observer of the bombardment.

Though off to an inauspicious beginning, the bombardment was devastating. General Fritz Bayerlein, a panzer division commander noted,

The planes kept coming, as if on a conveyor belt. . . . My flak had hardly opened its mouth when the batteries received direct hits which knocked out half the guns and silenced the rest. For an hour I had no communication with anybody, even by radio. By noon nothing was visible but dust and smoke. My front lines looked

161

like the face of the moon and at least 70 percent of my troops were out of action—dead, wounded, crazed or numbed.[15]

Numbed as they might be, many Germans miraculously survived and put up a determined defense. By the end of the first day, Collins' infantry had failed to reach their objectives. 'Lightning' Joe was now forced to make a bold decision. Should he commit the tanks or continue on with the infantry? On July 27, he unleashed his armor. The 'Rhinos' were of great assistance in clearing the terrain of obstacles. The armor rumbled its way south. Bradley was delighted with the progress. On July 28, Patton, anxious for a part in Cobra, was assigned to supervise the operations of Middleton's VIII Corps until his own Third Army could receive the green light, an event scheduled for August 1.

The lynch pin of the breakout centered upon the city of Avranches, lying between the See and Selune Rivers. It formed the hub of the road net from north to south and east to southwest. To Patton, this key city was more than a place to break through, he viewed it as a site to break out. Reaching Avranches on July 30, Patton pushed the corps through the gap. From there, the army could fan out south, east, and west in an operation resembling that of a shell burst. Field Marshal Gunther von Kluge, the German Commander in Chief West, succeeding von Rundstedt who had retired in early July, reported to German headquarters that, as a result of the enemy armored breakthrough, the whole western front had been ripped open.

On August 1, Bradley moved up to the command of the 12th U.S. Army Group. Now he was the equal of Montgomery, although the latter retained control of the ground fighting until Eisenhower established his headquarters on the continent. This was tentatively scheduled to take place around September 1. Succeeding Bradley at First Army was General Courtney Hodges and, of course, Third Army was officially activated under the bombastic Patton. Later, yet another army was added, the Ninth under General William Simpson.

Bradley's first directive as Army Group Commander was to send Hodges eastward to take the Vire-Mortain area while Patton was to secure the St. Hiliare-Fougeres-Rennes line. These were all necessary to protect the exit at Avranches, while also forming a line there for Third Army's westward movement into Brittany in an effort to secure vital ports.

Patton immediately ordered the VIII Corps to drive into Brittany. This area derived its strategic importance from the original Overlord assumption that the Allies would have to regroup on the Seine and there overcome a strong German position before pushing into Germany. With the arrival of bad weather, it was anticipated that Cherbourg alone would be unable to process enough tonnage to supply all the armies. Thus, possession of the Brittany ports was considered essential for the unloading of the Atlantic convoys.

Though caution was the prevailing feeling at Army Group headquarters, Patton was never one to worry about taking chances and usually, when given an order, interpreted it very broadly. Knowing that the defenders in Brittany were far from the cream of the German Wehrmacht, he threw caution to the wind and even though all Bradley had ordered was a bridgehead over the Selune, pushed Middleton's corps deep into the area.

On August 2, Bradley, hearing of Patton's order, went to Middleton's command post to discuss the operation. He found the VIII Corps commander furious over Patton's contradictory orders. Middleton wanted to follow Bradley's original decision and was not pleased with Patton's fire-eating brand of command. He was fearful that continuing into Brittany would expose his left flank and rear.

> I'm left with nothing, Brad, between my extended columns and the main force of the German Seventh Army to my rear.[16]

Middleton recognized the danger; the Germans viewed the move as a golden opportunity. On August 3, an Ultra picked up a conversation between Hitler and Kluge that read,

> The armored divisions which have up to now been employed on that front must be released and moved complete to the left wing. The enemy's armored forces which have pressed forward to the east, southeast and south will be annihiliated by an attack which these armored formations . . . will make, and contact will be restored with the west coast of the Cotentin at Avranches or north of that without regard of the enemy penetrations in Brittany.[17]

Thus, Hitler too recognized the possibilities for a major victory if the Germans struck from the east and recaptured Avranches, effectively isolating the American forces in Brittany.

Bradley was justifiably peeved at Patton and accused him of seeking headlines rather than using his head on tactics. He insisted that the neck of the peninsaul be blocked first, then the rest of Brittany would fall. Concurring with Middleton, Bradley went to Third Army's command post to confront its voltile commander. Encountering Patton who had just returned from the front, Bradley said,

> For God's sake, George, what are you going to do about that open flank of Troy Middleton's? I just ordered the 79th down there. I hate to bypass an Army commander on orders to a corps.[18]

Smiling sheepishly, Patton put his arm around Bradley's shoulder and said, "Fine, fine, Brad, that's just what I would have done."[19] That out of the way, Patton then described his operation.

Within a week, the Brittany coast was reached in a drive rivaling the German *blitzkreig* of the first years of the war. Unfortunately, Brest, the prize of the campaign, was stoutly defended by the Germans and would not be captured until September at a cost of ten thousand American casualties.

Patton's glory was not to be found in Brittany. The real war was further east. Bradley's first brush with the Third Army commander only served to confirm his previous fears of working with Patton. He had been apprehensive about accepting his former superior, fearing that he would not adjust to the reversal of roles. Fortunately, Bradley's opinion would soon be revised. Since the receipt on August 3 of the aforementioned Ultra intercept, the Allies were aware of Hitler's intention to mount a counteroffensive. On the morning of August 7, Field Marshal von Kluge launched a massive armored attack towards Avranches. The enemy managed to penetrate the gap between the XIX and VII Corps of Hodges' First Army. Mortain was overrun and the amassed weight of the offensive rolled westward towards its destination until it was halted by the combination of a determined stand by the 30th Infantry Division and Allied air attacks. Dubbed the 'Workhorse of the Western Front,' the 30th saved the day with their heroic defense.

Bradley, having anticipated the advance through Ultra, prepared to react. The offensive actually gave the Allies a golden opportunity to trap an enormous amount of German forces. By battling their way westward, the Germans were sticking their head in a noose. Instead of the Allies being cut in two, just the opposite was about to occur.

Bradley telephoned Montgomery and proposed another idea. Instead of attacking from Le Mans eastward towards the Seine as originally planned, why not turn ninety degress at Le Mans and allow portions of both First and Third Armies to drive around the German flank towards Argentan and Falaise, link up with the British and Canadians, and trap the entire German Seventh Army? Montgomery readily consented for he had already anticipated that very same move. He ordered General Simonds' II Canadian Corps to break through to Falaise and link up with Bradley's forces coming north. Bradley gave the task of linking up with the Canadians to Patton.

Right from the beginning, the Canadians ran into fierce opposition. According to Stephen Ambrose in his latest book, *Ike's Spies*, Montgomery disregarded Ultra information and attacked towards Falaise at the most inopportune time. Had he read his Ultra extracts, he would have seen that the 9th, 10th, and 12th SS Panzer Divisions were due to leave the Falaise area shortly and move towards Mortain. As it was, by attacking on August 8, Montgomery forced Kluge to cancel the order for the transfer of the Panzer Divisions. As Ambrose states:

> If Montgomery had only waited twenty-four hours, he could have had Falaise the next day.

As it was, the Canadians ran into the massed fire of two German armored divisions and made little headway.[20]

By August 12, the Canadians were still a long way from their objective. On the same day, the American XV Corps under General Wade Haislip reached Alençon. A wide gap existed between the Canadians and the Americans, a hole that had to be swiftly closed or the encirclement would fail. XV Corps moved towards Argentan.

Montgomery prodded the Canadian Army commander, General Crerar, to strengthen the attack towards Falaise. The staunch German defense was still standing firm. On the thirteenth, the Canadians mounted a large-scale attack. Simonds, the corps commander, ordered a division to push northwest in the hopes of drawing off some of the enemy strength from the sector of the main advance. Unfortunately, a copy of the plan fell into enemy hands and the Canadian effort was foiled. When August 16 rolled around, the Germans still held on to Falaise.

Haislip, meanwhile, after capturing Alençon, moved XV Corps towards Argentan which was reached on the evening of the twelfth. After securing the town, he pushed an armored detachment north towards Falaise, but was shortly ordered to halt. Why?

Patton had signaled Bradley that Argentan was secure and he was now making for Falaise. Authorization for a continuance of the advance was being sought. Patton stated, "We will drive the British back into the sea for another Dunkirk."[21] Bradley curtly responded, "Nothing doing" and ordered Patton to halt where he was, shut down, and build up a strong defensive line. Patton pleaded, ranted, and raged, but Bradley would not budge. He insisted that the boundary lines had been drawn and felt that Montgomery would not alter them. However, he failed to verify this fact with the field marshal. Post-war evidence indicates that Montgomery may have been agreeable to an alteration since his own forces were irrevocably tied down. The reason for the boundary in the first place was to prevent the converging forces from firing on each other's positions. Bradley felt that if Haislip strung out his forces further, he would be unable to establish a wall strong enough to prevent the enemy from making good their escape. He also obviously underestimated the amount of Germans remaining in the pocket. Whatever the reasoning, Bradley accepted complete responsibility for his actions and stated that at no time did the issue go beyond his headquarters. He explained that he preferred a strong shoulder at Argentan to a broken neck at Falaise. Not to be overlooked, however, is the fact that once more Montgomery failed to deliver.

As a result of the failure to close the gap at Falaise, a large portion of two German armies escaped the trap, albeit without most of their equipment which was abandoned. Nevertheless, as far as the Germans were concerned, the butcher's bill had been appalling and nothing now remained between the Allies and the Seine. Bradley was quick to recognize this fact and, a few days before the Falaise Gap was sealed, he granted permission for Patton to send most of Haislip's units dashing for that objective since reinforcements had moved into line as replacements for XV Corps.

The Falaise debacle continued to trouble Bradley. Should he have listened to Montgomery? Would so many Germans have escaped if he had allowed Patton to close the gap immediately? Unwilling to remain static, Bradley brought up units from other corps and allowed Patton to make for the Seine. Since little enemy opposition remained, Bradley realized that the road to Paris was now open. The entire incident marked the beginning of Bradley's disenchantment with Montgomery and the Englishman's boasts of rapid thrusts.

The German collapse far exceeded the Allies' wildest dreams; even Eisenhower had not expected this. He was now faced with a dilemma, how best to exploit the German collapse. The original plan called for a two-pronged thrust into Germany. Anticipating heavy resistance, tactic, named 'the broad front,' appeared the surest and safest method. Montgomery, however, wanted the 12th and 21st Army Groups to stick together and drive northeast into Belgium as a solid mass of some forty divisions. This single thrust, Montgomery emphasized, could drive into the Ruhr and knock out Germany's industrial capacity before heading for Berlin. The commander of this thrust would, of course, be Montgomery himself. The field marshal was acutely aware that on September 1, when Eisenhower officially established his headquarters on the continent, that it would be the Supreme Commander who would have the starring role and not Montgomery. Thus, if there was a way of retaining that position, he would do it. (For further coverage of this controversy, see the chapters on Eisenhower and Montgomery in Volume II of this series.)

Naturally, Montgomery was convinced that his strategy was the correct one. In effect, he was trying to retain full control and, failing this, he would try to convince Eisenhower to allow his 21st Army Group to make the major push in the north, relegating the 12th Army Group to one of support. Patton felt it was Sicily all over again where Monty had managed to convince his superiors to reduce Patton's Seventh Army to a role of supporting the British Eighth Army. This time,

Bradley sided with Patton in opposing Montgomery's machinations.

The news media played up the Bradley/Montgomery rivalry. Partisan writers backed their own champions and slanted articles to benefit the cause of their selected hero. Patton was a great asset to Bradley with his caustic tongue and biting comments about Monty's strategy. For the remainder of the war, both Army Group commanders continued to snipe at each other.

On August 23, a major meeting was held between Montgomery and Eisenhower. In no uncertain terms, the British commander presented his issues and demands. Eisenhower attempted to compromise. Montgomery's drive, he said, would be given priority because the V-1 launching sites and the port of Antwerp were in his sector. First Army, he went on, would be directed to thrust forward on Montgomery's right with its principal mission being the support of the British advance. Third Army was to continue eastward, but at a curtailed pace.

Patton was furious, Hodges angry, and Bradley dubious about the plan. The British chiefs were critical of Eisenhower's policy of splitting the forces. Brooke felt the plan would add three to six months to the war. Eisenhower's intended compromise failed to satisfy anyone.

Bradley agreed that the channel ports and V-1 sites were important. What he disputed was having to relinquish all three corps of First Army for Montgomery's use, instead of the one he was willing to give up. Furthermore, Patton, feeling short-changed since First Army was given priority to supplies and his army condemned to advance with empty fuel tanks, badgered the hell out of Bradley.

September found the Allies butting up against the

German border. The advance across France had been phenomenal, but the logistical situation was a nightmare. Supplies were still coming through the only available port, Cherbourg. From that point they had to be placed on trucks and moved to the front. Not only did the troops need supplies, but the liberation of Paris added that entire city to the logistical burden. It can be accurately stated that the rapid pace of victory contained within itself the seeds of its own demise. The Allied troops were so heady with victory they failed to notice that, when they reached the German border, the enemy appeared different. In a very short time, the Allies would come to understand just how much the enemy had changed.

As already seen, Eisenhower favored a broad front policy while Montgomery opposed it, feeling that one powerful thrust deep into the heart of Germany would result in final victory.

On September 4, the boom was lowered on the Americans as Eisenhower issued orders directing the forces north of the Ardennes. Montgomery's 21st Army Group and two corps of the U.S. First Army were to secure Antwerp, reach the area of the Rhine covering the Ruhr, then seize the great industrial area. Those forces south of the Ardennes were to proceed to the Rhine, and those in the north were to receive priority as regards to supplies.

Two days before issuing that directive, the Supreme Commander, returning from a visit to Bradley's headquarters, twisted his knee. This laid him up at a most critical time and prevented him from conferring personally with his commanders. Free from Eisenhower's influence, Bradley decided that Patton should not be held back, despite orders stating that the northern thrust was to be adequately supported. Amassing the little allotment of supplies sent to the First and Third

Armies, Bradley allocated one half to Patton and sent him moving to the Moselle River.

Meanwhile, Montgomery devised what was for him a most untypical plan; an airborne drop deep into enemy-held Holland along the main canals and bridges. If the operation proved successful, it could boost the Allies quickly over the Rhine and avoid a frontal assault on the main defenses of the West Wall (Siegfried Line). This operation was codenamed 'Market Garden.' Bradley's reaction to Montgomery's proposal was one of total surprise.

> Had the pious, teetotaling Montgomery wobbled into SHAEF with a hangover, I could not have been more astonished than I was by the daring adventure he proposed.[22]

Bradley was deeply affected by this operation. More supplies and the even more critical transports were diverted to support Market Garden. He called Patton on September 17 and informed him that the Third Army had been requested by Montgomery to halt all offensive action because of the need for complete support up north. Bradley was furious but Patton, with traditional bravado, told him not to worry. The Third Army commander went on to say that he would get so involved that they would be unable to stop him. He then told Bradley not to call him back until after dark on the nineteenth.

> This was a typical Patton dodge to involve himself in action although he wasn't authorized to do so. First, he would order a reconnaissance which, once it got itself involved with the enemy, would be progressively built up until Bradley found himself with a minor battle on his hands

and could report to Eisenhower that Patton would have to be supported or suffer a defeat.[23]

With Montgomery's subsequent failure at Arnhem, any possibility that the war would be over before Christmas was abandoned. The Germans had regained their balance and their former élan had returned. They managed to form a coherent line along the German frontier and everywhere the Allies hit they were repulsed by a very determined enemy. Patton was involved in a bitter struggle at Metz, Hodges was stalemated at the Aachen Gap, the recently arrived American Ninth Army fared little better just north of the First. The same situation prevailed in Montgomery's sector.

The problem of logistics continued to rear its ugly head. The need for a port nearer the fighting front was essential but, because of Montgomery's efforts at Arnhem, the clearing of the port of Antwerp was postponed. Now the Allies found themselves paying dearly for not having cleared the Schelde Estuary and making Antwerp available for use. The failure of Market Garden exacted a heavy toll.

It was clear that Allied strategy required reconsideration. Therefore, on October 18, Eisenhower met with Bradley and Montgomery in Brussels to discuss future plans. The Rhine was still the elusive objective, but Montgomery pointed out, if the Rhine was going to be reached at all, Bradley would have to avoid any major undertaking south of the Ardennes. Eisenhower did not concur completely, but he did agree that the major effort should be aimed towards the Ruhr in the north and that two armies should be used for this effort. This time, Bradley was given the starring role as his First and Ninth Armies were ordered to launch an offensive through the Aachen Gap at the beginning of

November. The First Army would aim for Cologne and Bonn, the Ninth Army for Krefeld. As for Patton, he was to hold steady until the logistical situation improved enough to permit him to mount a subsidiary operation aimed at benefiting the major effort further north. Montgomery was given the vital task of opening up the crucial port of Antwerp.

Patton was not happy with the prospect of inaction and convinced Bradley to give him the green light to proceed against Metz. Bradley agreed. The date for the offensive by First and Ninth Armies was set for November 5, Patton's five days later.

The fighting during that autumn of 1944 was marked by its ferocity. The bitter struggle at Aachen and the surrounding areas was only surpassed by the horror of the Huertgen Forest, a verdant hell. There, within the primeval pine woods, four American divisions were chewed up and decimated. Patton's forces met unexpected opposition at Metz and in the Saar-Moselle region. The frustration of these months of bitter fighting drained any bit of optimism remaining in the Allied High Command. One positive note, though, was the elimination of German opposition in the Schelde at the end of November which finally allowed use of the port of Antwerp.

Once again, Montgomery criticized Eisenhower's strategy. More than ever, he was convinced that the broad front strategy had caused the stalemate. Adopting a new approach, he told Eisenhower that, as the front was naturally divided by the Ardennes, this opened up the possibility of appointing one overall ground commander to control all operations north of Ardennes. Of course, the likely candidate for that auspicious position would be none other than B. L. Montgomery. Eisenhower refused to consider the proposal. Therefore, Monty remained convinced that disaster faced the Allies as long as the broad front policy remained in effect.

While the Allied commanders bantered back and forth, Adolf Hitler, a man whose bag of tricks was always full, devised a plan in which he placed his total hope for the solution of the war in the west. Hitler realized the importance of the Ardennes region; it was through here his great victory of 1940 had been accomplished and it was in this same area he placed his hopes for 1944. He was aware that the Ardennes was thinly held by only four American divisions. His fertile mind devised a plan to smash through the Ardennes and drive toward Antwerp which he felt would effectively cut the Allied forces in two. The determined fighting of October and November allowed the German leader time to prepare. The proposed offensive was so secret that those who knew of it did not even use the Enigma code to discuss the operation. The attack, when it came, would take the Allies completely by surprise. Though there were indications that the Germans were planning something, the Allied overreliance on Ultra and a gut feeling that the Germans simply lacked the ability to launch an offensive after months of bitter fighting, caused them to play right into Hitler's hands.

The Ardennes itself measured about sixty miles from north to south. It was beautiful country but militarily difficult. Omar Bradley deliberately kept the line thin in order to free troops for other operations under way to the north and south. The units holding the line were either new to combat or in urgent need of rest after the rigorous fighting in places like the Huertgen Forest. The front was the responsibility of Troy Middleton's VIII Corps of First Army.

Though most intelligence channels failed to warn Bradley of an imminent attack, Bradley himself considered the area a 'calculated risk.' General Strong, Eisenhower's British Chief of Intelligence had warned Bradley that the enemy might use his reforming Fifth and Sixth Panzer Armies for a spoiling attack in the Ardennes. Hodges' G-2, Colonel Dickson, noted a buildup in the Eifel and that high morale was evident among recently captured prisoners. In short,

> the fact that 600,000 Germans had been assembling and training for weeks, under the very noses of the Americans who possessed almost total air supremacy and had the most modern and sophisticated code-breaking computers and intelligence networks and were still caught flat-footed by the attack, was a scandal of considerable magnitude.[24]

Hitler's gamble depended on a variety of factors. First, he needed tactical surprise. Second, he required a long period of bad weather which would ground the Allied air forces. Above all, the Red Army had to remain inactive on the eastern front until he had destroyed the Allies in the west. When Hitler's blow fell on December 16, all those factors were present.

In the early morning hours of that day, the front before the Ardennes was rocked by heavy artillery fire. Then, out of the fog-shrouded forest recently blanketed by new-fallen snow, the Germans, alive with the vigor of youth, smashed into the weakly held American front.

That afternoon found Bradley at Supreme Headquarters in Versailles, studying the problem of logistics with Eisenhower. Suddenly, Brigadier General Edward Betts, the deputy Chief of Intelligence, came into Eisenhower's office and asked to see Major General Kenneth Strong, Ike's intelligence chief. Strong heard the news of the offensive, then reentered the office and announced,

> Gentlemen, this morning the enemy counterattacked at five separate points across the First Army sector.[25]

General Bedell Smith, Eisenhower's caustic Chief of Staff, reacted first by turning to Bradley and stating accusingly that he had warned of just such a possibility. In defense, Bradley shot back that he had, in anticipation of just such an eventuality, two divisions ready to intervene. He then went on to say that the enemy's attack in the Ardennes was simply a spoiling action aimed at forestalling Patton's pressure in the Saar and forcing the latter to divert forces to the Ardennes. Eisenhower retorted that this did not have the appearance of a local attack. If not local, said Bradley, then what was it? Ike was unable to clearly say since he was not sure himself.

Bradley was forced to send two divisions to help Middleton's VIII Corps defend the Ardennes. One of those two divisions, however, would have to come from Patton and Bradley knew that he would be unhappy at losing a division just days before a planned offensive. Eisenhower told Bradley to tell Patton that, "Ike is running this damned war."[26]

In misjudging the strength of the German forces, Bradley made probably his most costly error of the war. He freely admits in his memoirs that,

> In the face of this astonishing German build-up, I had greatly underestimated the enemy's offensive capabilities.[27]

However, he defends himself with,

> While I freely accept responsibility for our calculated risk in the Ardennes, I do not admit that there were any significant warnings given me which I chose to ignore.[28]

In that respect, he was partially correct. So secret were Hitler's preparations that no Enigma messages were sent regarding the operation. Too much reliance on Ultra had caused the Allies to lower their guard.

By nightfall of the seventeenth, Bradley began to change his mind about the intent of the German offensive. The next day, he cancelled Third Army's planned action in the Saar scheduled to begin on December 21 and ordered Patton to start planning a counterattack. Patton was a few steps ahead of everyone; he had already informed his staff to begin working on a plan.

Panic spread through Allied headquarters as the Germans drove a bulge into the American line. Middleton's front had virtually ceased to exist and heavy casualties were reported.

On the eighteenth, the very day that Bradley ordered Patton to plan for a relief operation northward, he and his aide, Colonel Hansen, left Versailles and drove to his main headquarters at Verdun before moving on to his advanced headquarters in the city of Luxembourg. This proved to be an error on Bradley's part for, by situating himself south of the major action, it caused him to jeopardize effective control of the entire battlefield.

On the morning of the nineteenth, Eisenhower called a conference of his senior officers at Verdun. Present were Bradley, Devers, and Patton. In the face of the crisis, Ike appeared cool and calm. He had to. The British had anticipated that the Americans would be unable to deal with the problem. Looking at the assembled officers, Eisenhower announced that the present situation was to be regarded as one of opportunity for them, and not one of disaster. In typical Pattonesque style, the general's response to Eisenhower's remarks was that we should have the guts to let the 'sons of bitches' go all the way to Paris! Then they would really be cut off. Patton's response to the crisis is an epic and covered in detail in the chapter on him. There is no need to repeat it here. In short, his conduct during the Battle of the Bulge is one of huge proportions and one that military enthusiasts will discuss for centuries. (See Map 8)

As for Bradley, the Bulge presented him with a personal command crisis. As the situation continued to deteriorate with each passing hour, Eisenhower felt that he had no choice but to give Montgomery command of all operations north of the weakened area. This included the First and Ninth U.S. Armies. Bradley was left with only Patton's Third Army to command. This decision held deep national ramifications. Since the battle zone was primarily American with hardly any British troops involved at all, the fact of the British field marshal commanding American troops in the crisis might suggest to the world an inadequacy in the American command and adversely reflect on Bradley's competence as a field commander.

Bradley protested vigorously to the proposed command structure, but Eisenhower stuck to his guns. Bradley was furious for he knew that his reputation was at stake. What he wanted was a clear presentation made to the press as to why the changeover in command was being made.

For unless the changeover were clearly explained by SHAEF, it could be interpreted as a loss of confidence by Eisenhower in me—or, more significantly, in the American command. If, as a result of the shift, the public were to lose confidence in me, Eisenhower would quickly remedy that situation by sending me home. But if his action were taken to mean repudiation of the American command, if it were inferred that we were bailed out by the British, the damage could be irreparable to our future role in the war.[29]

While Bradley wrestled with his command crisis, the fighting in the Bulge became more and more vicious. Two vital road centers took on great significance, St. Vith and Bastogne. Because of the mountainous terrain and the heavy amount of snow, the capture of these two towns was imperative to facilitate the sustained German movement westward.

Bastogne became very special to Bradley. In effect, Patton's drive to relieve that town was Bradley's sole command. He therefore took a personal interest in that operation since he knew his reputation was riding on the outcome. For him, the entire Battle of the Bulge was linked with the relief and defense of Bastogne.

Even when success was finally achieved on December 26, Bradley continued to interfere in Patton's plans. This was untypical of Bradley, but with his reputation damaged, he was desperate for a way to redeem himself.

By the end of December, another threat presented itself to Bradley in the guise of Field Marshal Montgomery. The debacle of the Bulge only confirmed Monty's feelings that Eisenhower's broad front policy was the cause of the crisis. He suggested a whole new command structure with himself as the commander of both the 12th and 21st Army Groups. In presenting his plan, Montgomery arrogantly implied that the current structure was to blame for the disaster and that a new one would avoid another catastrophe.

Eisenhower was furious at the insult and wrote back to Montgomery stating his anger. When Bradley heard of Montgomery's power move, he rushed to Supreme Headquarters and stated his opinion.

> You must know, Ike, that I cannot serve under Montgomery. If he is put in command of all ground forces you must send me home, for if Montgomery goes over me, I will have lost confidence in my command.[30]

On January 7, 1945, Montgomery held a press conference to explain his role in the battle. During that conference, Monty gave the impression that he was the only one who reacted positively to the German offensive. Immensely overstating his own contribution, he made himself appear a hero, the one everyone had turned to in an effort to save the day. By doing so, he slighted Bradley and implied the man's incompetence.

Not only was Bradley furious, but his staff was enraged as well. They implored their chief to make a public statement as to why SHAEF had divided the command. This Bradley did. In his remarks, he explained why Montgomery got control of the northern half of the Bulge and that it was only a temporary arrangement.

By doing this, Bradley violated SHAEF policy which directed general officers not to make public statements. Of course, this fact never seemed to deter Montgomery. Bradley also lacked the authority to state that the British commander's appointment was only temporary. But his hand had been forced. He wanted the public to know his side of the story.

Casting caution to the wind, he acted in an unusual fashion.

Besides explaining why Montgomery received command in the north, Bradley's press release also attempted to explain why the Ardennes sector was so lightly manned and why it was a calculated risk on his part. He then traced the countermeasures taken during the first four days of the battle prior to Montgomery ever becoming involved. This was the first the public heard that Montgomery's position was only temporary and that he had not received command until December 20, by which time the German spearheads had already been blunted.

This controversy between the generals threatened to destroy the working relationship so laboriously forged over the three previous years. As newspapers divided along national lines, the crisis approached a boiling point. Bradley and Patton both threatened to resign. Something or someone had to put an end to the crisis. And it was finally Winston Churchill who cleared the air by means of a balanced statement of the battle in a speech before the House of Commons. In the address, he praised Bradley's work during the counteroffensive. Thus, a command crisis was averted, but the scars remained.

Finally, U.S. Chief of Staff Marshall chimed in with his vocal support of Bradley. Eisenhower was directed to return First Army to Bradley's control, but Montgomery was allowed to retain Ninth Army.

Meanwhile, the Battle of the Bulge was fought to a foregone conclusion. The correct strategy for the Germans would have been to retreat from the Ardennes and defend the Reich from the Rhine, but the fanatical Hitler refused to heed his generals' entreaties of retreat. Every inch of German soil had to be held. Consequently, by defending the Bulge, the dictator reasoned, the Allied advance would be delayed. With that, the Germans signed their death warrant. By the middle of January, the pocket was sealed trapping eighty-five-thousand men and writing *finis* to Hitler's last gamble.

Bradley was now given a chance to redeem himself. This time, however, he would approach the command differently. He resolved to be less trusting of the British and made up his mind to seek less assistance from official channels. Although he was part of the team, he would conceal his plans from the British and report to Supreme Headquarters as little and as infrequently as possible.

With the situation in the Ardennes cleared up by mid-January, the next major objective for the Allies was the Rhine River. SHAEF plans called for the major Rhine crossing to be made in the north by Montgomery's forces. According to these plans, Bradley would conduct supportive crossings in the Mainz-Frankfurt area. This dual drive was designed to envelop the industrial Ruhr. After this area was secured, a thrust eastward to rendevous with the Russians was scheduled.

The British chiefs felt that Eisenhower's plans for a second crossing of the Rhine should be scrapped. Instead, they thought the other forces should pass over to the defensive upon reaching the river. Eisenhower did not agree. Perhaps he felt that U.S. public opinion would be against such a plan. Instead, he passed the British recommendation to General Marshall who applied pressure on the British chiefs by boldly stating that if Eisenhower's plans were not accepted, he would recommend his relief from command. The British gave in and Eisenhower was able to implement his own plan.

The Supreme Commander's strategy was composed

of three phases. In the first, Montgomery was to seize the west bank of the Rhine from Nijmegen to Dusseldorf while Bradley's forces conducted an active defense. In phase two, while Montgomery prepared to cross the Rhine with one of his famous set piece battles, Bradley would secure the river's west bank from Dusseldorf to Koblenz. As First Army struck for Cologne, Patton's Third would head for Koblenz. Phase three called for Montgomery's actual crossing of the Rhine while the U.S. Third and Patch's Seventh Army, part of General Devers' 6th Army Group, were to clean out the Saar-Moselle triangle and secure bridgeheads on the Mainz-Karlsruhe sector in preparation for a southern envelopment of the Ruhr.

Bradley was not entirely pleased with the Eisenhower plan for it continued to place too much emphasis on Montgomery's operations and the British commander still retained control of the Ninth Army. Bradley proposed an alternative. He suggested that the main thrust for the Ruhr be carried out by his own First and Third Armies driving straight through the Eifel to the Cologne-Koblenz area. This would give the decisive role to Bradley's Army Group while Montgomery held responsibility for covering the flanks. Eisenhower rejected the plan.

By February, it appeared as if Bradley was committed to the Eifel campaign. Although it would serve to lead Bradley to the Rhine, Montgomery was to have the major role. At that juncture in time, it seemed as if all the glory would be Monty's. The future, however, held a different destiny.

On February 4, Patton received a call from Bradley, informing him of the plans giving Montgomery the primary show. Patton was informed that he and Hodges were to swing over to the defensive while the British resumed the offensive in the north.

Bradley went on to say that this time the fault was not Ike's, but that the orders came directly from the combined chiefs themselves. Patton wasn't happy since he was convinced that his army had a better chance of crossing the Rhine. Taking a cue from Bradley's recent attitude towards Montgomery and SHAEF, in typical Patton fashion, he interpreted Eisenhower's phase one concept of active defense in its broadest sense and kept his scheme secret from everyone save Bradley. Let them find out what we are doing, he said, by looking at their maps.

Obviously, Patton was not content to have his army play a minor role. As February turned to March and Montgomery still had not reached the Rhine, the Third Army proceeded deeper and deeper into Germany. First Army was also making headway in their drive to the river. On March 7, a combat command of General Hodge's 9th Armored Division reached the Rhine near the small resort town of Remagen. There, to their amazement, they found a bridge over the river still intact, a rarity by that date. Frantic German efforts to destroy the bridge failed, thanks to the structure's sturdy construction and faulty dynamite. The bridge survived the blast. The Americans swiftly captured the span and, contrary to orders, Hodge established a bridgehead on the other side. (See Map 13)

Bradley was ecstatic. Eisenhower was also delighted and told Bradley to hold on to it. Though this deviated from the phasing plan, the Supreme Commander demonstrated his flexibility by not insisting on a crossing in Montgomery's sector only.

Now with the First Army having achieved a bridgehead on the river and Patton coming up rapidly through the Eifel on the left bank of the Moselle towards Koblenz, Bradley thought he

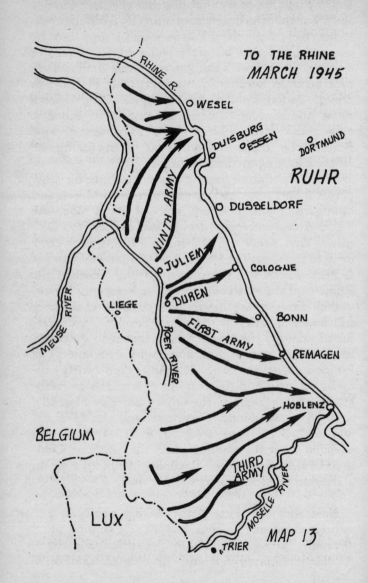

TO THE RHINE
MARCH 1945

RHINE R.

O WESEL

DUISBURG O ESSEN

O DORTMUND

RUHR

O DUSSELDORF

NINTH ARMY

JULIEM

COLOGNE

DUREN

BONN

ROER RIVER

FIRST ARMY

REMAGEN

MEUSE RIVER

LIEGE

KOBLENZ

BELGIUM

THIRD ARMY

MOSELLE RIVER

LUX

TRIER

MAP 13

saw a chance to give his own troops a chance to play at least an equal role with those commanded by Montgomery.[31]

Conscious that once Monty was across he was to divert his own strength to support that crossing, Bradley felt that it was imperative for him to obtain more Rhine crossings so that Ike might find it impossible to send his men in to support the British drive. If the First and Third Armies were heavily committed in their own sectors, it would be impossible for troops to be withdrawn. Bradley was taking a page from Patton's book.

He, therefore, gave Third Army a green light. Patton needed no urging. On March 14, he jumped off by crossing the lower Moselle southwest of Koblenz, then he headed for the Rhine. Five days later, Patton was within ten miles of Mainz. Bradley urged him to take the Rhine on the run.

The Germans anticipated a crossing at Mainz. Using deception Patton blanketed the river with smoke and, on the night of March 22, moved six battalions of the 5th Division across the Rhine at Oppenheim. It was a complete surprise. Though the Germans counterattacked, Patton held on and beat Montgomery across the Rhine by one day. That evening he excitedly called Bradley and shouted:

Brad, for God's sake. . . . Tell the world we're across! We knocked down 33 Krauts today when they came after our pontoon bridges. I want the world to know Third Army made it before Monty starts across.[32]

And the world was made aware of the event. Just as Prime Minister Churchill and the BBC were preparing announcements heralding Montgomery's move as the first major crossing of an enemy-held river in modern times, word came through of Patton's coup.

Bradley's improvisations yielded huge dividends. Eisenhower not only cancelled the order diverting his forces to Montgomery, but went so far as to order reserves to beef up the Army Group. Bradley had redeemed himself. A fourth star was added to his shoulder making him a full general.

In a lightning advance, the First and Third Armies continued eastward driving down the Frankfort-Kassel corridor in the direction that would take them east of the Ruhr. Ninth Army, still under Montgomery's command, meanwhile formed a left hand pincer around the north side of the Ruhr. On April 1, Simpson's 2nd Armored Division and Hodges' 3rd Armored closed the giant pincer by linking up at Lippstadt, trapping Field Marshal Model's Army Group B containing three-hundred-fifty-thousand men. Bradley was riding high.

The altered situation made Eisenhower revise his plans. With his armies successfully across the Rhine, he proposed to make the main thrust along the Erfurt-Leipzig-Dresden axis using Bradley's Army Group. Montgomery was to proceed to the Baltic while Patton advanced southeastward to meet the Russians in the Danube Valley.

To effect the final assault, Ninth Army was returned to Bradley on April 4. Now, one of the most controversial decisions of the war and one discussed at length in the chapter on Eisenhower, took place, the decision to halt on the Elbe. Churchill and the British chiefs reacted adversely to Eisenhower's decision to allow the Russians to capture Berlin. The Supreme Commander was completely confident that he had the backing of General Marshall in taking this course.

Ike's reasoning was that the greater part of Germany's industrial capacity remained in the area of First and Ninth Army. Rumor of a German National Redoubt also gave rise to fear of a last-ditch Nazi stand in the Alpine region. Militarily, therefore, those targets took priority. Berlin was simply a prestige objective. Besides, Bradley himself had said,

> I could see no political advantage occurring from the capture of Berlin that would offset the need for quick destruction of the German Army on our front. As soldiers we looked naively on this British inclination to complicate the war with political foresight and nonmilitary objectives.[33]

Forrest Pogue, Eisenhower's and Marshall's biographer, agrees that the military situation took precedence over the political.

Montgomery, of course, coveted Berlin, but Bradley was dead set against it for the reasons already stated. It was estimated a campaign to capture Berlin would result in at least one hundred thousand casualties, too many for a prestige target. Also, the Russians were to obtain their half of the city anyway, according to postwar plans for the division of Germany. In making the final decision, however, the fear of the National Redoubt was the determining factor for SHAEF. The war might be extended indefinitely should the Nazis lodge themselves in the mountains. Thus, the controversial decision to halt on the Elbe was made.

Little did Bradley know that the National Redoubt was only a myth, a plan without substance. Unfortunately, the fear of it was enough to make it an important factor in the strategic plans for the last few weeks of the war.

On April 4, Bradley issued his 'Letter of Instructions, No. 20.' This missive directed the recently returned Ninth Army to drive for a line south of Hanover about seventy miles from the Elbe. Then, it was to drive for the river and, if possible, seize a bridgehead over it (an order which appears contradictory to previous directives). Phase two of the instruction contained the possibility of an American drive on Berlin. Why would Bradley include this provision after what had already been decided? Perhaps there was still hope that America could wrest the political prize from the grasp of the Soviets. Anyway, the instruction was an enigma. Simpson, however, was eager for Berlin and was convinced that it was his for the taking.

By April 12, Ninth Army was ready to forge the Elbe. At 8 P.M. that evening, Simpson's army was across. With Ninth Army on the Elbe and the First past the Rhine and with the Ruhr systematically reduced, Bradley was anxious to push southeast and rout the enemy out of Bavaria. From there, he would push down the Danube Valley and head east towards Vienna. (See Map 14) Yet, Eisenhower hung the red light out in front of Simpson on April 15. It was Bradley who had to break the news. Though the First and Ninth Armies were ordered to hold on the Elbe-Mulde line, Patton was given the go ahead to launch a powerful attack into the Danube Valley.

On April 20, the Third Army, Bradley's last active command, began its southward movement. Plowing swiftly through Bavaria, it roared into Austria, exposing the National Redoubt as a myth. Czechoslovakia appeared ripe for the picking. Both Patton and Bradley desired a deep penetration into that country. Marshall intervened and put a halt to any potential political entanglements. The fear of an accidental clash with the Russians loomed large in Eisenhower's

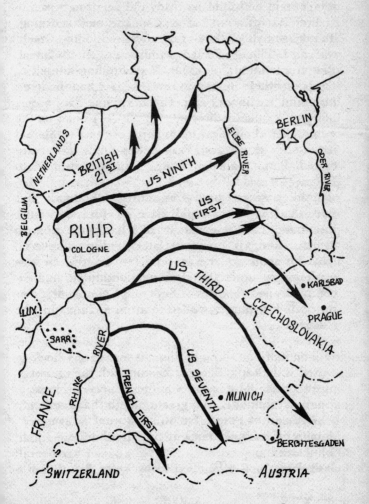

THE FINAL THRUST

0 50
MILES

MAP 14

NETHERLANDS

BELGIUM

BRITISH 21ST

US NINTH

RUHR

COLOGNE

LUX.

SARR

RHINE RIVER

FRANCE

FRENCH FIRST

SWITZERLAND

BERLIN

ELBE RIVER

ODER RIVER

US FIRST

US THIRD

KARLSBAD

CZECHOSLOVAKIA

PRAGUE

US SEVENTH

MUNICH

BERCHTESGADEN

AUSTRIA

and Marshall's reasons for keeping their hands out of Czechoslovakia. Eisenhower ordered Bradley to halt Patton while he waited to hear what the Russian intention was. Finally, on May 4, Bradley contacted Patton with the news that he could continue his forward move. Patton, flamboyant as ever and happy as a lark, said he would be ready the next morning.

True to his word, at 8 A.M. the next morning, Third Army's XII Corps advanced into Czechoslovakia. Though denied permission to enter Prague, Patton was intent, as usual, of embroiling himself to the point where he had to continue. He had made up his mind to liberate the Czech capital. His order, however, explicitly directed that he was to halt on the Pilsen Line about sixty miles north of the city. Should he disobey the order? Prague was ready to be liberated. Patton called Bradley. "Can you get me into Prague?" he said.

Bradley wanted to give an affirmative answer, but said that he first would have to find out what Eisenhower's attitude was. Bradley was not anxious to act first and ask questions later, a distinct reversal from his stance of the previous few months. He was unwilling to upset the close relationship he had recently developed with the Supreme Commander. For his part, Eisenhower wished to avoid a clash with the Russians.

'The halt-line through Pilsen is mandatory for V and XII Corps, George,' he said with the utmost emphasis. 'Moreover, you must not — I repeat not — reconnoiter to a greater depth than 5 miles northeast of Pilsen. Ike does not want any international complications at this late date!'[34]

Prague was not to be touched by Third Army. It was

to be left to the Russians.

At 4 A.M. on May 7, the telephone alongside Bradley's bed rang. It was Ike calling from Rheims with the news that the war was over. Bradley immediately called Patton, then Hodges, Simpson, and finally the commander of the newly formed Fifteenth Army, George Leonard Gerow.

With the war in Europe over, Bradley found himself scheduled to head to the Far East. Before that could happen, the war ended cataclysmically in a nuclear holocaust.

On August 15, 1945, Omar Bradley was appointed the Administrator of Veteran's Affairs, a post he relinquished on December 1, 1947, when he was appointed to the chief military post of the nation, that of Chief of Staff. In August of 1949, he was sworn in as the first Chairman of the Joint Chiefs of Staff. Exactly two years later, he was reappointed for two more years because of the crisis engendered by the Korean War. On September 20, 1950, he was given a fifth star making him the coequal in rank with Marshall, Eisenhower, and MacArthur.

After the mid-fifties, Bradley disappeared from the military scene. For some years after, though, he advised presidents and took part in many memorial services. His great contributions were, for the most part, behind him. He died peacefully on April 8, 1981, revered and respected by his associates as well as those who had served under him.

Omar Nelson Bradley's originality has been the subject of much criticism. How much of what Bradley said and did was actually Patton's idea? Colonel Codman of Patton's staff said that, as of August 1, 1944, Bradley had adopted practically all of Patton's ideas. Still other people praised Bradley for his keen ability. Eisenhower said of him:

A fine capacity for leadership and a thorough understanding of the requirements of modern battle. . . . The best rounded combat leader I have yet met in our service. While he probably lacks some of the extraordinary and ruthless driving power that Patton can exercise at critical moments, he still has such force and determination that even in this characteristic he is among the best. In all other things he is a jewel to have around.[35]

In a letter to Marshall, Ike summed up his evaluation by saying, "I consider Bradley the greatest battle-line commander I have met in this war."[36]

In summation, we consider Bradley a great commander for his steadiness and stability on the battlefield and for his concern with detail and the logistics of war. We concede he made errors in judgment such as those during the Battle of the Bulge. But his recovery was rapid and his refusal to panic during times of crisis were to his credit. After the Bulge, his campaigns in conjunction with Patton were bold and inspired. Bradley, the revered 'G.I.'s General,' will long be remembered as one of American's greatest.

Chapter 4

In May of 1942, a gaunt figure emerged from the Burmese jungle and entered the relative haven of Assam, India after weeks of travel by foot through some of the thickest vegetation in the world. Upon reaching New Delhi, he made his now famous statement:

> I claim we got a hell of a beating. We got run out of Burma and it is humiliating as hell. I think we ought to find out what caused it, go back and retake it.[1]

The speaker's name was Lt. General Joseph Warren Stilwell. Already in his fifty-ninth year, he had proven himself superior to most men thirty years his junior during the famous walkout from Burma.

In January 1942, Stilwell had been handed a mission to perform, one characterized as the toughest assignment ever given an American soldier. He was told to support China, but while he was given the job, he was hardly given the means. The theater he was sent to was low on the priority list, falling a distant third behind the European and Pacific theaters. Stilwell was made Chief of Staff to Chiang Kai-shek, a person whom he hardly respected and repeatedly referred to on his papers as the 'Peanut.' As an ardent Anglophobe, Stilwell was placed in the difficult position of maintaining constant contact with the

'Limeys,' as he was fond of calling the British. He was a man who personally nursed grudges, used verbal indiscretions freely, and disliked pomp and ceremony. In the 1930s, his saucy language earned him the nickname 'Vinegar Joe.' However, there was another side of the man which also caused him to be known as 'Uncle Joe.'

Stilwell's jobs were plural, his headaches multiple, and yet, against all obstacles, he managed to organize and command the first successful Chinese offensive of modern times against an extremely powerful foe. He proved to the world that the Chinese soldier, properly led, fed, equipped, and trained, could indeed get the job done. One writer has said,

> Only a most versatile soldier of high martial skill could have done what Stilwell did.[2]

Through a biographical sketch of his life, the authors will attempt to portray's Stilwell's command problems. Joseph Stilwell was a man who thirsted for action. At times, one might feel that he would have been more at home commanding at a battalion level rather than acting as theater commander. His command problems were immense, his answers to these problems prophetic, and, like the proverbial voice crying in the wilderness, his prophecies proved all too correct. What then was the background which spawned this enigmatic character?

The Stilwells trace their descent from Nicholas Stilwell who came to America from England in 1638, two years before England found herself embroiled in civil war. He acquired property on New York's three islands, Staten Island, Long Island, and Manhattan. Two of the Stilwells served during the American Revolution and one, Garrett Stilwell, rose to the rank of general. Joseph Stilwell's grandfather settled the family in Yonkers. His son, Dr. Benjamin W. Stilwell, obtained a law degree from Columbia University, but drifted from one occupation to another before settling down and distinguishing himself as one of Yonkers' leading citizens. He held many eminent positions as president of the Yonkers School Board and director of many of Westchester's county banks. Joseph was born on March 18, 1883, in Florida where his father, on one of his escapades, hoped to establish a lumber business. Young Warren (as the family called him) grew up under the constant gaze of his domineering father. Benjamin Stilwell chose Yale as the institution of higher learning for his children, but Joseph, who graduated from Yonkers High School at age sixteen, was deemed by his father too young to leave home and so had to spend an additional year in the local school system. This proved both a boon and a mistake. Having already graduated, Joseph found school boring and so, out of character from his previous years, he involved himself in many childish pranks which netted him more trouble than he bargained for. One joke, which got totally out of hand, persuaded Dr. Stilwell that the youngster required discipline. The father accordingly reasoned that the army was the only place for his unruly son.

Thanks to some wire-pulling, not the least of which was the persuasion of President McKinley, Joseph Warren Stilwell was appointed to the United States Military Academy upon the successful fulfillment of the necessary rigorous requirements.

Plebe year at West Point was an experience young Stilwell was eager to forget, but upon becoming an upper classman, he plunged himself into his studies with relish. He excelled in languages; in his other studies he managed satisfactorily. He also had a natural liking for athletics and enjoyed playing football, track, and basketball. Upon graduating in June 1904, he chose to serve in the infantry.

As a man of action, Stilwell felt that in the infantry he would get his share. As a shave tail 2nd Lt., his first assignment was in the Philippines as part of the 12th Infantry Regiment. Setting sail in October of graduation year, he embarked on a thirty-five day journey with only one stopover in Hawaii.

The Philippines at that time were seething with revolt. Ironically, the U.S. which prided itself as a symbol of freedom found itself putting down the rights of those citizens who desired self-rule. Many Filipinos resisted American rule, requiring the United States Army to ward off guerilla attacks by resisters armed with the dreaded bolo knife. In February 1905, Stilwell's unit, D Company of the 1st Battalion, was sent on its first expedition up the Gandora River on the jungle-covered island of Samar. This was Stilwell's first taste of the rigors and horrors of jungle existence. One experience almost cost the young officer his life, but his stamina saw him through the crisis. In his efficiency report from the company captain, he received a rating of excellent.

After fourteen months in the Philippines, Stilwell received orders early in 1906 directing him to return to West Point as an instructor in the Department of Modern Languages. At the Point, he taught English, French, and Spanish. During the fourth year in this assignment, he also became an Instructor of Tactics. Stilwell also found time to coach basketball, baseball, track, and football. A student of Stilwell's, the future General Jacob Devers of the class of 1909, said this of his instructor,

Sarcastic but in a way that made you want to
perform. I would have done anything for him.[3]

In the spring of 1910, Stilwell became engaged to
Winifred A. Smith and they were married the following October.

Not long after his nuptials, Stilwell and his young
bride set sail once more for the Philippines. Army
rotation regulations required officers to spend at least
two out of every six years with their regiment. Thus,
in January 1911, he rejoined his unit.

The second tour was confined basically to barracks
duty at Fort William McKinley near Manila. Promotion during peacetime was at a premium, but finally,
after seven years, Stilwell received 1st Lieutenant's
bars. He and his wife toured Japan extensively in
September of the same year. Then he saw Winifred
off to the United States before embarking on a tour
for the first time of the country of his destiny, China.

Stilwell's first glimpse of this vast country was
Shanghai, the great treaty port and center of foreign
influence in China. It was to a China rich in history,
but badly used by its inhabitants, particularly those
foreigners who raped its wealth and debilitated its
monarchy, that Stilwell came in mid-November of
1911. Only a month previously, Dr. Sun Yat-sen had
overthrown the decrepit Manchu Dynasty, thereby
establishing the Nationalist regime.

Stilwell remained in China for a mere seventeen
days which allowed him barely more than a passing
glance at that historic but troubled land. After
Shanghai, he continued by ship southward to Hong
Kong, the seething British colony of islands and
mountains. The mass of humanity and the thriving
foreign trade made a deep and lasting impression on
him. For the first time, he came into close contact

with British officers and his opinion was that "the English officer is a mess."[4] This prejudice remained with him for the balance of his life.

Leaving Hong Kong, he traveled to Canton where for the first time he was able to experience the true China with all its beauty and ugliness. From there he traveled up the West River on a British gunboat. Pirates, bandits, rebels, all the sights and sounds of revolution abounded around the young officer who was quick to absorb the experience.

Stilwell left China for Manila on December 9. The following month, he accompanied his regiment on their return to the United States where they were posted to the Presidio of Monterey in California. In August of 1913, Stilwell was again uprooted and returned to West Point to teach in the Department of English and History.

Desiring more out of his career, he transferred back to the Department of Modern Languages where he managed to contrive an assignment to Madrid in order to pursue the study of Spanish. Then, the following June, he heard of the assassination of the Archduke of Austria-Hungary by a Serbian nationalist. Within a month, all of Europe was engulfed in war.

For the next two years, while war raged in Europe, Stilwell went routinely about his teaching duties at West Point despite a yearning for action. Finally, in the summer of 1916, he was assigned as an instructor at a reserve camp in Plattsburgh, New York. His job entailed training civilians to become reserve officers in an effort to prepare the United States in case America entered the fighting.

In April 1917, President Woodrow Wilson, feeling justified in his action, declared war on the Central Powers. The United States with only one hundred and thirty-three thousand combat-ready men, went off to battle. The army faced a long and arduous task of creating a combat-ready force of decent size and training became the prime duty of every regular army officer. Stilwell, promoted to the temporary rank of major, was assigned to Camp Lee as brigade adjutant of the 80th Division. He arrived at his new post on August 25, but within four months, he received fresh orders to go to France where he was directed to report to the Commanding General, American Expeditionary Force, for intelligence duty. Though anxious for action, his knowledge of French netted a staff position.

When Stilwell arrived in France, he found an air of pessimism pervading the Allied camp. After four years of bloody warfare, the end of hostilities was still nowhere in sight. Already the flower of the youth of France and Britain had been slaughtered and a new harvest was being made ready for the meatgrinder. Albeit the United States was present, but its troops were few and badly undertrained and ill-prepared for continual warfare. In addition, Russia had withdrawn from the fray following their cataclysmic revolution. This resulted in the freeing of many German divisions for the western front, units that outnumbered and were vastly better-trained than those the United States injected into the war. Gloom thus found its way into the Allied camp, but not into the camp of the Americans. They were young, eager, and determined. They were also naive to the horrors of trench warfare.

Stilwell became Chief Intelligence Officer for the IV Corps and helped prepare the American forces for an offensive by accumulating as much information on battle tactics as possible. While visiting the battlefields, he witnessed first-hand the total desolation of war: villages in ruin, trenches scarring the once verdant fields, and the sickly sweet-smell of rotting flesh. He visited the staff headquarters of both the British and French. There he found the British snobbish and the French polite and helpful. He then attempted to learn all the various techniques utilized by the Allies. While at Verdun on one of his forays to the front, the Germans opened up their massive Ludendorff Offensive of March 1918. This represented the German's final all-out attempt at winning the war. One offensive thrust after another, lasting clear through July, saw the enemy push the Allies practically back to Paris, causing a great deal of fear and despair in the governments of France and Britain.

Remaining with the French, Stilwell personally observed the massive amount of devastation caused by the German offensive. His facility with the French language made it rather easy for him to be incorporated into the French XVII Corps staff, the first American officer to serve with that French formation.

Finally, on April 29, he returned to American headquarters. Though yearning for action, his lot was staff duty. Thankfully, he was transferred, not to a combat position but one which placed him at the heart of the planning for an American offensive, the reduction of the salient at St. Mihiel. For eight weeks, he prepared the intelligence reports for the operation. Traveling from one divisional headquarters to another, he garnered as much information as he could on the enemy situation within the salient.

For his excellent work, Stilwell was promoted to Lt. Colonel on September 11. The following day, the roar of the guns signaled the beginning of the American offensive. As the Germans were pushed back, Stilwell remained busy summarizing the successes. Even though it was a weakened German force they were fighting, enthusiasm ran high among the Americans.

Finally, on November 11, 1918, the western front fell silent. Stilwell found himself promoted to the temporary rank of full Colonel and awarded the Distinguished Service Medal for his excellent staff work. General Wells, the IV Corps Chief of Staff, had this to say about the new Colonel,

> Unusually intelligent. . . . one of the most capable G2 officers developed in the war.[5]

After the signing of the Treaty of Versailles the following May, the IV Corps was deactivated and Stilwell returned home in July. By September, during the general reduction of all officers who had received temporary ranks during the war, he found himself reduced to the permanent rank of Captain.

Upon his return from Europe, Stilwell took stock of his situation and decided that, it he were to remain in the army, he would have to concentrate more on advancing his career. On July 25, he went to Washington to appeal for an assignment that would be both interesting and challenging. Coincidentally, just at that time, the War Department desired to strengthen the American presence in China and Japan. Stilwell was therefore informed that the Military Intelligence Division was seeking officers who possessed proficiency in languages and who had prior service in the intelligence sector to travel to these countries for language training. Although he asked to be assigned to Japan, Stilwell found that all these positions were filled and so he settled for China, thus beginning an affiliation with that country that would last until 1944.

On August 6, 1919, Stilwell was appointed the first language officer for China representing the Army. The first step of the journey required the family to travel to the west coast where Stilwell was told to spend one year studying Chinese at the University of California at Berkeley.

Promoted to Major in July 1920, Stilwell and his family left for China on August 5. They arrived at the treaty port of Chinwangtao in September near where the Great Wall of China reaches down to the sea. Leaving this port, they traveled by rail to Tientsin and Peking, the fabled City of Emperors, which housed the famous Forbidden City with its beautifully constructed pagodas and artificial lakes.

The young major and his growing family (a fourth child was born to them in February 1921) settled into life in the famed city. He plunged into further study of the Chinese language. As language officer, he was placed in a position of assisting the Military Attaché in various projects, many of which involved social actions such as food relief programs and road building projects which would facilitate the movement of food to the starving populace. He also toured much of China which gave him a feel for the land and the people and cemented many friendships that lasted right up until the time of his death.

By 1923, his tour as language officer had come to an end. During those four years in China, he saw a country that most foreigners have never seen to this day. He traveled far beyond the traditional foreign haunts, treaty ports, legation quarters, and missionary compounds. He ate, lived, and slept as the Chinese did and knew the out-of-the-way hamlets and the shabby inns. He met the old, the sick, the opium dealers, the starving peasants, the bandits, and the warlords. His experience was invaluable and his stake in China's future firmly cemented.

On July 9, 1923, a few months after his fortieth birthday, Stilwell left China with his family and set off for home. He then went to Ft. Leavenworth, Kansas where he attended the Command and General Staff School. Attendance at that school was an essential requirement for any aspiring soldier hoping for the high reaches of command.

Upon completion of the course at Leavenworth, wanderlust seized Stilwell again and he applied for the *École de Guerre*, the French Staff College. Just then, however, he heard of an opening for a battalion commander in the 15th Infantry in Tientsin, China. It became an obsession with him to return to China. As the most qualified officer available, he was chosen for the vacancy and in August 1926, the Stilwell family again set out for China. His wife noted, "We all felt we were going home."[6]

The China that the Stilwells returned to was a different one than that they had left three years before. A disciple of Sun Yat-sen had come to the fore as the new voice of Nationalist China, his name was Chiang Kai-shek. As the head of the Whampoa Military Academy, he automatically headed the Nationalist, or Kuomintang, Army. All was relatively stable as long as Dr. Sun was able to control Chiang and the many factions within the Kuomintang, but when the illustrious doctor died in 1925, an immediate power struggle developed between its right and left wings. Chiang was the leader of the right with the Communists aligned on the left. Civil war was inevitable. Not only did Chiang wish to suppress the Communists, he also desired to unify China by incorporating the independent war lords under nationalist rule. This internal strife was also accompanied by a rising seige of xenophobia reminiscent of the days of the Boxer Rebellion. Foreigners began to fear for their lives.

The Stilwells arrived in China in the midst of this

entangled situation. The Kuomintang soldiers fought northward from their bases in southern China in an attempt to bring the northern part of the country under their domination. Being a battalion commander afforded Stilwell an opportunity to study the Chinese problems more deeply. He came into close contact with the 15th Division executive officer, one Lt. Colonel George C. Marshall. Though their tour of duty overlapped for a brief period of only eight months, it was enough time for the two of them to form a mutal respect. This bond between them would later prove beneficial for both, but more so for Stilwell.

Meanwhile, the foggy political situation caused a great deal of anxiety in Tientsin. The American legation there required first-hand information on the true strength of the Nationalist forces pressing from the south. They urgently needed a reliable appreciation before taking any action, such as evacuating all Nationals lest there be a repetition of the horrors which had taken place in the south. Major Stilwell was given the dangerous task of reconnoitering the situation. Apart from his great command of the language, his earlier forays into the interior of the country made Stilwell eminently suited for the assignment.

Therefore, he and his Chinese servant, Chao, set off on the perilous journey. It proved to be a most difficult one with their lives in jeopardy more than once. Stilwell endured days of hiding, was nearly executed and only saved by the quick action of his servant which allowed both of them to jump a train and flee to safety. When he finally returned, he was able to deliver a positive report on the conduct of the southern soldiers and concluded that victory over the northern warlords was inevitable. Stilwell's superiors were impressed with his courage and daring. His commanding officer said,

> Courage in battle when accompanied by comrades is often seen, but a much higher courage is required by any individual who attempts what Major Stilwell accomplished—the close contact alone and unaided with hundreds of ignorant anti-foreign Chinese troops of two contending armies.[7]

In January 1928, Stilwell was transferred from troop duty to general staff duty as acting Chief of Staff to the commanding General. In May of the same year, he was elevated to the rank of Lt. Colonel.

That same year, Chiang Kai-shek finally realized his goal by extending Kuomintang rule to Peking. The city's ancient name which means northern capital was changed to Peiping meaning northern peace. The capital of China, however, remained Nanking, further south where Chiang felt more secure. Stilwell, as the army's resident China expert, reserved comment on the Kuomintang. He was skeptical about its ability to bring real progress to China. This represented the first of many negative statements that would later flow from Stilwell.

In the spring of the following year, the Stilwells returned to the United States where he became head of the tactical section at Fort Benning's Infantry School, a position purposely reserved for him by George Marshall. During the four-year tenure at Benning, Stilwell acquired the famous 'Vinegar Joe' tag. Whenever stupidity or a poor performance by one of his students displeased him, he would caustically criticize the unfortunate young man. On one such occasion, a student drew a caricature of the abrasive Stilwell with a not too flattering expression rising out of a vinegar bottle with three X's clearly marked on the label. 'Vinegar Joe' he was dubbed and so it remained.

In May 1933, his tour at Fort Benning came to a close and he was reassigned to San Diego where he was directed to train the Organized Reserves of the IX Corps area. Though inwardly bored, he still took his job seriously and stuck with it for two years. Nevertheless, he yearned for a more fulfilling position. He was now approaching the age of fifty-two, not yet a full colonel, and his future failed to promise anything noteworthy. He began to harbor thoughts of retirement. During this period of despondency, a new door was opened to him; he was assigned as America's military attaché to China. The appointment was made official in January 1935 when he received the appointment from Secretary of State Cordell Hull.

Once more, it was a different China he set out for. Japan had seized Manchuria in 1931, thus strengthening her position on the continent while Chiang had pretty well eliminated the Communist threat by exterminating virtually all its strongholds. This necessitated a Communist withdrawal deep into the heart of China, the same retreat known in Communist folklore as the 'Long March.' Stilwell knew, as he returned, that China was yet to face its greatest trial, outwardly from Japan and inwardly from the Communists.

Newly promoted to full Colonel, Stilwell found himself back in Peiping during the first week in July 1935. A military attaché serves as an intelligence officer whose function it is to keep his War Department appraised of any significant military developments within the host country. The military attaché could use many various methods to achieve that goal, both official and unofficial. In this position, Stilwell became a close observer of the growing tension between China and Japan in the northern part of the country.

As he had done previously, Stilwell traveled from South China to Manchuria in an attempt to get a better feel for the situation. Traveling by bus, car, riverboat, and even on foot, he made his way northward. His mastery of the language gave him the ability to mingle with the population. On an inspection tour in the north, he found that Chiang's forces had no planned defenses against any possible Japanese encroachments. His reports on the Kuomintang's ability to deal with the military situation were laced with pessimism. In addition, he formed a very low opinion of Chiang Kai-shek's military ability which he noted in his private diary.

> He can have no intention of doing a thing or else he is utterly ignorant of what it means to get ready for a fight with a first class power.[9]

Stilwell was also disillusioned with the corruption he saw at the heart of China's government and lamented there were no other influential leaders able to take Chiang's place. His growing animosity to the Chinese leader's government would not be quelled, but continued to grow more and more as he observed the ineptitude with which Chiang was conducting matters.

Meanwhile, the European situation grew steadily more tense. Italy annexed Ethiopia, Germany marched into the Rhineland, civil war erupted in Spain, and fascism was on the ascendency. In China, the Communists continued to resist, albeit from their place of exile, but they continued to encroach further eastward and Chiang was intent on their destruction. Finally, there was the Japanese in the north.

Late in 1936, Chiang Kai-shek was kidnapped by

Chang Hsueh-liang while on a trip to Sian where he had gone to unleash the sixth anti-Communist offensive. The pretext for the kidnapping was to convince Chiang that he should abandon the civil war and ally himself with the Communists instead to form a united front against the Japanese. News of Chiang's death was expected momentarily. Fear of chaos ensued throughout China and in many foreign capitals. However, Chiang was spared for it appeared to all concerned that he was more valuable alive than dead, if only as a stabilizing factor. Even the Communists, although prodded by the Russians to believe otherwise, held misgivings. Only Japan reaped any benefits. The final outcome of this bizarre affair was the cancellation of the extermination campaign by Chiang, an increase in his prestige, and the formation of a nominal coalition between the Communists and Nationalists to aim their full force at the Japanese.

The West was impressed with what now appeared to be national unity. In reality, Chiang was more than ever determined to avoid, or at least postpone, conflict with the Japanese until foreign powers became involved, thereby bringing him enough assistance to defeat both his enemies, Japan and communism.

Stilwell, however, was not as gullible as the rest of the world. He saw what Chiang was doing and the realization would later bring Chiang and Stilwell to blows when they became directly involved with each other in 1942.

Japanese militarists, however, were upset with the appearance of national unity in China. They knew that they would have to strike soon. All that was needed was an excuse. Tragically for China, this excuse was given on the evening of July 7, 1937. While Japanese troops were conducting a military exercise near the eight-hundred-year-old Marco Polo Bridge, they were suddenly fired on by Chinese troops. War was declared immediately.

The atmosphere in Peiping was suddenly tense with the biggest problem being the anticipated reaction of Chiang. Stilwell himself attempted to investigate the situation only to be turned away because of heavy gunfire.

When the Japanese crossed the Great Wall, Chiang found himself with little option but to resist. He could not tolerate the loss of any more territory to the enemy. Within a week, the Japanese were in Peiping. Stilwell was thoroughly disgusted with the poor showing of Chiang's forces. Just as he had expected, the inept Chinese leadership and training methods left them wanting. Only the Communists impressed him as having adopted decent military tactics.

Chiang continued to resist.

From first to last Chiang Kai-shek had one purpose, to destroy the Communists and wait for foreign help to defeat the Japanese.[10]

Fortified with this belief, he drew the enemy towards Shanghai in the hopes that the foreign governments would intervene. The bloody battle of Shanghai lasted three months, but no friendly powers came to Chiang's aid and eventually the Japanese conquered the city and pushed the Chinese Army westward and southward.

Stilwell was able to record the atrocities the Japanese inflicted on the Chinese populace. Nanking headed the list by far as tens of thousands of hapless Chinese were indiscriminately slaughtered in an orgy of murder and rape. He hated the Japanese and found it very distasteful having to deal with them, but also knew that he had little choice since they were the new masters of the north and east of China.

In January 1938, after many months of haggling with the Japanese, Stilwell was finally granted permission to visit the battlefield. Once more he was able to record first-hand information which he continued to do intermittently throughout the year. He was able to form judgments which he took with him to the Chinese theater four years later. Stilwell found cause to criticize the defensive tactics of the Chinese, in particular their half-hearted defense which they were all too eager to abandon. He was appalled at their hoarding of reserves and the failure to commit their full strength. Had they done so, they could have enjoyed occasional success. But the Chinese repeatedly failed to take advantage of their greatest asset, superior manpower. Stilwell did note:

> The Chinese soldier is excellent material, wasted and betrayed by stupid leadership. Suppose the Chinese soldier were well-fed, well-armed, and equipped, well cared for and well-led.[11]

By the end of October 1938, the Japanese were in Canton, China's last remaining access to the sea. China was thus isolated from contact with the outside world by water and only one supply road remained open, a newly constructed trail in Burma which wound its way over some of the most difficult terrain on earth. The slender, precarious passage was China's only remaining outlet. Nevertheless, Chiang was determined to continue the struggle against Japan from his newly established capital in China's interior, Chungking.

On December 19, 1938, after months of travel and observation, Stilwell arrived in Chungking. There for the first time he met Chiang Kai-shek. Because his tour of duty was scheduled to end soon, Stilwell's stay in the capital was brief since he was faced with a long journey back to Peiping. In his diary, he noted that his fifteen-minute meeting with the Generalissimo was cordial. However, in summarizing his G-2 report a month later, Stilwell recorded,

> "Chiang Kai-shek is directly responsible for much of the confusion that normally exists in his command. . . . His first consideration is to maintain his own control over the best troops and material so that his position cannot be threatened."[12]

Obviously, Chiang placed his suspicion of rivals above the common cause. Distrustful of his subordinates, he never assigned good artillery to divisions. Instead, he kept the artillery under his own personal control. Then, of course, there was the ever-present danger of the Communists. These same circumstances came to haunt Stilwell four years later when he returned as Chiang's Chief of Staff and American theater commander.

Stilwell arrived back in Peiping after a short stopover in Kunming, the terminus of the Burma Road. The final months of his tour were bitter ones as protocol dictated that he kowtow to the occupying Japanese.

In May of 1939, he returned to the United States disillusioned and disappointed with his native land which had failed to lift a finger to aid China in its desperate plight. In fact, it continued to sell scrap iron to Japan which the Japanese fashioned into bombs and bullets which were then used to kill Chinese. Frustrated with his career, he returned, still a colonel, to a doubtful future. However, three days prior to his departure from China, an event had occurred which would drastically affect his life; his old friend George C. Marshall was appointed Chief of Staff of the United States Army. Stilwell's name was immediately submitted for promotion to Brigadier General. On August 3, 1939, the promotion was confirmed.

A month later, Germany unleashed its *blitzkreig* against Poland. Within forty-eight hours, Britain and France declared war. Hostilities had come again to Europe.

The American army Stilwell returned to was decidedly understrength and undertrained. Isolationism was the prevailing mood in America and nowhere was that attitude more starkly revealed than in the unpreparedness of its military. The newly promoted brigadier was assigned to command the 3rd Brigade, 2nd Division at Fort Sam Houston, Texas.

Over the years, Stilwell had been rather critical of the United States' Far East policy. Before traveling to Texas, he submitted his report on that area to Washington. More than ever, he felt that the government lacked the understanding of how developments in the Far East affected America itself. In his opinion, Washington's preoccupation with Europe at the expense of the Orient was a dangerous oversight. He was firmly convinced that war with Japan was inevitable. Marshall assured him that his reports were read and that the problems were understood. Not entirely mollified, Stilwell set off for Texas to take up his new command.

While the situation in Europe continued to grow more serious with each passing day, Stilwell was making a name for himself during corps maneuvers. His ability for aggressiveness earned him a second star in September of 1940.

The United States, meanwhile, shaken by the string

of Axis victories, decided to strengthen its defenses. In an effort to deter continued Japanese aggression in the Pacific, the fleet was moved from San Diego to Pearl Harbor in Hawaii.

On July 1, 1940, Stilwell was named Commanding General of the 7th Division stationed at Camp Ord in Monterey, California. Two months later, Congress passed the Compulsory Military Service Act and suddenly the ranks of the 7th Division were swelled by draftees. Over 85 percent of the compliment were recent inductees. He was therefore required to train men who, had they had their own way, would happily not have been in the military. Stilwell held battle maneuvers, intensified training, and staged parades, hoping to foster pride in the division. Using all the skills at his command, he managed to mold the division into a viable fighting force. The proof came in 1941 when the division excelled in simulated battle maneuvers. His ease among the enlisted men earned 'Vinegar Joe' a new nickname, 'Uncle Joe.' He also was known as 'Galloping Joe' because of his great capacity for walking. Soon that ability would save his life.

In the very same month that Stilwell became a Major General, the Japanese joined the Axis by signing the Tripartite Act. The sands in the hour glass continued to flow towards America's involvement in the war.

In October 1940, the Chinese presented Washington with a request for five hundred American planes manned by American pilots to fly against the Japanese. This request was prompted by Chiang's air advisor, Colonel Claire Chennault, a retired United States Army air officer. Chennault pledged huge dividends if he were given the tools to carry out an air offensive against the Japanese. In his appeal, Chiang also stated that the morale of China would be greatly uplifted by the arrival of the aircraft. Deep down, however, he harbored other ideas.

> While Chennault was pursuing brilliant visions of sinking the Japanese Navy, Chiang was interested in the strengthening of his own position that an air force with all its war material would provide.[13]

As usual, the Chinese leader's fear of the Communists exceeded his fear of the Japanese. In fact, the Communists had renewed their offensive against the Japanese in the hope of both safeguarding themselves against the Kuomintang and appealing to the people. In reality, Chiang did have much to fear from the Communists and these crosspurposes later caused Stilwell unlimited problems. In truth, therefore, the Chinese united front aimed at the Japanese was in fact a sham.

Chiang continued to pursue his desire for an American-run air effort. This air force, as conceived by Chennault, offered Chiang the short cut he needed to destroy the Japanese without loss of troop strength. These troops could then be kept in readiness for an advance against the 'hated and deadly' communists.

Chennault and T.V. Soong, Chiang's brother-in-law and envoy, traveled to America hoping to procure the desired aid. Though they managed to inspire enthusiasm in the United States, all they were able to obtain for their efforts were 100 P-40s. Though well below the number and not the type of aircraft desired, they were accepted and formed the nucleus of the famous 'Flying Tigers.'

The recruitment of pilots was much more successful because of the high monthly salary offered, $750.00 plus a $500.00 bonus for every Japanese plane shot down. The American Volunteer Group (AVG) reached Burma in November 1941 and began its extensive training under the redoubtable Chennault.

In addition to the formation of the AVG, China now found aid from another corner. In March 1941, Congress passed the Lend-Lease Act. An abundance of supplies now began to pour into China, rifles, mortars, machine guns, field guns, tanks, etc. This action cemented the United States to the Nationalist cause.

It quickly became apparent that China's coffers were bottomless pits. However, few in America understood except perhaps Stilwell, that much of the material was not to be used against the Japanese, but rather would be stockpiled by the Central Government and used against insurrection within China. The support continue to flow, but there were no guarantees forthcoming as to how it would be used.

Meanwhile, the war broadened when the Germans invaded the Soviet Union on June 22, 1941, opening up for Germany the spectre of a two-front war. Japan took advantage of this opportunity and moved into Indo-China in July. This incident forced the United States to freeze all Japanese assets in the country and to enact an oil embargo against the aggressors. Thus, another step towards war was taken.

In the interim, Stilwell's career took yet another upward turn when he was given command of the III Corps in the summer of 1941.

As summer turned to fall, Japan slipped closer to outright fighting with the United States. The Japanese desperately needed natural resources for their war machine, particularly oil and all of these were available in Southeast Asia and the Dutch East Indies. Japan realized that Britain and the United States would have to be challenged if it were to fulfill its destiny and continue to establish its Greater East Asia

Co-Prosperity Sphere. The big question debated in their highest circles was how to do it with the insurance of the greatest success.

The United States Pacific Fleet was by now in Pearl Harbor. That fleet presented Japan with its greatest threat; it was like a sword pointed at the very heart of the Empire. Admiral Isoruku Yamamoto, the Commander in Chief of the Combined Fleet, therefore proposed a secret attack on the naval and air bases at Pearl Harbor. That quick blow, he said, would buy the necessary time for Japan to consolidate its conquests. With the adoption of this plan, Japan was ready to move. Only the politicians could halt the attack if they could obtain, via negotiation, what Japan was ready to seize by force. The United States Intelligence Agency, having broken the Japanese code, followed enemy aggressive talk closely. America knew that Japan intended to move, but unfortunately, they did not know Pearl Harbor was the target until the 'Day of Infamy,' December 7, 1941.

That sunny December day, Stilwell and his wife were leisurely spending the day with an officer from Fort Ord when word of the daring attack was received. Stilwell suddenly found himself responsible for the southern sector of the Western Defense Command, covering the California coast down to the Mexican border. Although he knew that California was beyond the reach of the Japanese, a feeling of alarm and confusion reigned there. The general was painfully aware that American forces were woefully inadequate to repel an invasion if indeed one did come.

Stilwell spent the remaining days of that anxious December traveling up and down the coast, conferring with city leaders and helping them organize warning procedures. Meanwhile, as the fear of invasion prevailed in California, the Japanese Imperial Army and Navy scored resounding victories in the Pacific. The entire scene filled Stilwell with a sense of horror.

At 6:30 A.M. on December 22, the general was awakened by a call ordering him to Washington at once "to work on a war plan for some expeditionary force which implied I was to command."[14]

He and his Chief of Staff, Colonel Frank Dorn, reached Washington on Christmas Eve. Arriving at the War Plans Division, he was presented with the startling news that he had been chosen to command the first American offensive, a landing in French West Africa. Marshall had chosen Stilwell because of the great respect the Chief of Staff held for the general's abilities as a master tactician.

Stilwell soon learned that the destination of the offensive was far from conclusive. A top-level conference known as Arcadia was at that time in session with both Winston Churchill and Franklin D. Roosevelt present. Both leaders accepted the pre-war plan that, in case of a two-ocean war, the European enemy would be the primary target. How and when that target would be assaulted, however, remained vague.

While Stilwell and his staff grappled with potential European or Asian operations, the Japanese war machine continued its unrestricted advance. Hong Kong fell on Christmas Day, Manila a week later, and soon Thailand was occupied. The Japanese Army was advancing down the neck of Malaya towards the 'Pearl of the Orient,' the great British base at Singapore. Burma was being threatened and, with it, China's final remaining link to the outside, the Burma Road. The Chinese rejoiced over the news of Pearl Harbor for now they felt they were not alone in their struggle against Japan. Chiang issued a list of plans which he felt would bring the Japanese to their knees in 1942. Unfortunately, his plans were not in keeping with the

Europe-first strategy accepted by the combined Chiefs of Staff.

To Chiang, Burma now loomed as the land of great importance. It was the only route for lend-lease aid to flow into the country. Already, tons of equipment were in Rangoon awaiting shipment over the precarious route. Burma was also important to a number of other factions. To the British, it represented a buffer to India. To the Japanese, it represented a crucial area that could act to isolate China and protect its own conquests. Therefore, Burma was fated to be an important battleground.

Chiang Kai-shek and the British Theater Commander, Sir Archibald Wavell, met in Chungking to discuss aid to the Chinese and the Burmese situation. Wavell knew that the British did not possess the force necessary to halt the Japanese onslaught, but he was also unhappy with Chiang's plan. The latter offered Chinese troops to the British to help in the fight to keep Burma from the Japanese. Wavell, however, knew that China had traditional claims to Burma which they had never renounced. What guarantee was there that once the Chinese entered Burma they would ever leave? Feeling somewhat apprehensive, Wavell accepted only one Chinese division to aid in the defense of Burma. Chiang was infuriated with the British for this obvious insult which was but one of many he suffered at their hands. The alliance did not hold much prospect of success.

The United States was unhappy with the British snub of China; it felt tradition bound to fight for and with the Chinese.

America wore China like an albatross around her neck. Shantung, the unfulfilled nine-power guarantee, the important Stimson Doctrine, the scrap sold to Japan, the 'special' American relationship, the return of the Boxer indemnities, the theory of a strong China after the war—all were part of the burden, a compound of guilt, guardianship, and illusion.[15]

General Marshall knew it was important to keep China fully committed to fight alongside the Allies. He argued the necessity of building up China's confidence in British-American joint purposes in the Far East. The Americans felt that it was the British imperialistic ways that were getting in the way of true coalition warfare. The United States' opinion was that if China went under it would free untold numbers of Japanese divisions to attack Australia or even link up with a German advance through the Near East. The Americans also feared that the 'Wavell incident' would upset Chiang enough to cause the Chinese leader to seek an armistice with the Japanese (an unlikely eventuality).

President Roosevelt also had plans about China's role after the war. Roosevelt felt China would be needed to fill the void left by a defeated Japan. It was therefore important to prop up the current Chinese government militarily. Furthermore, if China was going to function as a great power, it must be treated as one, Roosevelt added. The British, however, felt that aid to China was a waste of valuable material that could be used more beneficially elsewhere. This divergence of opinion also caused Stilwell years of difficulty and frustration.

Washington felt that a high-ranking American officer should be sent to China. Chiang himself even recommended that very same thing. General Drum's name was tossed about, but it soon appeared that he was not qualified to deal with the Chinese, nor did he desire to go once he realized what the job entailed. On January 14, Stilwell was invited to the home of Secretary of War, Henry Stimson. After lengthy discussions during which Stilwell summed up the situation in China superbly, Stimson was convinced that he had found the right man for the job. He later said, "So I went to bed with a rather relieved feeling that I had discovered a man who will be very useful."[16]

The Secretary was thoroughly impressed by Stilwell's enthusiasm and knowledge and would, over the difficult years ahead, be one of the general's most ardent supporters.

Marshall also knew that Stilwell was the most qualified, but felt somewhat dismayed that the new command for his friend could wind up being a waste of one of America's most talented combat commanders. Never had one military figure ever accepted such a diverse and complicated assignment. First of all, he was to be the Chief of Staff to the Chinese Theater commander, Chiang Kai-shek. Second, he was to secure China as a base for early operations against Japan. Third, he was to insure that China would never make a separate peace with the Japanese. Then he was to supervise the disposition of lend-lease aid and also take control of all American air operations in China. Finally, he was required to arm, equip, and train the Chinese forces in China for offensive operations against the enemy. But the big question remaining, and one which haunted Stilwell as he pondered whether to accept this illustrious if somewhat dubious command, was what guarantee did he have that the Generalissimo would allow an American officer full control over the disposition of Chinese troops? That remained to be seen.

Meanwhile, the Japanese approached Singapore

while more of their forces were readying themselves for an advance against Burma, an operation that finally commenced on January 20, 1942.

Three days later, it became official that Stilwell was to be the one to go to China. When Marshall asked him, the general's reply was, "I'll go where I'm sent," but privately Stilwell noted, "The blow fell".[17] His private papers express his doubts; he looked upon himself as a goat being sacrificed on a pyre. He was haunted by many questions. Will the Chinese play ball or will they sit back and let us do it? Will the British (he called them "Limeys') cooperate?

The newly promoted Lt. General was designated Commanding General of the United States forces in the China-Burma-India Theater, Chief of Staff to the Supreme Commander China Theater, Supervisor of Lend-Lease, and U.S. representative on any Allied war council. His functions were to maintain the Burma Road, command Chinese forces assigned to him in the field, assist in improving the combat efficiency of the Chinese army, and increase the effectiveness of American assistance to the Chinese government. In all, Stilwell had eight different titles and functions. Before leaving for China, two more duties were heaped on his shoulders, the opening of an air route to supply China in the event the Burma Road was severed and the construction of a new road from India.

As Stilwell prepared himself, studying the latest reports, meeting with Stimson, the President, Marshall, and Harry Hopkins, the situation in Burma continued to deteriorate. By February 9, the Japanese had crossed the Salween River and were only a hundred miles from the Sittang River, the last natural barrier before Rangoon. In addition, they were ready to storm Singapore Island. On all fronts, the Japanese held the initiative.

On February 13, Stilwell and his staff left the United States. The trip took twelve days in all. They went through South America, across to Cairo, east thru Palestine, Iraq, and Persia, then to New Delhi. While in transit, Singapore fell to the Japanese on February 15. Now more than ever Burma loomed as the decisive field of battle. Should the Japanese manage to capture it, they would have an ideal base for action against India. Furthermore, if the Germans were successful in breaking through the Middle East into Asia, the Axis forces could then unite to conquer all of Asia. Meanwhile, the situation before Rangoon worsened.

In New Delhi, Stilwell attended a conference at general headquarters. He was appalled at the situation, especially the lack of a coordinate strategy. From New Delhi, the despondent general moved on to Calcutta where he met the disheartened commander of the American, British, Dutch, Australian Command, Wavell. On March 3, Stilwell and his entourage left Calcutta on the last leg of their journey to China's wartime capital, Chungking, where Stilwell was to establish his headquarters, report personally to the Generalissimo, and clarify his command status. (See Map 15).

En route to Chungking by air, Stilwell flew over the densely grown Brahmaputra delta and the verdant hills of Assam and over the mountains of Burma into Lashio. At Lashio, he met Chiang Kai-shek and his wife, Madame Chiang, who were there to give direction to their troops in Burma. The Generalissimo was cordial, but the meeting was brief. An hour later, Stilwell continued his journey to China and arrived at Kunming a few hours later where he remained overnight as a guest of Chennault. There, he settled an

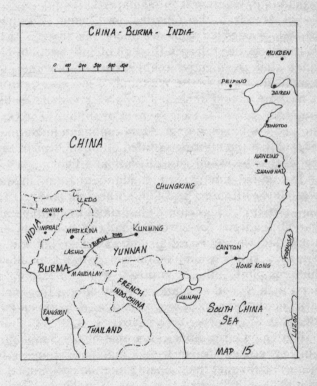

CHINA - BURMA - INDIA

0   100   200   300   400   500

MUKDEN

PEIPING

DAIREN

TSINGTOO

CHINA

NANKING

SHANGHAI

CHUNGKING

KOHIMA

LEDO

INDIA

IMPHAL

MYITKYINA

KUNMING

BURMA ROAD

LASHIO

YUNNAN

CANTON

BURMA

MANDALAY

HONG KONG

FRENCH

INDO-CHINA

FORMOSA

HAINAN

RANGOON

SOUTH CHINA

SEA

THAILAND

LUZON

MAP 15

issue with the commander of the Flying Tigers that was the cause of some concern in Washington, the incorporation of the American Volunteer Group into the American Army Air Force. Chennault was friendly and receptive to the proposal, but the pilots were not too pleased with the prospect of losing the higher pay and bonuses. The next day, after a two hour flight, Stilwell arrived in Chungking (the 'manure pile' as he would later describe it in his papers).

On March 6, he reported to Chiang Kai-shek. Stilwell wanted to convince the Generalissimo that Burma could be salvaged through offensive action. He knew that an offensive could serve two purposes, to keep China open to the West and, if successful, instill a measure of confidence in the fighting soldier. To his immense relief, Chiang agreed with him and expressed a willingness to give him command in Burma. Stilwell left the meeting satisfied and confident in the belief that he would go to Burma and fight.

But as the time passed, a summons from Chiang was not forthcoming and Stilwell became anxious. In the interim, he occupied his time by developing various strategies for Burma. Finally at the end of the third day, Chiang issued a command plan, but it was one that Stilwell could not approve of. It did not allow him complete authority, instead, it placed him on a level with the other Chinese commanders. This incident marked the beginning of a struggle between the two that would never be resolved.

During an after-dinner discussion of the campaign, Stilwell politely listened to Chiang's discourse. It became clear that the Chinese leader did not trust the British and felt that they would probably simply retreat and leave the Chinese units to fight it out on their own. It was also obvious that Chiang had no intention of risking his Fifth and Sixth Armies. His avowed strategy was the very opposite of that advocated by Stilwell. The American soon realized that the Chinese-British mistrust of each other's motives would be fatal to the future of Burma.

The Generalissimo, however, was willing to make some concessions, foremost being the turning over of the Fifth and Sixth Armies to Stilwell's control. Chiang even went so far as to suggest that Stilwell should become the Allied Commander in Burma. The delicacy of the situation, however, dictated ignoring that course.

By the time Stilwell entered northern Burma, Rangoon had fallen and the British and Indian troops were retreating to the west (See Volume II, *The British*, Chapter 6.) Northern Burma had to be held and plans were therefore organized along those lines. The Allied intention was to hold a line from Prome to Toungoo, about one hundred and fifty miles north of Rangoon. Stilwell's Chinese forces were to move south to Mandalay where they would build, along with the British and Indian units, an impenetrable barrier to the Japanese advance. Stilwell established his headquarters at Maymyo, northeast of Mandalay.

The first order of business upon arriving in Burma was to pay a courtesy call on the British Governor-General. The Englishman was completely astonished to hear that an American was the commander of the Chinese armies in Burma. The British were doubly perplexed when General Tu li-ming, the commander of the Fifth Army, called himself the Commander of the Chinese armies in Burma. When the Governor-General asked the Chinese general how both could hold the same title, the reply was,

The American General only thinks he is commanding. In fact he is doing no such thing. You see, we Chinese think that the only way to keep the Americans in the war is to give them a few commands on paper. They will not do much harm as long as we do the work.[18]

This, of course, posed a monumental problem. What was Stilwell's true position?

While at Maymyo, Stilwell met the new British military commander in Burma, General Harold Alexander, who had taken over Wavell's position when the latter reverted to Commander in Chief, India. Churchill had dispatched Alexander to Far East to help prop up the decaying situation. However, there was little he could do to save Rangoon.

The first meeting between Stilwell and Alexander was recorded by the latter.

> Friday the 13th. Alexander arrived. Very cautious. Long sharp nose. Rather brusque and standoffish. . . . Astonished to find me—mere me, a goddam American—in command of Chinese troops. "Extrawdinery!" Looked me over as if I had just crawled out from under a rock.[19]

Arrangements were made between the two commanders for unity of command. Stilwell reported to Marshall that he would be willing to serve under Alexander.

Now all Stilwell required was permission from Chiang to unleash the Chinese divisions. It must be understood that here Stilwell was up against a great cultural barrier. In the Chinese army, each division was usually based on a province whose divisional commander was often the local civilian governor. Many of the commanders were war lords who had served Chiang, but owed him only dubious loyalty. Their divisions were their only assets and sources of income. Therefore, they would be unlikely to attack any enemy with vigor. Loss of a division, beside signifying the loss of one's wealth, also meant a loss of face for the commander. Moreover, throughout history the Chinese forces had never fought a battle resulting in destruction of their forces. The old adage of living to fight another day was strictly adhered to by Chinese commanders. Another saying, just as meaningful, was 'Let others do the fighting.' Stilwell was up against culture and corruption.

Nonetheless, he believed that the Chinese would fight to save their own country. In order to persuade the Generalissimo, Stilwell, along with Shang Chen, Chief of Foreign Liaison, flew back to Chungking on March 17. For two days they argued. Shang Chen reported to the general staff and managed to gain from them an assurance that they would in turn urge Chiang to consent to Stilwell's orders. It appeared as if he would.

Meanwhile, Marshall managed to extract a concession from Churchill. Instead of unity of command in Burma, a dual command arrangement was organized between Alexander and Stilwell. This, Marshall felt, would insure Chinese participation. Roosevelt pressured Churchill to agree.

Chiang Kai-shek finally granted permission for the use of Chinese troops, but only if they were under Stilwell's command and used only in an emergency.

He did not desire to sacrifice his troops in a lost cause and he stated emphatically that his Fifth and Sixth Armies were not to be defeated.

Before Chiang could vacillate again, Stilwell flew quickly to Lashio where he signed the orders unleashing the Chinese divisions. Despair, unfortunately, was in the offing. The Chinese moved without any air support because the Japanese had already gained command of the skies. The enemy's northward offensive was launched in all its fury. Stilwell ordered the 22nd Chinese Division to attack and twice they refused. Every order Stilwell sent out had to be relayed first to Chiang through his generals, who then relayed the response back. Stilwell found his authority constantly challenged, every order was scrutinized. He was a commander tied down with fetters. If Chiang did not agree with Stilwell, he simply ordered something else not in conformity with the American's intention. The exasperated Stilwell was determined to reverse this situation. The Chinese just would not move, procrastination was the order of the day and while they delayed, the Japanese continued to move northward.

At Prome, the British corps commander, Lt. General William Slim, attempted to organize a counterattack, but morale among the British imperial forces was low and Prome had to be evacuated. This maneuver uncovered the Chinese flank, the very thing that Chiang had warned against. This was the first contact between Slim and Stilwell in the campaign. Slim was one of the few British commanders to regard 'Vinegar Joe' with respect. The feeling was mutual. In his own book, Slim said,

These were my first active contacts with Stilwell, who had arrived in Burma a few days after me. He already had something of a reputation for shortness of temper and for distrust of most of the rest of the world. I must admit he surprised me a little when, at our first meeting, he said, 'Well, General, I must tell you that my motto in all dealings is buyer beware,' but he never, as far as I was concerned, lived up to that old horse trader's motto. He was over sixty, but he was tough, mentally and physically; he could be as obstinate as a whole team of mules; he could be, and frequently was, downright rude to people whom, often for no very good reason, he did not like. But when he said he would do a thing, he did it. . . . He was a real leader in the field, no one else I know could have made his Chinese do what they did. He was, undoubtedly, the most colorful character in Southeast Asia — and I liked him.[20]

Meanwhile, Alexander went to Chungking where, to Stilwell's amazement, Chiang accepted the British general as overall commander. It appeared that unity of command was now a reality. Stilwell never did figure out Chiang's reasoning.

Stilwell left for Chungking on April 1 for a showdown with Chiang Kai-shek. He knew where the orders were coming from.

I have to tell Chiang Kai-shek with a straight face that his subordinates are not carrying out his orders, when in all probability they are doing just what he tells them.[22]

Chiang was the root of all his troubles. Had the Chinese leader not halted the movement of the 22nd Division, the Japanese could have been cut off around Toungoo. Instead, the Generalissimo ordered his forces to hold Mandalay.

During the course of their meeting, Stilwell informed Chiang that he was going to request to be relieved unless he was given an independent army under his command. Chiang and his wife did all they could to rectify the situation and even promised to go to Lashio to reinforce Stilwell's authority.

The Generalissimo and Madame Chiang arrived in Burma on April 5. There, Chiang assured Alexander that General Stilwell had full power to command the Chinese troops and then told the same thing to the Chinese troops themselves. In reality, most of the Chinese still considered the American's role to be advisory, but to Stilwell, it seemed that Chiang had finally swung around to his point of view.

Reporters on hand found Stilwell an excellent news item. 'Vinegar Joe' was rapidly becoming a celebrity.

He made good copy, and the press made the most of it, developing a picturesque stereotype, the crusty cracker-barrel soldier's soldier, tough leathery, wiry, down-to-earth, wise-cracking, Chinese-speaking, a disciplinarian loved by the troops, with lack of swank and a warm smile, an American 'Chinese Gordon,' an 'Uncle Joe.'[23]

The Japanese, meanwhile, methodically advanced up the Irrawaddy towards Mandalay. They envisioned a three-column drive up the three river valleys with the intent of enveloping and destroying the Allies between Lashio and the Chindwin river. But it must take place before the onset of the annual monsoon, due in mid-May.

All the fighting in Burma, both the Allied retreat and the subsequent advance to victory, as well as the Japanese operations, was dictated by the terrain and climate. In Burma, the mountain ranges stretched southward. In the west was a huge range that separated Burma from India, a formidable, jungle-covered bastion. Great river valleys existed between the mountain ranges, the Chindwin, Irrawaddy, Sittang, and Salween. These main rivers dominated the strategy of the Burma campaigns and provided the main highways and lines of communication. The monsoons came, twice a year around the middle of May and in October, bringing with them anywhere from two hundred to eight hundred inches of rain. In addition to the mountains and monsoons, the jungle presented a formidable obstacle. Thick, dank, and swampy, movement within it was reduced at times to a standstill. Men's clothes rotted from the humid heat and the unhealthy climate destroyed one's health just as readily. Malaria, dysentery, typhus, and cholera were endemic. Snakes, fire ants, leeches, and wild animals of all descriptions lurked within the tangled growth. Then, of course, there was the native population. Some worked with the Japanese, others against them. Depending on who they were working with, God help a captured enemy. Death by torture was usually in store. This then was the battleground.

As the Japanese advanced northward, Stilwell remained convinced that a counteroffensive would allow the Allies to retain their hold on central Burma. Chiang even sent the 38th Division fresh from China, to help hold Mandalay.

On April 3, Mandalay was bombed by the Japanese. Four hundred people were killed and destruction was widespread, including the hospital and railroad station. Acres of city streets lay in ruins as corpses of men and animals lay bloating in the tropical sun. When Stilwell arrived in the city on April 8, the area was still burning and the smell of death hovered over him as he conferred with General Sun Li-jen, the 38th Division commander. Chiang and Madame Chiang also came to Mandalay and were appalled at the sight. They used this as a reason to castigate the West for its unpreparedness and confused conduct in the Burma campaign.

Stilwell traveled from one divisional headquarters in the Fifth Army to another seeking to prepare them for a fight in the Pynmana area. At the headquarters of the Sixth Army, he laid down plans for a fight in the Lockaw area. He then went to Pynmana himself to visit the battle-torn 200th Division. Stilwell felt as if he were fighting with a blindfold over his eyes since his forces were devoid of aerial reconnaissance and had no idea of the enemy's line of approach.

On April 16, he wrote his wife and said, "We are about to take a beating."[24] Sensing the imminent loss of Burma did not prevent him from conducting a hard and fast campaign. Realizing its importance, he had already begun to formulate plans for its reconquest. He hoped to personally lead both Americans and Chinese forces to inevitable victory. The future plans called for the transfer of Chinese troops to India where they could be trained and equipped under American direction as a new model army.

On April 20, the decisive Japanese blow fell. They hit the Chinese divisions hard, smashing them, causing them to scatter and retreat. Shortages of every type of equipment hampered any type of defense. Military discipline dissolved. Stilwell personally took command of a Chinese company and achieved some local success, but all for naught. The Japanese continued their relentless advance ever northward. Stilwell concluded,

"It is an impossible situation which I will have to see through as best I may. CKS [Chiang Kai-shek] has made it impossible for me to do anything, and I might as well acknowledge it now.[25]

Stilwell now knew that the 'Peanut's' visit to Lashio

had been a farce. The higher commanders were just as impossible as ever to deal with and so was Chiang's interference.

Yet another problem encountered was Chinese hoarding. Always short of supplies, they hoarded whatever they had for use in some greater emergency. As an example, the Fifth Army had nine tanks, but the Generalissimo personally allowed the use of but one tank at a time, thereby reducing the effectiveness of concentration. The following conversation sheds light on the situation.

> At Toungoo, Alexander asked General Tu what had happened to his field guns which he had seen the day before, expertly dug in, well sited and carefully camouflaged. Tu said he had withdrawn them to safety. 'Then you mean that they will take no part in the battle?'
> 'Exactly.'
> 'But then what use are they?'
> 'General, the Fifth Army is our best army because it is the only one which has any field guns, and I cannot afford to risk those guns. If I lose them the Fifth Army will no longer be our best.'[26]

The Japanese continued to push towards Lashio and westward towards the Chindwin, threatening to envelop the Allies.

On April 25, Stilwell and Alexander held an important meeting. Stilwell appeared in his World War I campaign hat, looking "terribly tired" according to Dr. Seagrave, a physician who worked tirelessly among the Chinese soldiers. It was finally agreed that retreat was the only alternative. But was that now possible? The Chinese Sixth Army could move back to China, but Stilwell, with the 38th, 22nd, and 96th Divisions at Mandalay, would have to make for India.

Stilwell knew that had the Chinese troops been properly led, a retreat would not have been necessary. He proved this a week before when he led the 200th Division personally and recaptured Taunggyi, Ho Pon, and Loilem. Later on, he was awarded the Distinguished Service Cross for this feat. However, once he left the front line, the Chinese attack petered out.

From Mandalay, Stilwell went to Shwebo, fifty miles to the north. There he witnessed the humiliation of defeat with its accompanying fear and panic. It was not a pleasant sight to behold. On April 28, Lashio fell to the Japanese and the Burma Road was severed. In the west, Monywa on the Chindwin River sixty miles below Shwebo also succumbed. It became imperative for the British to cross the Chindwin at Kalewa before the Japanese arrived or their escape route would be cut.

On May 1, a plane was flown in to take Stilwell out of Burma. He staunchly declined the offer, saying that his sole idea was to go out with the Chinese troops. This, he felt, was his duty as commander. He offered no further explanation. This attitude appeared unorthodox like his refusal to wear insignia. Although he owed the Chinese no such loyalty, deep down he felt a sense of obligation. Therefore, he sent his headquarters group on the plane while he, with the balance of his staff, went sixty miles north to Wuntho. There, he hoped to re-establish some contact with the Chinese troops arriving. Unsuccessful, he decided to move his party westward over the hills to India.

His party consisted of approximately one hundred people. There were eighteen American officers, six enlisted men, and Dr. Seagrave's unit of two doctors and nineteen Burmese nurses. The group also included assorted Chinese, Indian, Malayan, and Burmese cooks and porters, and even a handful of British officers.

The proposed route would be difficult at best, through jungle, mountains, and rivers with the Japanese danger ever present. The Chindwin crossing at Homalin was the first goal along the route, with the mountains to Imphal their final destination.

To a man in his fifty-ninth year, a trek such as this could prove fatal, but Stilwell dauntlessly continued. Ever mindful of the approaching monsoon, the walkout became a race against time. En route, the party passed through the last vestiges of civilization. At Indaw, they saw the chaos of retreat and the magnitude of fear. From there, they headed westward into the unknown forest. In his last missive, Stilwell said,

This is our last message. We are armed, have food and map and are now on foot fifty miles west of Indaw. No occasion for worry. Chinese troops coming to India this general route. . . . Believe this is probably our last message for a while. Cheerio. Stilwell.[27]

He was amazing. Those men thirty years his junior found it hard to keep up with the general's pace. Malaria, dysentery, and sunstroke all plagued the hikers. The steaming May jungle wilted the retreating column. Ants, thorns, a rogue elephant, insects, leeches, leg sores, infections, and blisters hampered the group. Cutting food rations by one-half, Stilwell instilled strict discipline and set the example by standing last on the chow line.

When they reached the Uyu, a tributary of the Chindwin, the little band constructed rafts. Poling their way towards the Chindwin, they lived in constant fear that the Japanese would beat them to Homalin. When they finally reached this place, no food was waiting for them, but thankfully, neither was the enemy.

On May 14, the rains began signaling the monsoon's approach. For the next five days after the crossing of the river, they climbed and climbed, then began their descent on the other side of the mountains. The trails were so slippery that the climbers often stumbled. Many pushed themselves beyond endurance, but Stilwell prodded, pushed, and ordered. It was probably his fierce stubborness which carried them through.

Finally on May 20, Imphal was reached. Stilwell had brought them through without loss. Many came to hate his guts during the journey, but realized that they owed their lives to his persistence. Stilwell himself lost twenty pounds, his hands trembled, his skin was yellowish (he picked up jaundice), and his eyes appeared sunk in their sockets. But he was alive and determined as ever to return to Burma at the head of a victorious army. The question he would soon have to face was with what army?

From Imphal, he was brought by rail through Assam to Dinjan where he was met by a plane and carried to New Delhi. There, at a press conference, he gave his "hell of a beating" speech, already quoted. Later, he attempted to pinpoint why they had suffered this beating. He listed no air service, Japanese initiative, inferior equipment, inadequate ammunition, lack of transport, no supply set-up, 'stupid gutless command,' and interference by Chiang Kai-shek, among the chief reasons. Obviously, Chiang's suspicions of western intentions and his personal persecution complex contributed to the defeat as well. Finally, Chinese culture, which influenced fighting tactics, had a major impact on the conduct of operations. All in all, it was a combination of factors which ultimately proved decisive. Despite everything, Stilwell settled himself for the ordeal ahead. He was determined to correct these defects and revenge the humiliation.

Upon reaching India, Stilwell immediately submitted a plan for the reconquest of Burma. Foremost among his suggestions was the incorporation of American troops into the theater. This, he felt, was necessary for victory to become a reality instead of a dream. Neither the War Department and General Marshall was unable, however, to comply with his request. Europe needed all the troops available and the western front rated first priority. The only alternative was to carry out his plan for training the Chinese in India.

On June 3, Stilwell made the two-thousand mile trip from New Delhi via Assam, over 'the Hump' to Kunming, then to Chungking. Chiang was cordial, primarily because he still desired Lend-Lease aid and could ill afford to snub the United States. Now, more than ever, he emphasized his opposition to the strategy of attack that had brought disaster to his finest army, the motorized Fifth. He never anticipated this result when he placed the army in the hands of a foreigner. There is a Chinese proverb which states, "It was equally best, when defeat loomed, to succumb to the enemy without fighting."[28] Instead, the net gain for China had been more devastation, loss of its troops, total isolation, and Japanese occupation of Chinese soil. Adding insult to injury was the fact that the Allies failed to treat China as an equal. Chiang was troubled by such questions as, why was China not on the Munitions Control Board? Why were they not a member of the Combined Chiefs of Staff? The simple answer was that China was considered a poor security risk. For Chiang, this was a loss of face! Consequently, his attitude of letting barbarians fight barbarians stiffened.

This very attitude was diametrically opposed to the objective Stilwell had been sent to achieve. Lend-Lease's main reason was for China to use the material against the enemy. Chinese passiveness was not meant to occur. In a sense, Chiang had to be blackmailed to fight for his own country. Stilwell thus presented to Chiang a number of suggestions. First of all, the Chinese army system had to be reformed and the political commanders replaced by well-trained soldiers who wanted to fight. These reforms, Stilwell stated, would go a long way toward making the Chinese Army a superior fighting force. Stilwell and the Generalissimo debated endlessly. The American was frustrated.

Chiang was made to realize that if Lend-Lease aid were to continue, he would have to cooperate with Stilwell to some extent. Therefore, after lengthy discussion, Chiang agreed to allow Stilwell to command and control the training of Chinese troops in India. The provision was so many tons of aid per month flown to China over the Hump. So far, Hump tonnage had been poor and equipment was desperately needed, especially by Chennault and his air group.

Meanwhile, Chennault was making fantastic claims that his air strategy could singly destroy the Japanese by cutting their sealanes. The vital element, he emphasized, was supplies.

To Chiang, always looking for easy solutions and eager to have someone else do the fighting,

Chennault's thesis was compelling. He endorsed the plan. If given the supplies he needed, along with full authority to conduct the campaign as he saw fit, Chiang felt Chennault would be able to achieve the desired aims without the need to reform the army and disturb the dangerously delicate balance of cliques found there. Change would be very dangerous and perhaps even allow a rival to come forward from the army circles. Chennault's plan was simple and required little Chinese effort. Thus, Chiang prodded the United States to provide Chennault with all the material he thought necessary to fulfill his aims.

Other demands, however, continued to hamper the flow of supplies, the foremost being the requirements of the European theater. Stilwell had to report these facts to Chiang who became more and more infuriated and even threatened to make a separate peace with the Japanese unless tonnage increased. The Chinese leader asked pointed questions. Why couldn't Stilwell use his influence to obtain more aid for China? Could it be that Stilwell lacked influence? Was he really attempting to get all he could? Chiang was becoming increasingly disenchanted with his American advisor. Stilwell was angry with the criticism. In his own mind he knew he desired more aid and support for the theater. What infuriated him most was the charge that he was not doing his job.

The chasm between Chiang and Stilwell widened. Chiang was also displeased with the disposition of Lend-Lease aid. When this aid was given to England and Russia, these two countries were allowed to use it as they saw fit. However, when the aid arrived in China, it was Stilwell who determined its use. To Chiang, this lack of trust by the Westerners constituted additional loss of face. Unfortunately, it had to be so. The United States simply could not trust

Chiang to use the aid against the Japanese as he should.

While the debates and arguments continued between Stilwell and Chiang on one hand, and Chiang and Washington on the other, Stilwell continued to push forth the training program in India. His first priority was a location to use as a training area for the Chinese troops. Finally, after long and arduous negotiations with the British Colonial Government he was allotted a camp called Ramgarh which had been used to house Italian prisoners, approximately two hundred miles west of Calcutta. The British agreed to feed the Chinese troops if the United States equipped and trained them. In October, troops from China were airlifted to join those already in India after the great retreat of the previous sping.

Meanwhile, Stilwell came to understand more clearly the difficulty in reforming the Chinese army system. To reshape the army meant the elimination of incompetents, many of whom were close friends of Chiang. Removing them and placing more capable commanders in control could possibly give birth to a potential rival. Lurking in the background might be a budding Napoleon, readying himself for an opportunity to seize control of the army and, eventually, the government itself. Chiang always kept this possibility in mind and therefore continued to place obstacles in Stilwell's path. This frustrated the American to no end, since he felt the job at hand was the defeat of the Japanese and, in order to accomplish that feat, the army had to be strong, well-led, and well-equipped. With that hope and despite the constant procrastination of Chiang, the undaunted Stilwell proceeded with his plan, one he called the X-Y Plan. X represented the Ramgarh-trained troops and Y those trained in Yunnan. These Y or Yoke Forces comprised a potential army of fifteen divisions which Chiang promised would be ready by February 1943. This promise, however, was linked to the demand for massive Allied air cover and naval control of the Bay of Bengal in order to prevent Japanese reinforcements from coming through Rangoon.

The program at Ramgarh officially began in August 1942 with about nine thousand survivors of the Burma campaign. Stilwell personally visited the training camp that month and returned again in October when the airlift of Chinese divisions commenced. By the end of the year, thirty-two thousand troops were in training there. Stilwell's objective was to have two combat-ready divisions along with three artillery regiments and other auxiliary units ready for battle by February when the campaign to reconquer Burma was scheduled for launching. The American general felt right at home on the training field. He cajoled, exhorted, and screamed orders when necessary in his desire to create a crack fighting force.

That October, Wendell Wilkie, the former presidential candidate, making a world wide tour as a special envoy arrived in China. The Chinese made lavish plans to give him the red carpet treatment. During the visit, Chennault spoke at length with the envoy. He gave Wilkie a letter to deliver to President Roosevelt which boldly reiterated his boast of being able to defeat Japan in China if given the proper tools. Chennault's letter went on to complain that Stilwell's method of ground fighting were outdated. (Chennault should have studied the Luftwaffe's attempt to destroy Britain in 1940 totally by air. He could also have learned some lessons from the German air attack on Malta. Both proved unsuccessful due to the lack of follow-up by ground troops.) In essence, Chennault was undermining Stilwell with the hope of being appointed to succeed the general as American commander in China. Chiang, of course, was quite agreeable to this proposal since, as we have already seen, he was not completely sold on Stilwell's methods.

Meanwhile, Chiang himself was applying pressure to have Stilwell recalled and replaced by Chennault. Colonel McHugh, the Naval attaché in China, also endorsed Chiang's recommendation and stated so quite frankly in a letter to Secretary of the Navy, Frank Knox.

> Stilwell's insistence on the recapture of Burma was a personal ambition resulting from his defeat and represented a dissipation of strength preventing the effective employment of air power in accordance with Chennault's program.[29]

Knox forwarded the letter to Secretary of War Stimson who in turn showed it to Marshall. The Chief of Staff was furious. Meanwhile, the President read the letter with interest since he was also the recipient of Wilkie's reports and the personal letter from Chennault.

Roosevelt considered relieving Stilwell, but the opposition of Stimson and Marshall who restrained the President by informing him that the reopening of Burma was essential, won out. What was urgently needed was a supply route that could accomodate both land and air forces and the only way this could be accomplished, the officers said, was to move forces into Burma. In other words, the very thing that Stilwell proposed. Thus, Marshall and Stimson were able to preserve their comrade's position.

With that issue settled temporarily, Stilwell felt free to concentrate on the Burma campaign. Visiting New Delhi and Chungking, he made an effort to commit both the Chinese and British to the forthcoming offensive. Many problems developed; suspicion and fear held sway. Stilwell faced British and Chinese reluctance to be committed to a campaign whose intent was to defeat the common enemy. Eventually, pressure from Marshall settled the issue and the British became more cooperative.

Stilwell's Chinese forces were assigned the task of clearing the Hukawng Valley in northern Burma, with Myitkyina and its airfield as their primary objective. The British in turn would concentrate their efforts in southern and central Burma. Stilwell now assumed another responsibility, the construction of a road from Ledo through the jungles of the Hukawng Valley. The purpose of this pass was not only to supply the offensive but also to link up with the old Burma Road and open up land contact with China again. The British opposed the Ledo Road, but eventually agreed to the concept albeit reluctantly. The frustrated Stilwell wrote his wife, "It is no fun bucking two nationalities to get at the Japs."[30]

Chiang, who was more changeable than a chameleon, waxed enthusiastic about Stilwell's project. On November 3, he agreed to release fifteen divisions on the Yunnan side for the forthcoming offensive. What was behind this sudden change of heart? The reason lies with the return home to China of T. V. Soong who, prior to leaving the United States, was involved in lengthy discussions with Stimson and Marshall. These two informed Soong that cooperation with Stilwell would insure a continued abundance of Lend-Lease aid. For now, Soong became Stilwell's ally, at least until the following year when he became the driving force seeking Stilwell's dismissal.

Sea and air superiority in the Bay of Bengal, which Chiang insisted on as a prerequisite for commitment of Chinese forces in Burma, was not met. Again, the priorities of other theaters took its toll on the CBI (Chinese-Burma-India). To the Generalissimo, it smelled once more like neglect of China and, on January 8, he changed his mind once more and formally declined to undertake any offensive. He was determined not to be pushed into any action unless the Allies proved their full commitment. He said,

> If the navy is unable to control the Burma seas the campaign had better be postponed until autumn.[31]

Disgusted, but reluctant to give up, Stilwell continued to plan. On January 16, he was surprised to receive the Distinguished Service Cross for his action the previous April resulting in the capture of Taunggiyi. In his usual sarcastic manner, the occasion is noted with a few choice words, "We all had a drink."[32]

At the Casablanca conference in January 1943, it was decided that a Burma offensive, Operation Anakim, should be initiated in the fall. Marshall expressed reasons why this operation should indeed go forth and demonstrated that it could serve to commit the Chinese to fighting and would force the Japanese on the defensive in China. The latter was really the crux of the issue. The United States Pacific campaign was scheduled to get underway soon and could be exposed to disaster if China reached a private agreement with the Japanese that would free thousands of enemy troops to man the Pacific Islands. In addition to other reasons, this one important issue dictated that the United States prop China up militarily.

Meanwhile, the limited British offensive in the Arakan Peninsula proved a dismal failure (see Volume

II in this series, *The British*, Chapter 6). It was but another demonstration of the futility of ground operations and served to pour fuel on the seemingly endless debate over Chennault's proposals. Should he be given priority and the starring role in the CBI at the expense of ground operations? Roosevelt and Churchill both questioned the wisdom of Burma's reconquest and leaned towards Chennault's plan. The President made it quite clear to Marshall that in 1943 more emphasis should be given to air operations in addition to a land campaign in Burma. In keeping with that, in March the Fourteenth Air Force was created under Chennault who was accordingly promoted to the rank of Major General.

All the while, Stilwell continued to train and equip the Chinese forces for an anticipated November campaign. At Ledo, work on the road progressed despite difficult terrain obstacles and an unbearable climate. Mountains, deep canyons, and torrential rains made work on the road a herculean task. The arrival of the monsoon in May 1943 did not help.

In April, both Stilwell and Chennault were summoned to Washington to discuss CBI priorities. Marshall informed Stilwell that he was to go to the White House and present arguments to the President against the major air offensives advocated by both Chiang Kai-shek and Chennault. If the Frenchman was allowed his way, the entire air tonnage over the Hump for May and June would go to him to the neglect of the ground troops. Stilwell prepared a memorandum where he again emphasized the importance of reopening Burma and raising the combat efficiency of the Chinese Army. He elaborated on the one great danger of the air offensive. If Chennault's raiders really began to hurt the Japanese, it could result in swift retaliation from enemy ground forces who might easily overrun the Chinese airfields. If the Chinese ground troops were untrained, who would protect and defend the airfields against the Japanese attacks? This was the reason, he argued, why his program for the preparation of Chinese divisions was necessary and why a land supply route through Burma was essential.

Stilwell met with the President on April 30, but made a bad impression. So much so, in fact, that Roosevelt mistook him for being ill. Stilwell failed to argue for his program. Why? This was the enigma of the man. Could it be that by doing so he would be promoting himself, something he was against? Perhaps it was his hostility towards Roosevelt. He never liked the President and made some rather derogatory statements about him in his own private papers. Perhaps it was his feeling that he knew his plan was right and thus it required no explanation; it stood on its own merit. It might have been the innate hostility he felt emanating from Roosevelt and the President's predetermined inclination towards Chennault's plan that caused Stilwell to become tongue-tied at the critical moment. Whatever the reasons, he was unable to put into speech what he so eloquently put in writing.

> The creation of an effective ground force would be of far more lasting and effective benefit to China than increased air activity without a foundation. . . . Air coverage over nothing is in my opinion of little value.[33]

It was left to the Trident Conference scheduled for May to decide the fate of Anakim. Wavell, Stilwell, and Chennault were all present. Naturally, European theater strategy received priority, but the CBI also had its say.

Marshall was unhappy that Roosevelt had aligned himself with Chennault's policy for he considered the latter unfit for independent command, lacking the essential logistical knowledge. Besides, Marshall personally did not like the man.

At Trident, Roosevelt and Churchill both voiced opposition to Anakim. Admiral King, the Chief of Naval Operations, cast his lot with Stilwell and added weight to the argument. Finally, Stilwell presented his platform followed by Chennault with his. The debate intensified. After the heated exchanges ended, Roosevelt's view prevailed for the time being. The major effort would be allotted to increasing the Hump services so that additional supplies could be provided for Chennault. In the interim, the Anakim operation would be shelved while a more limited operation against the Japanese-held airfield at Myitkyina took place. This expedition would serve to benefit the Hump operations since this airfield posed a distinct threat to the aircraft flying the Hump runs. The revised North Burma Campaign was given the code name Saucy.

Now more than ever, Stilwell faced an enormous task. While in Washington following the Trident conference, he gave a series of speeches to an audience of influential Senators and publishers in an effort to inform them of the realities in China. He must have resembled an Old Testament prophet spreading gloom and doom. The general also spoke at length with Churchill who promised to replace Wavell and various other British commanders in the near future.

Stilwell returned to China via London and Cairo in June to face the Generalissimo and make one final effort to gain approval for China's participation in a Burma campaign. But Roosevelt's decision to favor Chennault steeled Chiang in his resolve to neither fight nor reform. Stilwell felt lost.

It was obvious the Chinese promise to fight was only made in order to insure the continuance of Lend-Lease material. Chiang's pledges were not the equivalent of intended performance, but rather a method of condescending to another person. Yet, Stilwell continued to push ever onward in the hope that Chiang would finally realize that fighting in Burma was the best way of protecting China's future. Once more, Chiang agreed to take part in the campaign, but this time he put it in writing and signed it. That event took place in July. With his objective accomplished, Stilwell left for India to make preparations for the campaign.

Meanwhile, in August, another high-level conferences was held, the Quadrant Conference. The American and British leaders gave serious thought to the strategy of a direct attack on Japan. Chennault's bombing thesis was again brought up, specifically the supplying of the bombing offensive. Differences in strategy were evident between the Americans and British. The United States insisted on the reconquest of Burma as an initial step toward providing an effective land route to China while the British tended to view any Burma offensive more in the vein of the recapture of Rangoon and Singapore. Disagreements were conveniently shelved, but accord was reached on the establishment of a new command structure. A Southeast Asia Command was established, separate from the Pacific theater as well as those of India and China. As far as the British were concerned, it was basically established in order to concentrate on the reconquest of their lost possessions in Southeast Asia. Admiral Lord Louis Mountbatten, the dashing Chief of Combined Operations and cousin to King George VI, was named Supreme Commander of this new theater. Stilwell was appointed his deputy. This now made the general accountable to Mountbatten in Burma, Chiang in China, Auchinleck in India, and Marshall in the United States, all at the same time.

There was one new development in the theater which pleased Stilwell immensely, the introduction of American troops. Stilwell had hoped for many American divisions to fight hand-in-hand with the Chinese. To his dismay, the effort proved much less successful than he had hoped for. Only a small commando force of about three thousand jungle-trained volunteers were brought to India. They were given the code name Galahad and modeled on the British Long Range Penetration Group, the Chindits, under the inspired leadership of General Orde Wingate. This force had already seen action behind the enemy lines in central Burma. Though the first Chindit operation was a failure, its method of guerilla tactics, involving severing the enemy's line of communications, seemed correct and another effort was already being prepared in connection with the forthcoming campaign. Force Galahad, the American contingent under the command of General Frank Merrill was also, unfortunately for Stilwell, placed under Wingate's operational control. This force became popularly known as 'Merrill's Marauders.'

Stilwell went to meet the dashing Supreme Commander when he arrived in India. He noted in his diary that event and called Lord Louis a "good egg."[34] Though Stilwell was senior in rank to Mountbatten, he was nevertheless willing to work under him.

Stilwell returned to Chungking in the middle of October and was stunned to find that the Generalissimo had demanded his recall on the grounds he had "lost the confidence of the troops."[35] The driving force behind the effort was T. V. Soong who, for a few months, had been agitating to get rid of Stilwell so that he could advance his own position by being placed in charge of Lend-Lease aid. Stilwell noted his appreciation of Chiang's decision.

> It may be with me out, nobody else will push the campaign. Neither the Limeys nor the Peanut wants to do it, so everything will be jake. Or it may be just the suspicious, jealous Oriental mind, listening to lies and thinking that it won't do to let a damned foreigner gain any more influence. Or he may be afraid to let the thing grow and upset the equilibrium of mediocrity through which he retains control.[36]

As far as Stilwell was concerned, this hit the nail on the head. Chiang hated being forced into action. Furthermore, his insistence on reforming the army, he realized, exposed the inadequacies of the regime for all to see which in turn made Chiang lose face.

Mountbatten, influential people at court and in the army, all rushed to Stilwell's defense. Their combined efforts managed to reverse Chiang's decision and, in particular, the influence of Madame Chiang and her sister Ella. However, Stilwell was required to see Chiang in person and admit he had made mistakes and had only one aim, the good of China. Though Stilwell was made to eat crow, the Generalissimo had to eat more. T. V. Soong was sent into exile.

Within a month, Chiang's whole demeanor changed radically. The cause of that pleasant occurence was an invitation for him to attend the high-level conference in Cairo. To the Generalissimo, this meant that he was finally being granted equal status among the Allies. In addition, the Allies had included China as one of the signatories of a Four Power

Declaration that pledged united action after the war to establish an international peace organization. Chiang's goodwill overflowed upon Stilwell and he asked the General to accompany him to Cairo where his services would be required to explain military plans to the Combined Chiefs.

Meanwhile, the campaign into the Hukawng Valley was just about ready to commence. The overall plan called for a three-phase advance through the Hukawng and Mogaung Valleys to Myitkyina and was to be coordinated with the British offensive further south.

Chiang and Stilwell both departed amicably for Cairo. Roosevelt, Churchill, and the Combined Chiefs of Staff were all present for the meeting. A number of pre-conference discussions were held. Chiang and Roosevelt covered many points regarding China's role after the war.

The military discussions lasted for three days. Various proposals were made, including a naval and amphibious venture, codenamed Operation Buccaneer, aimed against the Andaman Islands. It was felt that his operation would prevent the Japanese from reacting strongly to the land offensive. Debate about strategy went on. National interests often received priority and led to some rather heated exchanges.

The Cairo conference ended without reaching any clear-cut, definitive solutions. Mountbatten had this to say about the conference.

[It] was the first experience of Roosevelt, Churchill and the Combined Chiefs of negotiating with Chiang Kai-shek and they have been driven absolutely mad.[37]

Nothing firm had been achieved. Chiang still continued to vacillate for he had little faith that the British were truly committed to the amphibious assault he considered essential. It was the old problem again; he would not use Chinese troops without a firm British commitment to the enterprise. Stilwell was left unsatisfied with the lack of concrete results, particularly regarding his desire for a commitment of significant American strength to the theater. He also wanted Roosevelt to agree to his assuming the position of Field Chief of Staff of a combined Chinese-American command.

Chiang returned to China, but Stilwell remained behind to await the return of Churchill and Roosevelt from Tehran where they had gone for a conference with Stalin. The Tehran Conference was the first meeting of the 'Big Three.' There, the Allies cemented plans for Overlord, the cross-Channel attack, and Anvil, a coordinated invasion of southern France. This gave Churchill the opportunity he needed to press for the cancellation of Buccaneer. The Prime Minister convinced the gathering that the landing craft was needed for Anvil. Russia also agreed to enter the war against Japan three months after the conclusion of the European war. Churchill became increasingly convinced that a campaign in China was no longer necessary.

The American Joint Chiefs of Staff opposed the cancellation of Buccaneer. Roosevelt, though visibly discouraged by the unsuccessful meeting with Chiang in Cairo, still felt that American public opinion was on the side of China, thus obligating the United States to fight for and with them until Japan was beaten. Consequently, the American chiefs remained committed to a campaign in Burma. Roosevelt made no secret of the fact that he felt a moral obligation to

Chiang Kai-shek. Churchill, on the other hand, felt no such duty.

The Chinese 38th Division, while advancing into the Hukawng Valley, met unexpected Japanese resistance and its commander refused to move forward despite orders to the contrary. The British heard of this and used it to justify their position that the Chinese simply would not fight and, thus, any operation designed to include the Chinese was sheer lunacy.

On December 5, Roosevelt called off Buccaneer. No sooner had China been recognized as one of the great Allied powers than her allies were breaking promises to her. Of course, this placed Stilwell in a most embarrasing position. How could he now deal with the Generalissimo? When Roosevelt returned from Tehran, the two met to discuss this reversal. Nothing substantial came of the meeting and Stilwell was left pretty well on his own to deal with a sticky situation.

Chiang Kai-shek, having returned home proud of his new-found position of world leader, now faced the humiliation of learning of the cancellation of Buccaneer. As compensation for this loss of face, he demanded a high price. If America did not meet that price, China would surely collapse, he stated, thus freeing thousands of Japanese to pounce on the Pacific islands and present grave difficulties to American Pacific forces. Once more, Chiang resorted to blackmail as a means of achieving his aims.

Washington was becoming increasingly disenchanted with Chiang as each day went by. When Stilwell returned to Chungking, he attempted to explain the reality of the situation. The Generalissimo was told in no uncertain terms that any aid which the United States sent to China must be used for the war effort, and China would have to fight to open a route for that aid. Consequently, Stilwell placed emphasis on the Burma campaign. It had to be fought. Although Chiang was reluctant to agree, he gave in and told Stilwell that he could use the Ledo forces in India as his own, but that the Y Forces in Yunan could not be used in Burma unless the British took the Andaman Islands or Rangoon.

On December 19, 1943, Stilwell was confirmed as commander of the Ledo Force, now redesignated the New First Army.

> First time in history. G-mo gave me full command of the Ledo (X force) troops. Without strings—said there would be no interference and that it was 'my army.'[38]

The following day he returned to India, happy to be away from the 'manure pile.'

Stilwell then went to Burma, resolved to show the world what well-fed and trained Chinese soldiers could do. The capture of Myitkyina, he hoped, would shame Chiang into attacking with Y or Yoke forces from Yunan.

Joe Stilwell was a peerless commander, a trait which suited him well for his unique position. Here he was, the American Theater Commander, Chief of Staff to Chiang Kai-shek and Deputy Commander to the Supreme Commander of SEAC, handling a job normally the responsibility of a battalion commander. Direct supervision was necessary, however, for he realized that only his personal leadership could prod the Chinese into action. For the next seven months, from January through July, he remained in the jungle with the exception of a few brief jaunts to New Delhi and Chungking. Stilwell's primary goals were to open the land route to China and to prove his old belief that the Chinese soldier could be the equal of any in the world. His target was Myitkyina and its important airfield. Many deemed the task impossible, but the undaunted Stilwell was determined to prove him wrong.

The Ledo forces advanced down the partially completed Ledo Road. By the end of December 1943, the Chinese 22nd Division was ready to make its move into the Hukawng Valley. Once they did this, the American Galahad Force would become operational. When all this was accomplished, Stilwell could then establish the NCAC (Northern Combat Area Command) that included the Chinese divisions and Galahad Forces.

The terrain given to the NCAC was some of the worst in Burma. The jungle was so thick that progress was reduced to something like one mile an hour. The ridges were sharp and frequently caved in as a result of the heavy rains. Disease was endemic to the hot, steaming bush. The Japanese opposition was the formidable veterans of the 18th Division. Stilwell commanded three Chinese divisions, the 22nd, 38th, and 30th, about thirty-five thousand men in all. In addition, he had Force Galahad.

Thanks to the untiring effort of the air forces, the Allies were gradually gaining control of the skies. This was a necessity since the tactic adopted by Stilwell was to supply his troops by air drop. Stilwell's main strategy called for the well proven hook combined with an end run envelopment, the same tactic used with huge success by the Japanese in 1942 during their own conquest of Burma.

His design was to engage the enemy frontally while launching the real attack through the jungle from the flank, and at the same time dispatching an enveloping arm through the hills aimed at a point behind the enemy with the object of establishing a roadblock to cut off his retreat.[39]

Stilwell did all that was possible to build up the morale of the Chinese troops who felt jusitifiably inferior next to the Japanese. If they could but achieve some victories, it would instill a measure of confidence in their ability and leadership.

Headquarters for the first phase of the attack was Shingbwiyang. The move commenced on Christmas Eve with Stilwell present at his command post observing the day's fighting. After a week of determined struggle, the Chinese attained their first goal, Yupbang, deep in the Hukawng Valley. For the first time, they had defeated the Japanese in Burma. Stilwell's presence at the fighting front and his insistence upon living among the men made a deep impression on the Chinese. He expected no special favors because of his rank, slept on a cot or in a hammock, washed and shaved from his helmet, and stood in line to eat the same food as his men. It was quite a contrast to some of the Chinese commanders who lived remotely. Here was a soldier they could identify with.

The Chinese troops were now proving their worth. In truth, being better fed, armed, and cared for did indeed make a difference. Added to that was the superior training they had received. These troops were rapidly reversing the world's opinion of their fighting quality. This did not mean, however, that all problems were eliminated. Hardly. Stilwell still had to prod, cajole, and kick a few 'butts.'

The command situation itself also caused problems. Stilwell was a man holding many positions which at times conflicted with each other. In this particular campaign, he found himself answerable to the British. While he normally did not get along with many English officers, he totally disliked the commander of the ground forces, General Sir George Gifford. The American, using his prerogative as Deputy Supreme Commander, subordinated himself for the campaign to General Slim, the Fourteenth Army Commander who, though British, Stilwell respected. As he said, "I would fight under a corporal as long as he would let me fight."[40]

Nevertheless, Stilwell faced British opposition to a full-scale Burma operation. In fact, the British felt that Stilwell's goal of reaching Myitkyina was completely unrealistic. Instead, the eyes of the British gazed more at Singapore and Hong Kong as opposed to Burma. Fortunately, the American Joint Chiefs looked favorably on Stilwell's strategy. Roosevelt had to prod Churchill continuously. What finally convinced the British to commit themselves wholeheartedly to the Burma campaign was the Japanese themselves who, on March 7, launched an offensive over the Burmese border towards Imphal and Kohima in Assam. Before they were able to launch a full-scale attack, they were forced to defend themselves against a major onslaught by the warriors of Nippon.

While the Japanese and British went at it furiously in India, Stilwell's forces advanced through the dense jungle towards Myitkyina. There was an overriding fear that an enemy success would serve to isolate the Chinese forces in Burma. What was desperately needed was the presence of the Y forces from Yunnan, but Chiang still refused to allow them to enter combat under the pretext that China was too weak and her economy too damaged to undertake a major campaign.

Despite this, Stilwell pushed his men further south

toward his objective by way of Shaduyup and Kamaing. On March 27, he journeyed to Chungking for a conference with the Generalissimo. Though he was unable to convince the Chinese leader to release the Y force, he at least managed to extract a promise of reinforcements for the final drive. A promise which, incidentally, Chiang kept.

While the Chinese forces pushed south and 'Merrill's Marauders' hooked behind the Japanese lines, to the south the Chindits were protecting Stilwell's flank from attack. Though they lost their leader, Wingate, who perished in a plane crash, the Chindits still managed to perform their main task.

After weeks of difficult fighting in horrid conditions, by the end of April Stilwell was preparing to make his final thrust towards Myitkyina. The battered and disease-riddled Galahad forces formed the vanguard of the advance. Only fourteen hundred of the original three thousand remained, the balance having been evacuated due to various jungle-related illnesses or from sheer exhaustion. Stilwell informed Merrill, who himself had suffered a heart attack during the campaign, that he was aware he was pressing the men too hard, but there was no other option. He also told Merrill that once the airstrip was seized, he would authorize the evacuation of the Marauders to begin.

The Galahad attack toward the objective caught the Japanese completely by surprise and, on May 17, the airstrip was taken. This was the first important Japanese position to be recaptured in southeast Asia. Mountbatten, taken aback at Stilwell's achievement, sent the latter a congratulatory message on accomplishing what most considered an impossible feat.

Though the airstrip was won, the town itself remained in Japanese hands and they defended it strenuously. The campaign continued on into June and sapped the strength of the remnants of Galahad who came to hate Stilwell as much as they hated the enemy. The whole campaign settled into a bitter struggle with rage running rampant. Food was short, disease was widespread, and the enemy was as determined as ever to recapture the airfield. It became a battle of slit trenches, machine guns, mortars, and grenades.

In order to maintain an American presence, Stilwell continued to use the Marauders far beyond the time they were to be relieved. Stilwell seemed "bloody and utterly coldhearted, without a drop of human kindness."[41] Eventually, he also became embroiled in a bitter controversy with General Lentaigne, Wingate's successor as commander of the Chindits, who also felt his forces were totally played out through sickness and exhaustion and could not possibly continue to protect the flank.

Incredible as it seems, in the midst of this struggle on May 11 Y Force, renamed the Chinese Expeditionary Force, crossed the border into Burma.

In addition to his concern over Myitkyina, Stilwell received distressing news from China. The Japanese had launched a major offensive, Ichigo, aimed at the destruction of Chennault's air bases which proved how perceptive Stilwell had been. On June 3, Chiang summoned him to Chungking because of the danger to the Fourteenth Army air bases. The future boded ill.

By midsummer, Stilwell could boast, however, of some very significant results in Burma. The northern part of the country as far south as the Irrawaddy River was now reconquered with the Ledo Road following in the wake of the advance. The Chinese Expeditionary Force (Y) and the NCAC had yet to link up, but that was contingent upon whether the impetus of the attack could be maintained by the Chinese. At Myitkyina, the enemy was finally showing signs of weakening from attrition. In India, the Japanese gamble had failed. Though they fought on into July, low on supplies and suffering from disease, the Japanese commander had no other option but to order a retreat. The ill-fated offensive had cost the Japanese between eighty-five and ninety percent casualties. Only in China did the enemy make significant gains. This caused Washington to become alarmed and demand some action to forestall the annihilation of the air effort by the loss of American bases.

While Stilwell was involved in the Burma campaign, the situation in China had eroded from the effects of economic stagnation, rising disunity and discontent within the government, and the Japanese offensive. In China's history, there is a concept known as the Mandate of Heaven. In short, it means if a government is successful, it has the mandate but, if unsuccessful, the commission is no longer there and must be sought somewhere else. Many of the former warlords holding nominal loyalty to Chiang's government were rapidly becoming demoralized by the corruption and inneffectiveness they saw in the army. Morale was breaking down and some were advocating reform or an overthrow of the corrupt regime. Although the Communists in the north were efficient, they were Communists and many of the war lords feared their rising power. All in all, the situation was not good.

Stilwell found himself placed in the unenviable position of trying to save the very government he had come to despise. Appeals came from many corners. As the Japanese progressed towards the air bases, it became obvious that the fliers alone would be unable to stop them. Ironically, Chennault now appealed to

Stilwell for more planes and supplies; Chiang applied pressure to allow him to receive increased tonnage. Stilwell consented, providing the War Department did, but Marshall refused. He felt that the already enormous effort to sustain Chennault had not been worth it. All the earlier matériel had failed to reap the promised benefits and Marshall was not willing to squander anymore. Instead, the Chief of Staff leaned towards the establishment of B-29 air bases on the newly secured Mariana Islands in the Pacific. From these areas, B-29s could reach and bomb vital Japanese war industries and devastate their cities. That, Marshall concluded, would accomplish more than Chennault's efforts. The air commander and Chiang were furious and took their wrath out on Stilwell.

Chiang and Chennault both pleaded their anti-Stilwell case to Vice President Wallace when the latter arrived in China in June as Roosevelt's personal envoy to persuade Chiang to negotiate with the Communists and combine their forces peacefully for the common good of the country. Instead, Chiang fulminated against Stilwell while Chennault added his venom. The Frenchman was convinced that if Stilwell were relieved, the air war in China would be successful. T. V. Soong also added his voice to the plea. Wallace concluded that Stilwell should be replaced with Chennault. Later, however, he decided that General Wedemeyer would be a more suitable choice. To the Vice President, it appeared obvious that Stilwell had lost Chiang's confidence and he informed the President of that fact. Not once, however, did Wallace see fit to consult Stilwell.

Marshall blocked Wallace's proposal. The Joint Chiefs were dismayed over Chinese intransigence in the face of the renewed Japanese effort and were fearful that the enemy might entrench themselves so deeply in China that even their defeat would not prevent years of prolonged war in the country's interior. In fact, the Joint Chiefs were thinking of enlarging Stilwell's authority. In the face of China's apparent paralysis, they desired that their representative be placed in command of the total Chinese military effort. This would force Stilwell to leave Burma which, by the way, would make Mountbatten happy since a seething conflict had erupted between the two over the American's handling of the Chindits and his lack of tact when dealing with the British. Marshall proposed to promote Stilwell to full General and make him Field Chief of Staff, an idea that had originated in the latter's fertile mind a year before.

Roosevelt accepted the recommendation even though it represented a reversal of his opinion about how Chiang should be treated. The President in his message to the Chinese leader said,

> The critical situation which now exists in my opinion calls for the delegation to one individual of the power to coordinate all Allied military resources in China, including the Communist forces. I think I am fully aware of your feeling regarding General Stilwell, nevertheless. . . I know of no other man who has the ability, the force, and the determination to offset the disaster which now threatens China."[42]

Roosevelt pulled no punches. Here was an American President dictating to a Chinese leader, implying the latter's inadequacy to deal with a difficult situation.

Chiang had no intention of yielding to the Roosevelt's demand, yet he did not wish to lose American aid upon which he was so dependent. He, therefore, was forced to walk a tightrope. He attached three conditions to his acceptance of Stilwell as commander. The first said that the Communists were not to come under the American's leadership until they accepted the authority of the Central Government. Second, the limits of Stilwell's position were to be clearly defined, and finally, Lend-Lease aid was to be entirely under the authority of the Chinese government.

Stilwell was mildly enthusiastic about the new position though, as a realist, he knew that Chiang would interfere and undercut any real authority. Yet, he made his plans in the hopes that the critical military situation would mitigate Chiang's interference to a certain extent.

Meanwhile, on July 30, Stilwell was compelled to leave Burma for Ceylon where he assumed temporary command of the Southeast Asia Theater while Mountbatten traveled to Burma. In Stilwell's absence, the appointment to command in China was hotly debated. In addition, after seventy-eight days, the siege of Myitkyina finally ended with complete victory at last achieved.

On August 7, Stilwell's promotion to full General became official. Chiang, in the meantime, still expressed misgivings about accepting him, or for that matter any American, in charge of all military operations in China. Primarily, Chiang was worried that the 'foreign' military commander would give American aid to the hated Communists. The Lend-Lease problem was an obsession with the Chinese leader. Thanks to Chiang's evasiveness, Washington decided to send General Patrick Hurley and Mr. Donald Nelson to China to act as intermediaries between the two nations. Stilwell noted,

Hurley and Nelson arrived full of P. and V. They are going to pound the table and demand: 1. Real unification in China. 2. Unification of command. Then and only then will they talk about what the U.S. will do for China economically.[43]

One of the responsibilities of the envoys was to push for immediate confirmation of Stilwell's position.

On September 4, 1944, Hurley went to New Delhi to meet with Stilwell. He told the general that he was going to hit Chiang with two forceful demands. The first condition was that China become one nation and that Chiang work with the Communists in a united front. The second condition demanded that China prove its desire to help defeat Japan by appointing Stilwell Commander of the Chinese Army. If Chiang refused, the United States, he said, would shift its effort to Russia in the struggle against Japan. Chiang gave his verbal approval when Hurley pressed the demands.

With regard to the Communists, Chiang still maintained his position that they should be incorporated into the Chinese Army under the overall authority of the Central Government before Stilwell could assume command. This, however, was an impossibility since the Communists had little respect for the incompetent Chiang government.

Stilwell's concept of what his command should include was more than Chiang could accept. In addition to leading the campaign against the Japanese, Stilwell also felt that, as head of the military forces, he should have the authority to activate new units, disband old ones, and transfer personnel from one to another without regard to the jurisdiction of commands or of provincial and war area boundries. This was far more authority than Chiang was willing to allow any one person. But how could he avoid agreeing to this kind of leader without compromising Lend-Lease aid?

While waiting for Chiang's response, Stilwell traveled to the eastern front where he saw first hand the destruction caused by the Japanese offensive and the incompetence of the Chinese leadership. Because of this havoc, Chiang demanded that the Chinese divisions at Myitkyina advance immediately against Bhamo. If Stilwell would not allow this, he stated, he would withdraw the whole of Y force from the crucial area of Lungling on the Burma Road. This threatened action caused an uproar in Washington. Stilwell received a message from Roosevelt which scathingly chided the Generalissimo for his actions and flatly stated that Stilwell should be given unrestricted command. That message arrived on September 18. During the previous two days, Hurley had spent many exhausting hours trying to hammer out the details of Stilwell's assignment. Finally, the President, exasperated over the whole situation, forcefully called Chiang's hand. A letter was sent to the Chinese leader and Stilwell, aware of the dispatch's content, eagerly delivered it personally. He noted,

At long, at very long last, FDR has finally spoken plain words, and plenty of them, with a firecracker in every sentence. 'Get busy or else.' A hot firecracker. I handed this bundle of paprika to the Peanut and then sank back with a sigh. The harpoon hit the little bugger right in the solar plexus.[44]

Chiang gave no indication of emotion as he read the stiffly worded message. Stilwell was in utter ecstasy. He wrote his wife,

I've waited long for vengeance, at last I've had my chance. I've looked the Peanut in the eye and kicked him in the pants.[45]

Privately, the Generalissimo was outraged and shocked by the harsh wording of Roosevelt's message. He was acutely aware that he could not accept the American's demand for, if Stilwell were imposed on him without his consent, it would consititute a great loss of face. In addition, the Communists were to be treated as equals, something Chiang had worked against for years. The entire future of the Kuomintang was at stake. Thus, Chiang adopted a hard-line stance and said that because of the September 18 message he now found an excuse for not allowing Stilwell to assume command.

Outwardly, Chiang cooperated with Stilwell while secretly plotting with the aid of T. V. Soong for Stilwell's recall. Finally, on September 23, the Generalissimo flatly refused to authorize Stilwell's command. The American, he said, was the source of all his frustrations. Hurley did his best to intervene, but Chiang remained adamant. Rationalizing his refusal with the fact that Stilwell had personally delivered Roosevelt's letter, Chiang insisted that this action showed that the American ignored his rank. He went on to state that by refusing to order the attack on Bhamo Stilwell had disobeyed a direct order. Therefore, a man who did this was totally unacceptable as Field Commander of the Chinese forces. A mutiny could result. He went on to state that Stilwell

had no intention of cooperating with me but believed that he was in fact appointed to command me. . . . he was unfit for the vast and complex duties which the new command will entail.[47]

He also said that Stilwell's retention would cause irreparable injury to Chinese-American military cooperation. The way Chiang worded his response to Roosevelt's message (Stilwell was sure T. V. Soong wrote it), it assured the President that Chiang would be willing to assign any American but Stilwell to command the army.

Roosevelt, upon receipt of Chiang's reply, expressed a degree of sympathy with the Chinese leader's position. Though he had lost respect for the Generalissimo since the meeting at Cairo, he knew that he could not impose an American commander on a foreign country against the explicit wish of a Chief of State. Since Chiang held himself open to the basic appointment, Roosevelt decided to sacrifice Stilwell. However, Marshall continued to support his friend.

Unfortunately, an official version of the President's feeling was conveyed by Harry Hopkins to H. H. Kung, a Chinese financier, who in turn transmitted it to T. V. Soong in Chungking. Soong then informed Chiang that the President was willing to recall Stilwell.

Armed with the knowledge of Roosevelt's feelings on the matter, Chiang informed the Chinese Central Executive Committee that Stilwell had to go. This was the first time this group had heard the idea expressed. The Generalissimo told them that it was a matter of China's sovereignty to have as its military commander someone affable with the government. China would not be treated as a second class nation, nor would it be a puppet subjected to a new form of imperialism. If an American commander were named, he said, he would be allowed to have contact only with those Chinese forces placed at his disposal by Chiang himself.

Roosevelt replied officially on October 5. Marshall had managed to modify the President's stance by getting him to agree to Stilwell's retention as commander of the Chinese forces in Burma and Yunnan while relieving him as Chiang's Chief of Staff. The Generalissimo refused to accept the compromise and emphatically declared that Stilwell had to go.

> So long as I am Head of State and Supreme Commander in China it seems to me that there can be no question as to my right to request the recall of an officer in whom I can no longer repose confidence.[48]

He then went on to say that Chinese losses in the east were Stilwell's direct responsibility since the latter had drained Chinese strength for use in the Burma campaign. The American general, according to Chiang, bore the sole burden for his country's inability to resist the Japanese offensive. How twisted could the truth be?

When Hurley received Chiang's written demand for Stilwell's recall, he endorsed it on the basis that the two antagonists were totally incompatible and duly informed the President of the fact. Marshall made one last effort to save Stilwell, but to no avail. Roosevelt issued direct orders that Stilwell be recalled on the grounds that he and the Generalissimo were completely incongruous.

The axe fell on October 19. General Wedemeyer succeeded Stilwell as Chief of Staff to Chiang and commander of American forces in China. Stilwell remained in Chungking for a brief two days. Marshall hoped to avoid having his friend issue any sarcastic statements once the press got wind of the situation. There were two reasons for Marshall's attitude. The

Presidential election was less than a month away and 'Vinegar Joe's' bitterness could cast aspersions on Roosevelt. Second, he didn't want Stilwell saying anything that could hurt his chances for a possible reassignment.

Prior to his departure for the United States, Stilwell sent farewell messages to a number of persons within the theater. Surprisingly, Chennault was the recipient of a friendly message praising his achievements. Letters were also sent to various Chinese commanders who had worked with Stilwell over the years. The lone Englishman included in the correspondence was General Sir Claude Auchinleck whom Stilwell considered a friend.

Ironically, Chiang sent Stilwell a message offering him a distinguished Chinese decoration, the Special Grand Cordon of the Blue Sky and White Sun, the highest Chinese honor for which a foreigner could qualify. Stilwell refused, but protocol did call for him to accept an invitation to tea. Chiang and Soong were gracious hosts and polite exchanges were made before the American departed with the statement that China's good had always been his motive.

On October 21, under a gray sky, Joseph Stilwell departed China. His return resulted in an abundance of articles and editorials being published blasting the situation there. The truth of the moribund Chiang Kai-shek regime was exposed to the American public. At a news conference, Roosevelt stated that Stilwell had been relieved because of a conflict of personalities, but the press refused to swallow it. A *N. Y. Times* editorial saw through the President's rhetoric.

It is scarcely conceivable that more tactful representatives, if tact was what they lacked, could have overcome the disorganization and corruption which have hamstrung the Chinese war effort.[49]

Stilwell was brought secretly to Washington on November 3. In a sense, he was an embarrassment to the administration, a visible symbol of a wasted effort.

Marshall informed Stilwell that he was to take a month off. For the newly unemployed general, it was an inauspicious homecoming. In fact, Stilwell was treated more like a prisoner in protective custody rather than a returning commander. He was bursting at the seams to tell his side of the story, but was kept hermetically sealed.

Late in January 1945, Stilwell was appointed commander of the army ground forces. This job involved training soldiers for combat, but for a man who thrived on the battlefield, it held little charm.

In contrast to his peers, the American people looked upon Stilwell as a celebrity. Wherever he went, police escorts awaited him. He gave dozens of speeches and appeared at countless meetings and testimonials. One unique prize was bestowed upon him, though it must have been bittersweet at best. The Ledo Road was finally completed along with a pipeline in January 1945. It was renamed the Stilwell Road in honor of the man who had always believed it could be built, the man with the indomitable will, Joseph Stilwell.

Privately, the general still predicted disaster for China. However, the instrument of the country's doom was not the Japanese, but the government itself. Stilwell was convinced that civil war would rend China after the defeat of the enemy.

During the first two months of 1945, Stilwell devoted many hours to the recording and editing of the massive official record of his command, "History of the CBI Theater." The completed work filled an entire trunk and was delivered to the War Department during the first week in March. The central thesis was this:

> In supporting China without exacting a commitment to action in return for Lend-Lease, the United States had conducted a vacillating policy which drained public funds into a futile transfusion.[50]

The perceptive report concluded with condemnation of Chiang Kai-shek's government and a prediction of its downfall, which proved to be uncannily accurate.

As the war progressed towards its inevitable conclusion, Stilwell's yearning for action increased and he continued to hold out hope that he would again receive a combat command before the war's end. Meanwhile, the Philippines were retaken by MacArthur, Nimitz's forces had assaulted Iwo Jima in February and Okinawa in April, and the B-29 air offensive (based in the Marianas—not in China) was taking its toll of Japanese cities. Then came the dramatic conclusion of the war in Europe on May 7. Japan now stood alone and Stilwell's hopes began to fade.

As American forces continued to battle on Okinawa, it became obvious that the United States no longer required an invasion of China. It was concluded that whatever Japanese forces remained in that country would be withdrawn to protect the home islands. Those that were not could be easily handled by the Russians when they fulfilled their commitment to declare war on Japan three months after the conclusion of the war in Europe.

Once Okinawa fell, all that remained was the invasion of the Japanese homeland. General MacArthur was designated commander of all American ground forces for the proposed invasion. Stilwell knew if he were to receive any combat assignment at all, he would have to act fast. Therefore, he arranged for a Pacific mission under the guise of surveying the needs of army commanders in relationship to the functioning of the army ground forces. Stilwell arrived in Manila on May 25 and was cordially received by MacArthur. For the next month he traveled everywhere, meeting with the various army leaders and making suggestions.

On June 18, MacArthur offered Stilwell a position as his Chief of Staff, but the latter declined and held out for his real wish. He even went so far as to tell MacArthur that he would be willing to take a division. MacArthur stated that he would like Stilwell for command of the Tenth Army, but would first have to convince Admiral Nimitz, who controlled the fighting on Okinawa where the Tenth was embroiled in a bitter campaign. Stilwell left for home, but during a stopover in Guam he received word that General Simon Bolivar Buckner, the Tenth Army Commander, had been tragically killed in action. He quickly dispatched a message to MacArthur stating that he was en route to Honolulu and could be reached there if his services were required. In Hawaii, Stilwell received the eagerly anticipated message. He got Tenth Army.

On June 23, Stilwell assumed his new command. Though the Okinawa campaign was virtually over except for some mopping up, he looked forward with anticipation to the scheduled invasion of Japan. Then the scientists intervened and ended the war much quicker than any military man could have. On August 6, an atomic bomb was dropped on Hiroshima. This was followed three days later by another bombing, of Nagasaki. In between, the Russians entered the war. All hope for an invasion of Japan vanished and the

Emperor, in an unprecedented move, brought the war to a conclusion on August 14, 1945.

Stilwell attended the formal surrender ceremony on the battleship *Missouri* in Tokyo Bay on September 2. Five days later, he presided at the surrender of the Ryukyu Islands where he deliberately kept the Japanese waiting ten minutes before making his appearance.

Upon hearing that the Tenth Army would not take part in the occupation of Japan but would instead be returned to the United States, Stilwell again made an effort to find some way to remain. He had hoped to reenter China, but those hopes were dashed to the ground by Chiang Kai-shek who feared his influence. Stilwell was destined never to see China again.

He returned home on October 18 and was temporarily assigned to duty in Washington as president of the War Equipment Board. That assignment lasted only a few weeks and in January he was reassigned as Commander of the Sixth Army in charge of the Western Defense Command with headquarters at the Presidio of San Francisco, a few hours from his home in Carmel.

From afar, Stilwell watched China move inexorably toward civil war. Meanwhile, in Washington, the China lobbyists spewed their venom at Stilwell and those who agreed with him, blaming them for China's plight. People like Chennault used these opinions to elaborate how Stilwell had destroyed any chance of their achieving victory by not following the theory of air power. In the 1950s, Senator McCarthy would even go so far as to brand Stilwell a Communist sympathizer. Stilwell failed to live long enough to witness any of these unfortunate developments.

By the summer of 1946, his wife noticed a marked change in her husband's health. He appeared sickly and complained of weakness. For the rest of the season he suffered from chills, dizziness, and bouts of exhaustion. On October 3, the General underwent an exploratory operation which revealed that he was suffering from cancer of the stomach. Unfortunately, the disease was already in an advanced state and had spread to the liver. The sands of time were running out for 'Vinegar Joe.'

Though he was the holder of the Distinguished Service Cross, Distinguished Service Medal, and the Legion of Merit, Stilwell had always desired one award, the Combat Infantry Badge, an award usually reserved for enlisted men. On October 11, 1946, he was awarded the badge. Unfortunately, he never lived to view it for on Columbus Day of that year shortly after noon, General Joseph Warren Stilwell, 'Vinegar Joe,' 'Uncle Joe,' 'Galloping Joe,' passed away in his sleep.

In accordance with his wishes, there was no public funeral. Instead, his body was cremated and his ashes scattered over the beautiful blue Pacific near his beloved home in Carmel.

General Joseph Stilwell deserves more than a great deal of credit for accomplishing what he did. He was unquestionably handed the most frustrating task of any leader during World War II. Never, however, was a personality less fitted for a task. Here was an officer in possession of one of the great military brains of the period, plunged into a world of diplomatic intrigue and political maneuvering which was, in many respects, alien to his temperament. He was a mover of men. An 'Uncle Joe' to his soldiers, he who inspired them, worked, slept, and suffered along with them. He was more at home in a tent eating K rations that at the conference table. As his name implies, 'Vinegar Joe' was hardly a diplomat, yet he was forced to walk a diplomatic tightrope between the corrupt government of Chiang Kai-shek and the imperialistic-minded British. Still, he knew what to do and analyzed the situation correctly. If his solutions had been applied, perhaps the history of China would have been written differently. Had Chiang allowed him to reform the army and establish the ninety combat divisions he envisioned, possibly the Nationalist Army could have prevented the Communist takeover.

Stilwell's mission in China was America's supreme attempt to make up for the many years of Western exploitation. Yet, the effort failed because the goal the United States strove for was unachievable and because, basically, the driving force was not Chinese. America backed a government which, during the war, became increasingly unpopular to its own people. Its corruption was exposed for all to see and the Mandate of Heaven slipped from its grasp only to be snatched up by the eager hands of the Communists. Stilwell foresaw this all too clearly and expressed it in his diary. Thanks to this journal, we can see the raw Stilwell, the unpolished, brash, at times vulgar man. Yet, we can also see the prophetic genius who plainly predicted what millions of others failed to see. History will forever record the exploits of the man who, against all odds, accomplished what so many thought impossible.

Only a most versatile soldier of high martial skill could have done what Stilwell did.[51]

Chapter 5

In the brief span of five years, the fame of a relatively obscure American army officer soared to such unimaginable heights that it provided a springboard to America's highest office, President of the United States. That officer's name was Dwight David Eisenhower.

Probably no other soldier could have filled the role he was destined to play more successfully than Eisenhower. He saw his renown rise to rival that of his more illustrious colleague and former chief, General Douglas MacArthur. Of all the Allied commanders of World War II, only Britain's Sir Harold Alexander approached the much admired 'General Ike' in respect, admiration, and personality.

But Eisenhower's genius did not lie in the field of daring tactics or grand strategy. Instead, he was the unrivaled master of coalition warfare, the one key ingredient essential to the Allied defeat of the Axis nations. What other commander in history has had to lead such a diversified retinue of personalities, i.e., the impulsive and volatile Patton, the arrogant and snobbish Montgomery, the vain and glory-seeking Mark Clark, and the passive, reticent Omar Bradley? Not only were these subordinates diametrically opposed in character, at times they appeared to be fighting for varied and selfish goals. Ike was required to mold these men into a winning team. In addition to the varied individualism of his subordinates,

Eisenhower found himself commanding a multi-national force of Americans, British, French, Poles, Dutch, and Belgians, to name but a few.

At war's end, he commanded no less than eight field armies consisting of three army groups. Yet, to the top-ranking military professionals of the Allied high command, it seemed as if Eisenhower had sprung from nowhere. In a sense, they were absolutely correct.

Since tactics and battlefield command were for the most part the domain of the local army and group commanders, can Eisenhower truly be considered one of the great commanders? Unquestionably. By virtue of the aforementioned alone, he must be considered so. Furthermore, not only did he design and implement grand strategy, his side emerged victorious. Certainly he made his share of errors, but then again so did Lee, Napoleon and Wellington. All shared one fatal flaw—they were human.

To be sure, there were controversies during Eisenhower's tenure as Supreme Commander. The Chief of the Imperial General Staff, General Sir Alan Brooke, disagreed with Eisenhower's strategic concepts, as did Field Marshal Montgomery. The two formed an alliance which resisted the general almost every step of the way and they made no secret of the fact that they considered him an amateur.

Montgomery himself was another matter. Vain, arrogant, with an over-inflated estimation of his own talent and importance, Monty contested almost every directive from his commander and agitated constantly for the appointment of an overall ground commander, namely himself. Kay Summersby, Ike's chauffeur, and a British subject called Montgomery "a supercilious, woman hating martinet."[1] Throughout the war, the Supreme Commander called him a "thorn in my side."

Then, of course, there was George Patton. Eisenhower and Patton were old friends from their early days together in the newly established tank service. Unfortunately for their later relationship, Patton was headstrong, rash and prone to acting first and considering the consequences afterward. Time and again, Patton placed a strain on their friendship until finally the rupture was too severe to repair. Although Patton remained loyal to his chief throughout the war, this did not prevent him from criticizing many of Eisenhower's decisions and taking liberties with commands. For his part, Eisenhower suffered as much as he could before being forced to abandon his support of Patton after the latter's actions continued to be a source of embarrassment.

These then were but a few of the diversified personalities Eisenhower had to handle during the war. There were others, DeGaulle, Giraud, Churchill, King, and Roosevelt among them. Yet, Eisenhower handled each one in turn, usually with a smile and a smooth manner.

The roots of the Eisenhower family can be traced to southern Germany. In the seventeenth century, religious persecution forced the family to flee their homeland and settle in Switzerland. In the 1700s, the family uprooted themselves once more and set sail for the new world where they settled in Pennsylvania. During the westward migration of the 1800s, Dwight's grandfather traveled west in a covered wagon with other Mennonites, a religious sect. There the family finally settled in Kansas and set about the task of raising a family. One of the sons became a construction engineer and followed the westward progression of the railroads as they opened up the frontier. When the rails moved into Texas, the family followed their livelihood and there, in the small town of Denison,

Dwight David was born in 1890, the third of seven sons. Two years later, the family returned to their home in Abelene, Kansas.

The Eisenhower family was a close-knit, hard-working, religious group. Although monetarily poor, the family was rich in spirit; bible reading was a way of life in the household. Dwight had nothing but the fondest of memories of his childhood. He was a happy child, a good student, an above-average athlete excelling in football and baseball, and an industrious youth. Since the family was poor, Eisenhower was required to work during his early years in order to aid in support of the home. After graduation from high school, he continued to work locally since the family situation precluded any hope of higher education. Finally, at the suggestion of friends who were impressed by the young man's academic ability and honesty, Eisenhower decided to take an examination for one of the country's military academies. To a young man growing up on the great plains of America, the thought of going to sea aboard gigantic dreadnoughts was appealing. Unfortunately, by the time Eisenhower managed to take and pass the required examinations, he was too old for Annapolis whose age requirements were younger than West Point. Not to be deterred in his quest for an education where one not only learned, but was paid a salary for doing it, Dwight applied for one of the few remaining appointments to the United States Military Academy. He was one of the fortunate ones selected and at the age of twenty-one, set out for New York in the summer of 1911.

At West Point the future officer shined academically, but he also found time to pursue two other loves, baseball and football. Despite the harsh discipline at the academy, Eisenhower found himself enjoying the atmosphere. His outgoing, warm personality and his optimistic outlook on life secured him many friends. This popularity with people was perhaps his greatest asset in life. One of the cadets attracted to Eisenhower was another young midwesterner, Omar Bradley. At graduation in 1915 Eisenhower stood in the top third of his class.

The newly commissioned 2nd Lt. was assigned to the 19th Infantry at Fort Sam Houston, Texas. There he met, courted, and married Mamie Doud, daughter of a local businessman, the year after graduation.

During this time, Europe was embroiled in devastating war. Like all young officers, Eisenhower was eager to lead troops on the battlefield. His hopes were dashed when he was sent off to Camp Meade, Maryland, where he spent the duration of the war training troops in the newly created tank force. This marked his first exposure to the use of these vehicles in combat and he remained a proponent of armored warfare, although not as vocal as Patton or the German generals. Disappointed with his lot, he nevertheless threw himself into the task with zeal. Before war's end, he had risen to the rank of temporary Lt. Colonel. However, with the advent of peace, he reverted to his permanent rank of captain.

Tragedy soon stalked the young couple. A son, David Dwight, had been born in 1917 during the stay at Ft. Meade. In 1921, the boy contracted scarlet fever and died, leaving a void in the young couple's life. Happily, the following year, another son, John, was born and survived to attend West Point and become a United States ambassador.

After World War I, Eisenhower continued to hold a series of staff positions for which he was ideally suited. Since the recently concluded conflict had been billed as the 'war to end all wars,' Eisenhower reassessed his career and determined that the best he could possibly hope for was to one day command troops and retire as a colonel.

Eisenhower remained at Ft. Meade until 1922 when he reached a turning point in his career. That year, he was appointed to the staff of General Fox Connor in Panama. Connor was one of America's most capable officers. He had worked closely with Pershing during the war and was well known on the battlefields of Europe. He was a forward-thinking and progressive officer. No other individual exercised such a dramatic influence on Eisenhower's career during the early years as did General Connor. Eisenhower idolized him and eagerly learned all that he had to offer. In later years, Eisenhower said of his mentor, "Fox Connor was the ablest man I knew."[2] The two officers spent many hours together discussing military history and modern strategy. Connor repeatedly stressed to his young protegé that coalition warfare was perhaps the most difficult type of command.

In 1924, Eisenhower left Connor's influence to attend the army's command school where he graduated first in his class of 1926. This achievement brought him to the attention of another up-and-coming officer, George C. Marshall.

In 1928, Eisenhower graduated from the Army War College where once again his intellectual achievements brought him to the attention of his instructors and fellow students. With completion of the course, Eisenhower was anxious to put his newly-acquired knowledge to use and rightly expected an important post. Once more he was disappointed. Instead of attaining his cherished goal, he was sent off to France in charge of revising the army's guidebook to American battlefields. Little could he realize how valuable his knowledge of the French countryside would later become.

In 1929, Eisenhower returned to the U.S. and found himself posted to Washington, D.C. as a staff officer working on a plan for industrial mobilization in the event of war. During this time, he was instrumental in the establishment of the Army Industrial College.

The year 1933 saw another dramatic moment in his career. He was selected to be a member of the unit of the Chief of Staff of the Army, General Douglas MacArthur, thereby beginning a relationship that would last for six years. MacArthur and Eisenhower worked closely together for the next two years and when the general's term of office was up, he selected Eisenhower to accompany him to the Philippines, there to build up that country's army and defensive system.

Although MacArthur viewed his exile as a homecoming and an opportunity not to be wasted, Eisenhower viewed it as the final step before ending his career. When he was appointed MacArthur's special aide two years previous, Eisenhower was enthusiastic since MacArthur's star seemed to be on the ascent and the coattails loomed large. Now both men found themselves sent off to the far reaches of the Pacific. (See MacArthur, Chapter 6)

Upon arriving in the Philippines in October 1935, Eisenhower found himself and Major James Ord in charge of developing a defense plan in case of war. For the next few years, the staff was frustrated in their efforts by a lack of funding. Eisenhower constantly urged his chief to return to Washington and plead for financial aid and arms. During the tenure of the assignment, Eisenhower found himself daily becoming more and more disenchanted with MacArthur's theatrical flair and sense of self-importance. The year 1936 saw MacArthur appointed a Field Marshal in the Philippine Army and Eisenhower promoted to Lt.

Colonel in the U.S. Army. Nevertheless, his sense of dissatisfaction with MacArthur increased as time went on.

Two years later, Eisenhower returned home on a visit and assignment for his chief. It was an ideal opportunity to use his contacts and avoid returning to the Philippines. This was not Eisenhower's style, however. His sense of duty and loyalty were too strong, so he returned to his post, though it was a frustrating, humdrum existence.

On September 1, 1939, Germany invaded Poland, thus setting off what everyone had thought impossible just a few years previous, World War II. This time Eisenhower was determined not to miss the boat. He therefore informed MacArthur that he wanted to be sent home forthwith. When he approached the Philippine President, Manuel Quezon, with the same request, Eisenhower was offered a commission in the Philippine Army on what amounted to his own terms. The generous offer was politely but firmly refused and Eisenhower set sail for home.

He found himself assigned to the 15th Infantry at Ft. Lewis, Washington, which was not exactly the ideal post. Training troops proved a dreary task since America was not taking any drastic measures to increase the size of the army.

However, that summer things changed dramatically. America suddenly decided to prepare herself and the draft was instituted. Overnight the Army was transformed into a beehive of activity and Eisenhower found himself Chief of Staff of the 3rd Division. A few months later, in March 1941, he assumed the same title with the IX Corps and was promoted to Full Colonel. Events were moving rapidly. A few months later, Colonel Eisenhower moved on to the headquarters of Third Army in San Antonio where he shortly became

Chief of Staff to that unit's commander, General Walter Krueger. Soon came the opportunity to prove his worth.

The army's summer maneuvers of 1941 proved highly successful and since Eisenhower, using every bit of knowledge acquired from Fox Connor, was instrumental in planning and developing Third Army's strategy, his reputation was assured.

Eisenhower's contribution to the exercise was not lost on the current Army Chief of Staff, General George C. Marshall. The latter added another credit in the ledger on Eisenhower's side. Shortly afterward, his first star was forthcoming.

Training and preparation for war accelerated as America was drawn closer to the conflict raging overseas. On December 7, 1941, Eisenhower was listening to the radio when a bulletin was broadcast announcing the infamous Japanese attack on Pearl Harbor. Throughout the country, various commands began feverish preparations for war and Third Army was no exception.

On Friday, December 12, a bone-weary Eisenhower retired to bed after leaving strict orders that he was not to be disturbed. Shortly after dropping off to sleep, he was awakened by his aide with a message that there was an important phone call. Greatly agitated at what he thought was insubordination, Eisenhower picked up the phone and was astonished to hear on the other end the voice of Colonel Walter Bedell Smith, Secretary of the General Staff, calling from Washington. After confirming his identity, Smith said,

The Chief says for you to hop a plane and get up here right away. Tell your boss that formal orders will come through later.[3]

'The Chief,' of course, was Marshall.

Eisenhower wasted not a moment and arrived in Washington the following day. Upon reporting, he found that Marshall wanted to take advantage of Eisenhower's knowledge of MacArthur and the Philippines. Consequently, Eisenhower found himself assigned to the War Plans division for the Far East. At that point in the war, Marshall was prepared to make every effort to save the Philippines despite the existence of the 'Rainbow Five' plan which stated that in the event of a two-ocean war priority was to given to defeat of the European enemy. Since America was unprepared to take a hand in Europe immediately, the Philippines was the only place where the enemy could be contested.

The chapter in this volume on MacArthur examines the Philippine debacle in detail and it would be repetitious to rehash it here. Eisenhower's role was significant. He, too, firmly believed that the Philippines could be salvaged and clung to the theory that no effort to do so should be spared. Working late into the night every night, he attempted to accumulate everything available for MacArthur's use. For morale purposes alone, Eisenhower was convinced that the Philippines should be saved. He was supported by Marshall. While efforts proceeded to procure all available aid for MacArthur, Eisenhower proposed that a massive buildup begin in Australia. This, too, coincided with Marshall's thinking and plans were made accordingly.

It soon became obvious that America was woefully ill-prepared to wage war. Reinforcements and materiel for MacArthur were in dreadfully short supply. Eventually, the Japanese stranglehold around southeast Asia constricted until American defeat became a foregone conclusion. Marshall, and finally Eisenhower, were forced to concede the inevitable. It was simply a matter of a distinct lack of men and material. Although MacArthur thought he had been abandoned to his fate, Marshall and Eisenhower were genuinely concerned and did everything in their power to help the American forces in the Philippines. Finally, the war department found itself with little choice but to implement 'Rainbow Five.'

Although he still continued to divert as much as possible to the beleagured Philippines, all efforts proved vain in the face of the Japanese onslaught. Eisenhower even went so far as to consider ordering Stilwell to fly reinforcements in from Burma, but this idea was discarded quickly as impractical. Eisenhower deeply regretted his inability to aid his former chief but, in reality, the turn of events were far beyond his own control. He had done all that was possible.

On February 6, Eisenhower took command of the War Plans division from his old friend, Leonard Gerow. Despite having a hard task master for a boss, Eisenhower soon developed a deep and lasting admiration for the Chief of Staff. In turn, Marshall was suitably impressed with the younger man's performance. The two were able to work closely with each other in spite of their contrasting personalities. Where Eisenhower was warm, friendly, and outgoing Marshall was a cold, stern introvert. One day, as Eisenhower was leaving Marshall's office, the Chief of Staff decided to test his subordinate's attitude towards advancement.

The men who are going to get the promotions in this war are the field commanders, not the staff officers who clutter up the war department. Take your case. I know that you were recommended by one general for division command and another for corps command. That's all very well but you are going to stay right here and fill your position and that's that.[4]

Eisenhower sensed that he was being tested and quickly retorted,

General, I want you to know that I don't give a damn about your promotion plans as far as I'm concerned. I came into this office from the field and I am trying to do my duty. I expect to do so as long as you want me here. If that locks me to a desk for the rest of the war, so be it.[5]

He had passed the test with flying colors. Within a month, Eisenhower found himself sporting a second star, denoting his rank of Major General.

The Combined Chiefs of Staff had developed a number of strategies, foremost of which was 'Bolero,' a buildup of American troops in England in anticipation of an eventual assault against German-held Europe. Consequently, Eisenhower threw himself wholeheartedly into the plans for this attack. He continued to work long hours and shunned any attempt at relaxation. During the first few months of the war, only once did he leave his office early. That event took place upon receipt of the news of his father's death. Eisenhower was devoted to his father and made this notation in his diary.

His finest monument is his reputation in Abilene and Dickinson County, Kansas. His word has been his bond and accepted as such; his steady honesty, his insistence upon the immediate payment of all debts, his pride in his independence earned him a reputation that has profited all of us boys. My only regret is that it was always so difficult to let him know the great depth of my affection for him. . . . I'm quitting work now, 7:30 P.M. I haven't the heart to go on tonight.[6]

Work continued to go at a feverish pace and Eisenhower's easy-going manner was instrumental in greasing the wheels of the War Plans division so that tasks proceeded smoothly and in a swift and efficient manner. Among the officers serving in Washington at the time were men destined to play prominent roles in the conflict. Matthew Ridgeway, Albert Wedemeyer, and Thomas Handy were among Eisenhower's colleagues. Not all Eisenhower's new acquaintances made a favorable impression, however, Admiral Ernest King, Commander in Chief of the U.S. fleet was among these latter. After a few meetings with the admiral, Eisenhower was able to comment,

(He) is an arbitrary, stubborn type, with not too much brains and a tendency towards bullying his juniors. One thing that might help win this war is to shoot King. He's the antithesis of cooperation, a deliberately rude person, which means he's a mental bully.[7]

Early in May, Eisenhower was directed to concentrate his efforts on the question of the command for Bolero. General James Chaney had initially been appointed interim commander in the United Kingdom. Eisenhower insisted that any commander in chief of an area, be it Europe or the Pacific, be invested with authority over every branch in his command, i.e., army, air forces, and navy. Working under the assumption that Marshall would be named to command the cross-Channel invasion, Eisenhower recommended that the head of Bolero be someone who could work easily with the new theater commander and urged that this man be appointed at the earliest possible moment.

Marshall was delighted with Eisenhower's grasp of the situation and on May 21 he sent Ike to England to brief Chaney on recent developments and obtain first-hand knowledge of how the buildup was proceeding. Accompanied by his close friend, Mark Clark, Eisenhower set off. The two generals arrived in London on May 26. They were assigned a driver, Miss Summersby, who was disappointed at having been assigned to a two-star general since she felt that major generals seldom got important jobs.

A few days later, Eisenhower had his first meeting with General Bernard L. Montgomery, then commander in chief of Southeast Command. After reviewing a field exercise, the guest officers settled to listen to Monty's explanation of the maneuvers. Casually, Eisenhower took out a cigarette and lit it up. The ferret-like British general sniffed, looked around, and asked who was smoking. When Eisenhower admitted to being the culprit Montgomery rebuked him sharply. "I don't permit smoking in my office."[8] Nevertheless, Eisenhower formed a favorable opinion of the quaint little general. After several meetings with the British chiefs, Eisenhower also found himself deeply impressed by the head of Combined Operations, Admiral Lord Louis Mountbatten. Their close friendship and admiration for each other lasted until both men's deaths. On a negative note, Eisenhower and the Chief of the Imperial General Staff, General Alan Brooke, failed to hit it off. Both officers were thereafter unable to discard their animosity towards each other. Neither did Chaney manage to make a favorable impression.

Eisenhower thought the latter lacked control of the situation and that everything appeared a bit disorganized. Upon returning to Washington, he immediately recommended that Chaney be replaced by General McNarney, Marshall's deputy. The Chief of Staff promised to take the matter under consideration and directed Eisenhower to begin laying down plans for the new commander of the European theater's use.

The key feature of the finished plan was the emphasis once more that the new commander have authority over all branches of the armed services. Eisenhower also added the recommendation that Clark be given command of the first corps to be established in England.

As soon as the plan was completed in mid-June, Marshall glanced at it and asked Eisenhower when he would be available to implement it.

Eisenhower was thunderstruck. He had resigned himself to spending the war in Washington with OPD and had no idea that Marshall had been grooming him for command.[7]

Before leaving for Europe, Eisenhower wished to assure himself that his new command would receive the priority as per prior agreements. Even though he preferred to concentrate on the Pacific, the new Chief of Naval Operations, Admiral King, gave his verbal assurances that he would do all within his power to cooperate.

On June 24, 1942, Eisenhower and his hastily assembled staff arrived in London. The first order of business was to make it clear that all decisions regarding the theater were to be funneled through his office; there were to be no exceptions. He also let it be perfectly plain that his command was to be a unified, allied arrangement and that failure to act with this in mind would result in severe reprisals. For example, one high-level officer was reduced in rank and sent home for calling his English comrade an unflattering name. The English officer in question took no offense and appealed the verdict to Eisenhower. Ike replied that calling any one a 'son of a bitch' was alright, but that the American had used the term 'British son of a bitch' and this was unacceptable. The verdict stood.

Still another initial move was to totally integrate all departments. Where one section chief was American, his deputy would be British, or vice versa. If the war effort was to be an allied one, Eisenhower was determined that it would not fail through lack of sufficient effort on his part.

As Bolero proceeded, it soon became obvious that the proposed cross-Channel attack (Sledgehammer and/or Roundup) could not possibly take place during 1942. As a result, efforts were made to concentrate on the next best thing, a proposed invasion of North Africa (Gymnast, later Torch). However, before agreeing to the proposal, the American Chiefs of Staff demanded guarantees that Torch would not compromise Bolero. Finally, early in the fall, during a series of conferences in England, the American Joint Chiefs gave their approval for Torch. The British suggestion that one commander be appointed for both Torch and Roundup was also accepted. Ironically, it was Ernest King who pressured Marshall into appointing Eisenhower to this position. Not that Marshall needed much convincing, but King's advocacy of Ike was probably the determining factor.

During the period of debate regarding the relative merits of Torch and Sledgehammer, Eisenhower made two important additions to his staff. One of these was Commander Harry Butcher whom King readily agreed to assign as Eisenhower's naval aide. The most vital appointment, however, was the selection of General Walter Bedell Smith to be Chief of Staff. For the balance of the war, Smith was the indispensable right hand of Eisenhower, one which the Supreme Commander could ill afford to do without. The two formed a unique and contrasting team which made Eisenhower's mammoth task that much easier. The contrast between Smith and his boss was evident to all. In Eisenhower's own words:

> (He was) a master of detail with clear comprehension of the main issues. Serious, hard working, and loyal, he proved equally as capable in difficult conferences as he was in professional activities. Strong in character and abrupt by nature, he could achieve harmony without appeasement.[20]

For the next three years Smith proved the most valuable member of Eisenhower's immediate staff.

With the issue of the North African venture settled, Eisenhower found himself slated to command the operation. Once more, he was pleasantly surprised since never before had he commanded troops in combat, but by this time he was Marshall's protegé and the Chief of Staff threw all his weight behind the selection of his hand-picked subordinate.

It was agreed that under Eisenhower the British would provide the leading commanders of the various forces involved, with the exception of the American effort in Morocco. Because events necessitated the hasty dispatch of Alexander and Montgomery to Egypt to deal with the crisis there, command of the ground forces in Tunisia fell to the colorless but efficient Scot, General Sir Kenneth Anderson. Each one of the British commanders made a distinct impression on Eisenhower and later he remarked of Anderson,

> He was not a popular type but I had real respect for his fighting heart. Even his most severest critics must find it difficult to discount the smashing victory he finally achieved in Tunisia.[11]

The deputy for air, Air Marshall Arthur Tedder, eventually became one of Eisenhower's closest friends and confidant.

> (He was) not only a brilliant airman but a staunch supporter of the 'Allied' principle as practiced in that command.[12]

But it was for the naval commander that Eisenhower reserved the most glowing tribute. Few other individuals earned Eisenhower's respect as did Sir Andrew Cunningham.

> He was a Nelsonian type of admiral. He believed that ships went to sea in order to fight and destroy the enemy. He always thought in terms of attack, never of defense. He was vigorous, hardy, intelligent and straightforward.[13]

Eisenhower was indeed fortunate to have Cunningham as a member of the team. 'ABC' as he was affectionately known was probably the outstanding Allied naval personality of the entire war.

To head the American effort, Eisenhower's choice was George Patton, an old aquaintance from tank days and a friend of long standing. Although not keen on Patton's flamboyant showmanship, Eisenhower considered him a brilliant commander and admired his fighting qualities. Just as Bolero was a test of Eisenhower's organizational skills, North Africa would prove a test of two further essential skills, diplomacy and command.

With D-Day set for early November, the Allies desired to avoid unnecessary bloodshed by seeking the cooperation of the French forces in Algeria. The resident American diplomat there, Robert Murphy, secured the assistance of a few high-ranking Vichy officers who agreed to collaborate with the Allies. However, they stipulated that the Allies must provide a known Frenchman around which the French troops could rally. Murphy assured Eisenhower that General Henri Giraud, recently escaped from a German prison camp, was available for the role. On the other hand, the Allies toyed with the prospect of dealing with Admiral Jean Darlan, Commander in Chief of the French Navy and a member of the Vichy cabinet. DeGaulle and his Free French were conveniently ignored for the time being.

Darlan was a complex character. An avowed Anglophobe, he nevertheless despised the Germans as well. As a member of the Vichy government, he was highly distrusted in the west. However, he was the highest ranking French official available no matter how distasteful his politics might be. Finally, the Allies settled on Giraud since the Admiral was not considered trustworthy.

Eisenhower dispatched Mark Clark on a secret and dangerous mission to Algeria in an attempt to feel out the French commanders. Clark received assurances from them that they would offer only token resistance to an invasion, just enough to save face before laying down their arms.

After moving his headquarters to Gibraltar shortly before the invasion day, Eisenhower met with Giraud and was appalled at the price the French General demanded for his cooperation. Giraud insisted he be given overall military command of Torch and absolutely refused to consider anything less. Eisenhower and his staff pleaded, threatened, and cajoled, but to no avail; Giraud would not budge. As the hour for the invasion approached, Giraud remained adamant. Naturally, Eisenhower was just as emphatic in his refusal of the general's demands.

On November 8, Allied troops waded ashore in North Africa at Oran, Algiers, and Casablanca. After their token resistance, the French commander in Algiers, a willing collaborator, General Mast, ordered his units to cease fire. Unfortunately, Darlan just happened to be present in the city and immediately countermanded the order. Every Frenchman in North Africa was directed to resist the Allied landings to the best of their ability at all points. Murphy managed to make contact with the admiral and attempted to reason with him, but Darlan flatly refused to deal with anyone but Eisenhower or his representative.

The next day the Germans began dispatching reinforcements to Tunisia and met with no opposition from the French troops. Once again, Eisenhower called on Mark Clark and sent the latter into Algiers to attempt to deal with Darlan. When Clark arrived, he was informed that Marshal Pétain, titular head of the Vichy French government, had agreed to allow the Germans free access to all areas in return for their help in repelling the invasion. Darlan insisted that he was powerless to act without Pétain's authority.

The following morning, Clark again met with Darlan and threatened to throw the admiral in jail. General Alphonse Juin interceded and convinced Darlan that further arguments were futile. The little admiral gave in, but the damage had already been done. The Germans were pouring into Tunisia in force. Even though Darlan ordered them to resist on November 11, the French forces were totally inadequate and unable to deal with the German buildup.

Meanwhile, as the jockeying for political position was in full swing, General Anderson sent his leading elements forward into Tunisia. Montgomery had won a spectacular battle at El Alamein and Rommel's forces were retreating across Libya towards the Mareth Line in Tunisia. The Allies hoped to prevent the German forces from linking up, but thanks to Montgomery's lethargic pursuit and German General Walther Nehring's masterful makeshift defense on Anderson's front, all hopes of a quick victory vanished.

Eisenhower now knew that any chance of seizing northwest Africa by surprise was lost. Tunis was the sought after prize, but the inadequacy of his own force, the refusal of the French to cooperate, and Hitler's determination to hold onto the land by pouring reinforcements in thwarted the likelihood of an easy triumph. Victory would be costly.

On November 13, Eisenhower himself flew into Algiers to meet personally with Darlan and confirm the deal that Clark had already concluded. By this time, he was working from a position of strength. Churchill and the anti-Nazi fanatics in America exerted pressure to dump Darlan in favor of Giraud. However, Eisenhower knew that the Admiral's influence with the French was immense, so he disregarded the critics and struck a bargain whereby Darlan would become the civilian head of French North Africa. Furthermore, only the man on the spot knew that Giraud's name was virtually worthless as long as Darlan remained available. Thus, Eisenhower asserted his authority and let it be known that as long as he was in command things would be his way. By choosing Darlan over Giraud, he demonstrated a willingness to make prompt decisions without concern for his own career. Unfortunately, the entire controversy was academic since Darlan was assassinated on Christmas Eve.

The military situation in North Africa was another tale. Anderson made little headway in the race for Tunis. Transportation was scarce, the distance was great, there were no advance airfields available, the supply lines were much too long, and the Axis forces contested every step of the way. Although Anderson continued to apply pressure, it was to no avail. He simply could not achieve a breakthrough.

Eisenhower sensed that the entire campaign was suffering from an overall lack of direction. Clark was supposedly his deputy and, by virtue of that, was technically responsible for coordinating the effort. But, he was busy in Algiers with the political situation. In addition, Clark was an ambitious man whose entire stint in World War II seemed to be an effort on his part to further his own cause and enhance his reputation at the expense of the overall picture. He was certainly not a team player. Although a close friend of Eisenhower, he was at the opposite end of the spectrum from his chief and was the antithesis of everything Eisenhower had stressed from the very beginning.

Clark wanted command of the troops in Tunisia who were operating under Anderson which led him to an anti-British attitude.[14]

Dissatisfied with results thus far, Eisenhower moved his headquarters to Tunisia on November 23 so that he might provide the urgently required leadership. As soon as he arrived there, Eisenhower took control of the battle and began to straighten things out. Tedder was brought in to coordinate the air effort. When he found out that vehicles were being held back for lack of available rail space, Eisenhower exploded and ordered them forward under their own power. Then he set out for the front where he spent two days meeting with Anderson and various other commanders before concluding that Anderson suffered from a shortage of every essential needed for victory. Eisenhower ordered the British First Army commander to regroup and consolidate his gains before resuming the offensive. The rainy season then set in, turning the countryside into a quagmire and effectively halting any proposed offensive. The battle settled down to a stalemate. The overall goal of Torch was a failure. To add to the Allied woes, after finally getting Darlan and his political ambitions in line, Eisenhower was shocked on December 24 to receive the news that the Admiral had been murdered. Giraud was finally elevated to the top spot.

While both sides continued to probe each other's positions, Rommel's defeated troops were making good their escape from the British Eighth Army. Early in February, Panzerarmee Africa reached the Mareth Line in eastern Tunisia and Rommel, confident that Montgomery would not launch an offensive immediately, turned on the Allied formations in his rear and, in conjunction with Nehring's successor, General Jurgen von Arnim, launched an impressive counterattack against the American II Corps near Kasserine. The Battle of Kasserine Pass was the American's first full-scale battle of the war and it was a dismal failure.

During a visit to II Corps during the second week in February, Eisenhower had been critical of the corps' dispositions. The commander, General Lloyd Fredendall, had split his forces, divided his units, and was exercising command from far behind the front. Eisenhower recommended that the tactical placements be corrected, but failed to express sufficient concern since his intelligence chief had stated that the Germans would not attack especially strongly in that sector. On February 14, the attack hit with full fury while Eisenhower was en route to his headquarters. Upon learning of the attack, he immediately scraped everything available together and dispatched it to the front. But Fredendall's faulty dispositions threatened to bring on a disastrous defeat.

Finally, as the crisis deepened, Eisenhower sent for General Ernie Harmon of the 2nd Armored Division and ordered him to the front in an attempt to salvage the situation. Fredendall, who had been squabbling with his subordinates, briefed Harmon, turned the battle over to him, and went to bed.

By February 24, the crisis had passed. Rommel had managed to break through Kasserine Pass, but lacked sufficient strength to exploit the victory and was forced to withdraw. Eisenhower had been reluctant to relieve Fredendall during the heat of battle, but lent a sympathetic ear when Harmon recommended that very thing. The Supreme Commander then sent his newly arrived 'eyes and ears,' General Omar Bradley, forward to size up the situation. On March 5, Eisenhower traveled to the front and asked Bradley's conclusion. The latter replied that the command situation was pretty bad and that a change in command was required. Eisenhower replied that Bradley's observations were just what he had suspected all along and that he had already ordered Patton up from Morocco to relieve the hapless Fredendall. As for himself, Eisenhower had learned a valuable lesson. Never again would he hesitate to remove a commander if there were any doubts of the man's ability.

In January, the Casablanca Conference had decided that Sicily and Italy would be assaulted next. After the conference, Marshall, worried about the strain from the massive responsibility Eisenhower had assumed, ordered the latter to relax more frequently and offered to have Bradley lend a hand. Decisions at the summit meeting had also led to Alexander's being named overall ground commander directly under the Supreme Commander. However, Alexander had not assumed his new command by the time of the Kasserine battle and was thus unavailable to help out. He did arrive shortly thereafter so, in effect, victory in North Africa was really his instead of Eisenhower's, although the latter remained closely on top of events. The only time he interceded was when Patton and later Bradley thought that II Corps was being slighted in favor of the British during the final drive to victory.

Alexander can be excused for being skeptical about the ability of the Americans to fight after their performance at Kasserine, but he nevertheless agreed to allow them a larger share of the battle.

As the North African campaign approached its inevitable conclusion, planning began for the invasion of Sicily. Eisenhower agreed that Patton and Montgomery should lead the assaulting armies under Alexander's overall command. However, a controversy developed over where and when to land. The Combined Chiefs wanted the invasion to begin in June, but Eisenhower was not happy with the state of readiness for an amphibious operation and he ordered the date set back to July in order to allow for more time to train the forces involved.

Where to land was perhaps the greatest problem. Originally, the planners recommended that Patton and Montgomery land at Palermo and near Syracuse, respectively. Montgomery disagreed and forwarded his own proposal, calling for Patton to land on the southern coast of the island as well to protect the rear and flanks of the British while Montgomery's forces struck for Messina. Tedder and Cunningham opposed this plan on the grounds that it would result in a dangerous concentration of force open to Axis naval and air attacks. Patton opposed it on the basis that again the Americans were relegated to a secondary role. Unfortunately, Montgomery managed to sell his version to Bedell Smith and Alexander. Patton was furious when Eisenhower too swallowed Montgomery's plan. The angry American general exclaimed, "This is what happens when your commander in chief ceases to be an American and becomes an ally."[15]

Eisenhower's direct contribution to the plan was his insistence on the neutralization of the Axis air fields on the island of Pantelerria.

Despite Churchill's adamance, Eisenhower refused to commit himself to any operations beyond the conquest of Sicily. The Prime Minister pushed for an invasion of Italy itself to insure the retention of Allied power in the Mediterranean. However, Eisenhower ordered plans devised not only for Churchill's proposal, but the invasion of Corsica and Sardinia as well. Above all, Eisenhower did not wish to compromise Roundup.

To casual observers of the command arrangement, it appeared as if Cunningham, Alexander, and Tedder were actually giving the orders. But, Eisenhower was in constant touch with his subordinates and was always ready with suggestions for change when he felt they were justified. Although it was a unified team effort, never once did the service leaders express doubts about who was in overall command. Eisenhower's word was final.

Alexander was one of those opposing the decision to capture Pantelerria. His arguments were based on the fact that the island was heavily fortified. Eisenhower was not to be deterred. He was convinced that the island would make an ideal forward air base so he ordered Tedder to bomb it into submission. On June 7, Eisenhower and Cunningham boarded a British cruiser and sailed right into the island's harbor where the ship duelled with the island defenses. The lack of heavy opposition convinced Eisenhower that Alexander's assessment was incorrect and that the island was ripe for picking.

On June 11, the assaulting force arrived off the shore of the island.

Eisenhower fretted all morning but the finale was an anticlimax. Shortly after noon, Cunningham sent word to Algiers that Pantelleria had surrendered before a single British soldier set foot ashore. The Italians had cracked. There was one casualty. A British Tommy was bitten by a mule. The Allies rounded up 11,199 prisoners of war.[16]

Eisenhower was beside himself with glee and eagerly anticipated the launching of Husky, the invasion of Sicily, set for July 10.

Storms seemed to plague Eisenhower throughout his career. Rain had halted Anderson in Tunisia and foul weather would later play a key role in the invasion of Normandy. So, too, did a storm threaten the invasion of Sicily. High waves and heavy winds prevailed off the island's coast during July 9. From his command post on the island of Malta in Cunningham's headquarters, Eisenhower nervously consulted his meteorologists who indicated that favorable conditions might be in store for the next day. A postponement would mean a two or three week delay. The decision was Eisenhower's alone to make and he chose to proceed as planned. The landings were successful.

Since Alexander held overall responsibility for the ground effort in Sicily, which he in turn entrusted to Patton and Montgomery, Eisenhower found himself with little to do but become anxious, offer advice, and deal with the many political problems still existing in North Africa.

One day, Lord Louis Mountbatten stopped by before taking up his new position as Supreme Commander, Southeast Asia. The two were close friends and Mountbatten asked Eisenhower's advice on being an allied commander. Eisenhower told Mountbatten that the key to success was the

> earnest cooperation of the senior officers in the theater, cooperation which depended upon self-lessness, devotion to a common cause, generosity in attitude and mutual confidence.[17]

Eisenhower firmly believed this was the key to success. Yet, one must wonder where he came up with these conclusions since his most visible subordinate, Montgomery, possessed none of these traits.

Although Eisenhower himself took little active part in the campaign other than to provide guidance, he monitored it closely and was unquestionably on top of the situation. In addition, he was occupied with overseeing the planning for an invasion of the Italian mainland.

Because he remained in close touch with the action in Sicily, it did not take him long to become unhappy with what appeared to be excessive caution on the part of the Eighth Army commander. However, he chose to leave this problem in the hands of Alexander and was for the most part pleased with the progress of the campaign.

Patton's entry into Messina on August 17 marked the end of the Sicilian campaign. Although Eisenhower wished to follow up immediately with an invasion of Italy itself, lack of shipping prevented this. In the interim, Mussolini had fallen on July 25 and was replaced by General Badoglio. Eisenhower wanted to broadcast a surrender offer immediately, but was dissuaded by his political adviser, Murphy, who stated that this was beyond the scope of Eisenhower's responsibility. Nevertheless, a plan was drawn up in the event the Italians asked for an armistice on their own. Eisenhower had few qualms about dealing with the avowed Fascist Badoglio. If he could deal with Darlan, he reasoned, he could deal with Badoglio.

The launching of Avalanche, the invasion of Italy, was scheduled for September 10, but Eisenhower disagreed with his planners and ordered it to begin three days sooner. The major question remaining unresolved was where to land. At the same time, what Eisenhower had been hoping for appeared to become a reality. The Italians contacted the Allies and agreed to meet and discuss terms. Bedell Smith and Eisenhower's intelligence chief, Strong, were sent to Lisbon to meet with the Italian representatives on August 19. After a tentative agreement was reached, the principals returned to their respective commands. Unfortunately, Eisenhower was not empowered to act without concurrence of the Combined Chiefs of Staff who imposed additional demands. Eisenhower protested and insisted that the Italians would not accept the new terms and shortly thereafter, he was proved correct. A few days later, the chiefs themselves relented and authorized Eisenhower to accept an armistice based on the original terms.

On August 31, Smith and Alexander met with the Italian delegates again. The two Allied generals were informed that the Italian Government would not announce an armistice until the Allies had landed with overwhelming force. The Italians further demanded that a strong force be sent to Rome to insure that the city (and the government) would not fall into German hands since the German forces in Italy were numerous and, in effect, the country was under occupation. Smith recommended transporting the entire 82nd Airborne Division to Rome, but insisted that any further effort was beyond the realm of possibility.

After conferring with Badoglio and the King, the Italian delegates signaled Allied headquarters that they were ready to conclude an armistice. This decision was no doubt hastened by Montgomery's crossing of the straits of Messina on September 3. That same day, General Castellano, representing the Italian government, signed the treaty on behalf of his country. It was agreed that formal announcement would wait until September 8. By then, the 82nd Airborne would be ready to occupy Rome with Italian assistance.

On September 7, Eisenhower sent the 82nd's General Maxwell Taylor on a secret mission to meet with Badoglio in Rome. Taylor was to insure in his own mind that all preparations were in readiness. When he met with Badoglio, the Italian leader wavered and said that he could not guarantee Italian assistance for the airborne landing and renounced the armistice. Taylor radioed his findings to Allied headquarters.

Eisenhower was enraged. He called for Castellano and informed the hapless delegate that, come what may, he would announce the armistice on schedule and the Italians could suffer the consequences. It was common knowledge that Montgomery had crossed to the mainland at Messina, but the scheduled landing of Mark Clark's Fifth Army at Salerno still remained a secret. The Italians were therefore unaware that another force was approaching their homeland even as Castellano was suffering tirades at the hands of Eisenhower. Early in the evening of September 8, just as he had threatened to do, Eisenhower went on the air.

> The Italian Government has surrendered its armed forces unconditionally. As Allied Commander I have granted a military armistice. The terms have been approved by the Allied governments and the Italian government has bound itself by these terms without reservation. The armistice became effective this instant.[18]

The Germans wasted no time in disarming the entire Italian Army. Their commander, Field Marshal Kesselring, had anticipated the move and had made the appropriate preparations. Consequently, the Italian surrender was of little benefit to the Allies.

Although Eisenhower had appeared candid and forthright to the Italian delegation, there were many items he refused to reveal to his would-be allies. Foremost among them was the fact that, even as the final negotiations were taking place, Fifth Army was at sea—destination Salerno. (See Map 16)

The following day, Clark launched a second invasion in the Gulf of Salerno. Ultra intercepts had deluded the Allies into believing that Salerno was weakly held by portions of two German divisions. However, of all the landing points the Allies might have chosen, Kesselring accurately guessed their intent and, while Clark's forces were disembarking from

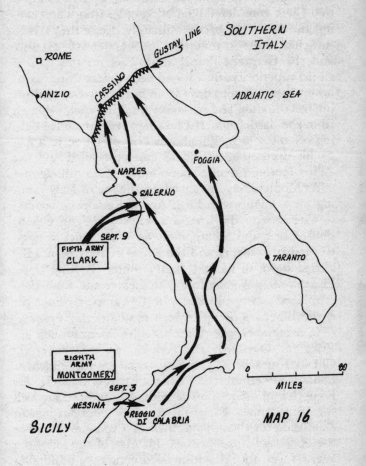

ROME

ANZIO

CASSINO

GUSTAV LINE

SOUTHERN ITALY

ADRIATIC SEA

NAPLES

SALERNO

FOGGIA

FIFTH ARMY
CLARK

SEPT. 9

TARANTO

EIGHTH ARMY
MONTGOMERY

SEPT. 3

MESSINA

REGGIO DI CALABRIA

SICILY

0   80
MILES

MAP 16

their ships, Kesselring was rushing reinforcements into the area. Fifth Army soon found itself locked in a life or death struggle for survival. Intense German counterattacks threatened to eject Clark's troops from the beach. At one point, the situation became so grave that Clark considered reembarking his troops and calling the operation off. Fortunately, Kesselring lacked sufficient units to maintain the unrelenting pressure and the Germans shortly drew back in the face of Allied superiority. But, it had been a near miss. Eisenhower spent anxious days at his headquarters monitoring the situation and nervously awaiting each dispatch from the battlefront. If Clark had recommended calling off the attack, Eisenhower was prepared to abide by his decision. Alexander's calm prevailed and the Allied foothold soon became too large to dislodge.

As Montgomery advanced up the toe of Italy, aiming for a linkup with Fifth Army, Kesselring decided to withdraw to the first of a series of defensive positions. Clark and Montgomery were not quick enough to catch the enemy and the battle of Italy eventually settled down to its first dreary winter. By that time, Eisenhower was gone from the theater and from then on played but a token role in the campaign since his entire time was occupied with the battle for France.

In September, the Allies began to intensify their activity for Overlord, the code name for the cross-Channel attack. A planning team for the endeavor had been established under British General Sir Frederick Morgan. This team had been hard at work for some time. Early in the fall, Morgan began clamoring for the appointment of a commander since the operation was scheduled for May of the following year. Never once did it cross Eisenhower's mind that he would be chosen for this post. When the cross-Channel attack was first discussed by the Combined

Chiefs of Staff, Churchill promised Brooke command of the operation. However, by 1943, it was obvious that the American effort would dwarf the British one, so any thoughts of having a British leader were out of the question. Brooke's hopes were dashed which may explain his later coolness to Eisenhower. Everyone in the Allied camp assumed that the position would quite naturally go to Marshall. The American Chief of Staff desired the appointment even though it was beneath his dignity to lobby for it. Eisenhower wanted to remain in the Mediterranean and heartily endorsed the selection of Marshall. Immediately after the conclusion of the Sicilian campaign, he had prepared an evaluation of the American commanders for Marshall's use in selecting subordinates for the invasion.

Clark, Bradley, and Patton were included in Eisenhower's evaluations. The Supreme Commander said that Patton was great in the field, but had problems dealing with subordinates. As already seen, Marshall was still unaware of the slapping incident, but he was not high on Patton anyway. Marshall always felt that Patton was too temperamental to hold any position higher than army command. Of course, Clark received a glowing report. Eisenhower is considered to have been a brilliant judge of character who chose his subordinates wisely. Yet, his high regard for Clark remains a puzzle since the latter certainly did little to earn this esteem. The only logical conclusion is that Eisenhower and Clark were close friends and the former was fiercely loyal. In all fairness to Clark, however, it must be said that he had performed valuable services on Eisenhower's behalf during the dealings with the French in North Africa. The highest praise was reserved for Omar Bradley. Eisenhower was impressed by the latter's outstanding performances in

Tunisia and Sicily. In concluding his assessment, Eisenhower said that Bradley was, "the best rounded in all respects of the three."[19]

For a British commander, Eisenhower did not hesitate for a moment in forwarding the name of Sir Harold Alexander.

> "He is broad-gauged and should perform excellently. . . . He works on the Allied basis."[20]

The wisdom of this choice was, of course, obvious. The failure of Alexander to secure the primary British command was one of the great Allied blunders of the war. In fact, Alexander would have made an ideal alternative to Eisenhower as Supreme Commander, even more so than Marshall or Brooke.

As they will, rumors abounded about the shakeup in the Allied command for Overlord. The most prominent one had Eisenhower returning to Washington as Marshall's replacement. This rumor received additional credence when the Combined Chiefs of Staff agreed that, since an American was to command the invasion, command in the Mediterranean would pass to a British officer. Eisenhower was horrified at the thought of returning to Washington. Conscious that he could no longer remain in the Mediterranean, he decided to ask Marshall for command of a group of armies under the former's direction.

Roosevelt could not make up his mind who to appoint. At the Tehran conference in November, Stalin attempted to prod the President into naming a commander, but Roosevelt avoided the trap. He simply could not decide. One fact was certain however. It was no secret that Roosevelt was reluctant to part with Marshall as Chief of Staff. The general was considered much too valuable in his current position and his dominating presence was urgently required as a member of the Combined Chiefs of Staff. Therefore, only one logical choice remained — Eisenhower. At the conclusion of the Cairo conference during the first week in December, Roosevelt confided his choice in a wire to Stalin. Eisenhower was directed to meet Roosevelt in Tunis on December 7. After the general settled into the car beside his Commander in Chief, the President turned and said, "Well, Ike, you are going to command Overlord."[21]

Eisenhower was taken aback. His rise had already been meteoric. When the war began he had been an obscure staff officer in the backwaters of the Philippines with the rank of Colonel. Now he found himself entrusted with the most prestigious command on the Allied side.

Little time was wasted in assembling his team. Smith, of course, would be chief of staff. Churchill pressed for Smith's retention in the Mediterranean since he had been present in the theater from the beginning. But, this was one issue that Eisenhower refused to concede. He would have Smith for chief of staff and no one else would do. Thanks to Eisenhower's earlier hearty endorsement, Bradley had already been named to command the American First Army. Ike planned to make Bradley an army group commander as soon as possible with either Hodges or Simpson stepping in as a replacement. Another army was slated for Patton's command. Despite Drew Pearson's exposure of the slapping incident and the resulting controversy, Eisenhower continued to admire the battlefield qualities of his errant bad boy. Over Marshall's objections, Eisenhower insisted that Patton be a member of the team. Tedder, too, was selected for a high role. Months before receiving his new appointment, Eisenhower had recommended that the

British air marshal be given command of the air forces for Overlord and Tedder had returned to England. Now he was named Eisenhower's deputy.

Only in the selection of the key British commander was the Supreme commander disappointed. When he still believed that he would remain in the Mediterranean, Eisenhower had recommended Alexander for the British command in Overlord. He was impressed with Alexander's ability and also felt that if he were going to continue to command the Mediterranean, Alexander could handle Montgomery.

Yet, to his acute dismay, he himself was shortly to have to handle the difficult Montgomery. Although Alexander was probably Churchill's favorite field commander, the Prime Minister insisted on Montgomery for Overlord because the latter had made a name for himself through his cultivation of the press whereas Alexander preferred to take a back seat. Montgomery's name and popularity could not be ignored. In addition, not only did Montgomery lobby for the appointment, but he was supported by Brooke who had Churchill's ear.

With the addition of Admiral Sir Bertram Ramsey for naval operations, the team for Overlord was completed. Before leaving for England, Eisenhower made one additional recommendation that confirmed his excellent judge of character. General Jacob Devers was suggested as the new American commander in the Mediterranean even though Eisenhower did not particularly care for him. However, Ike was big enough not to allow personal feelings to stand in the way.

After a brief two week leave in the United States, Eisenhower arrived in England in mid-January to formally assume command of SHAEF (Supreme Headquarters Allied Expeditionary Force). Morgan's original draft of a plan was reviewed by both he and

Montgomery who reached the same conclusion; it was way understrength. Salerno was still fresh in Eisenhower's mind and the last thing he desired was a repeat performance.

Morgan explained that available landing craft allowed for only a three-division landing. This force would then be required to establish a strong beachhead to allow for further buildup before breaking out into the French countryside. Eisenhower directed the planners to strengthen the overall plan and ordered Montgomery to get involved directly.

The lack of sufficient landing craft plagued commanders in all theaters during the war. MacArthur, Slim, Nimitz, Mountbatten, and Alexander all lost their share of sleep over the severe shortage. Assault craft was shifted from one theater to another as situations demanded and very often plans for major operations were scrapped due to the critical deficit. Units had already been diverted from the Mediterranean to begin training for Overlord and only with the greatest reluctance did Eisenhower agree to part with them briefly for support of the Anzio operation. In order to allow more time for American shipyards to produce additional craft, he directed that Overlord be put back one month till June. But the cross-Channel attack was not the only operation whose fate hinged on the availability of landing craft. Anvil was also compromised.

When serious discussion for Overlord finally began, the Combined Chiefs decided to support it with a simultaneous landing on the southern coast of France, 'Operation Anvil.' During those early stages, no one was conscious of the impact the shortage of material would have. The British had always opposed Anvil in favor of a stronger effort in Italy and the Mediterranean, preferably in the Balkans. Now they saw their opportunity.

All through the spring, the issue was hotly debated by the British chiefs on one side and Eisenhower as spokesman for the American chiefs on the other. Marshall doggedly refused to concede the plan.

During this period, Eisenhower diligently scraped together every available landing craft. After adamantly refusing to cooperate, King relented and agreed to the temporary transfer of some from the Pacific, but only on the condition that they be used for Overlord and Anvil, not to further British ambitions in the Mediterranean.

When the final Overlord plan was devised, it called for a landing at five beaches on the coast of Normandy. Eisenhower had ordered Montgomery to work directly in the planning since he was to be the overall ground commander temporarily. In typical Montgomery fashion, the finalized plan contained enough strength to insure initial success. Unfortunately, the increased dimensions of Overlord would require even more landing craft than originally estimated. Therefore, Eisenhower, conscious that Marshall would never agree to the complete abandonment of Anvil, sought a compromise. Overlord would have priority and Anvil could still be attempted, but only after the Normandy invasion was securely established ashore. This seemed to satisfy Marshall but Montgomery, Churchill, and the British chiefs continued to voice their opposition. However, they also respected Marshall. The latter held the threat of an increased American effort in the Pacific at the expense of Europe over the heads of his British colleagues. Thus, Anvil was granted a reprieve.

The planning for Overlord and Anvil were not the only items making demands on Eisenhower's already scarce time. The selection of commanders for the various corps and divisions was of high priority.

Among the men finally chosen were J. Lawton (Lightning Joe) Collins, Wade Haislip, Leonard Gerow, Troy Middleton, and Walton Walker to head corps. With the enormous amount of divisions envisioned for the battle for Europe, Eisenhower was bound to make a few miscalculations in his selection of divisional commanders. However, his batting average was remarkably high and he did not hesitate to correct his mistakes by removing any man who failed to live up to expectations, be it prior to or in the heat of battle. Ike went one step further with this doctrine and impressed it on all his army and army group commanders.

George Patton provided his share of woes during the buildup for Overlord. Once more his mouth ran ahead of his brain and he caused a major controversy when he addressed a ladies meeting in the small town of Knutsford. Marshall wanted to relieve Patton on the spot, but he eventually yielded to Eisenhower's pleas and agreed to leave any disciplinary action to the direct superior. Patton offered to resign and stated that all he wanted to do was fight. Butcher's diary suggests that this was all a show on Patton's part, designed to impose on Ike's generosity. Patton was a polished actor as well as a brilliant commander.

Nevertheless, after severely chastising Patton and losing his temper in the bargain, Eisenhower let the humbled offender off the hook with these words, "You owe me some victories. If I am right the world will consider me a great man."[22]

Eisenhower had a temper alright, but it was one of the best kept secrets of the war. Thanks to his outgoing, warm personality and his ability to charm reporters, the other side of the man was overlooked. However, Patton, Smith, and Bradley were all witness to the ire in Ike's character at one time or another.

They knew how explosive he could be when pushed to the limit.

The finalized Overlord plan called for Miles Dempsey's Second British Army to land over three beaches near Caen, Sword, Juno, and Gold. Bradley's First American Army would land over Utah and Omaha beaches at the base of the Cotentin Peninsula. In addition to the assault from the sea, an airborne drop the night preceding the invasion was incorporated into the overall plan. (See Map 17).

The final days were spent in a hectic pace. Eisenhower barely found time to catch his breath as he attended conferences, visited various commanders, met with the troops, and kept himself abreast of political developments. His overwhelming burden was not made easier by the presence of Churchill and his constant interference. Roosevelt and Marshall were miles away and could therefore exercise little direct influence on the day-to-day operations. The Prime Minister, however, was close at hand and thought nothing of sending for Eisenhower late at night or during the small hours of the morning to propose some hairbrained scheme or treat the general to a dissertation on plans for operations. Foremost, of course, was the Prime Minister's opposition to Anvil. Since responsibility for the greatest military operation in history rested squarely on Eisenhower's shoulders and failure would be his fault, the very last thing he needed was additional grief in the personage of Churchill.

Nevertheless, there were brief intervals of relaxation. Worried lest their chief suffer a breakdown from exhaustion, the staff encouraged him to spend as many weekends as possible away from the awesome workload and a suitable cottage was rented some miles from London where Eisenhower played golf, went

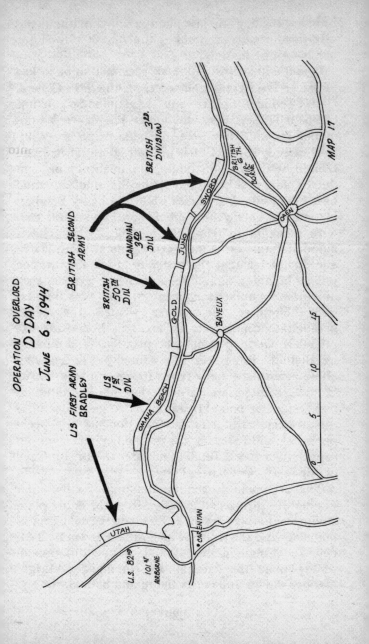

OPERATION OVERLORD
D-DAY
JUNE 6, 1944

BRITISH SECOND ARMY

BRITISH 3RD DIVISION

CANADIAN 3RD DIV

BRITISH 50TH DIV

SWORD

JUNO

GOLD

BRITISH 6TH AIRBORNE

CAEN

BAYEUX

MAP 17

US FIRST ARMY
BRADLEY

US 1ST DIV

OMAHA BEACH

UTAH

CARENTAN

U.S. 82ND
101ST
AIRBORNE

0   5   10   15

horseback riding, or just plain relaxed. Without this diversion, the strain would simply have proved too much for one man.

One final piece of the puzzle remained to be locked in place. The strategic air forces of America's General Carl (Toohey) Spaatz and England's Sir Arthur (Bomber) Harris were not under Eisenhower's command. Instead, they were independent posts responsible directly to the Chiefs of Staff. Both airmen had their own theories on how the war should be conducted, foremost being the notion that soldiers should be used to guard air bases while the heavy bombers blasted the enemy into submission. Therefore, they were reluctant to relinquish control of their closely guarded domain to a mere army general. Both Harris and Spaatz felt that the best way to aid the invasion was by bombing targets deep in enemy territory such as cities, manufacturing centers, and fuel installations. However, Eisenhower wanted the heavy bombers to concentrate on areas in Normandy like railheads, German troop concentrations, and military installations. In addition, he wanted just as heavy an effort against the same type of targets in the Pas de Calais to substantiate the deception that Patton would invade at that point. In his effort to gain control of the strategic air forces, at least for the few weeks preceding and following the invasion, Eisenhower was supported by both Tedder and later the British Chief of Air Staff, Sir Charles Portal.

The argument waxed intense until finally, after Eisenhower threatened to resign from the entire plan, a compromise was reached. Eisenhower could control not command the strategic air forces. His deputy Tedder, an airman himself, would assume this responsibility since the tactical air commander, Leigh-Mallory was an unpopular figure and both Harris and

Spaatz refused to allow him to command their squadrons.

Finally, June approached. All last-minute preparations were completed and the massive undertaking prepared to jump off. Then, hours before the operation was scheduled to begin, the weather turned sour.

The Allied planners had determined that they required just the right combination of favorable tides and full moon for the operation. These conditions prevailed at only two times during the month of June, from the fourth thru the sixth and later during the middle of the month. Without the proper tidal conditions and a relatively calm sea, the transports and landing craft could not accomplish their task. Unless there was sufficient moonlight, the air forces would be unable to drop the paratroops and succeed in their bombing missions. June 5 was therefore designated as the date for the invasion.

On the evening of June 3, Eisenhower's chief weather forecaster, Captain Stagg, predicted that June 5 would be stormy with high winds. Eisenhower decided to wait before making a final decision. Troop and supply convoys began assembling in the English Channel and Irish Sea. Early the next morning, Ike met with his key commanders and solicited their opinion. Leigh-Mallory and Tedder leaned towards a twenty-four-hour postponement. Incredibly, the usually over-cautious Montgomery voted to carry on as planned. Stagg predicted a two-day period of clear weather beginning late on the fifth. Eisenhower decided to heed the meteorologist's forecast and postponed the effort for a full day. He was gambling that Stagg's forecast was accurate and decided to bet all on one cast of the die.

After dinner on the fourth, the key commanders again assembled to hear what Stagg had to say. The weather was horrid. Rain was wind-driven in torrents against the building and few could fathom any type of military operation taking place in those conditions, let alone predict that the weather would soon turn favorable. The weatherman again confirmed his earlier forecast, stating that a high was moving in from the north and that a thirty-six to forty-eight hour period of clear weather could be expected.

Once more, the group was polled for their opinion. The air men again emphasized that clear weather was absolutely essential the success of their effort. Admiral Ramsey warned that any additional delay would require those ships already at sea to be recalled, resulting in their being unable to resume until the eighth. This would thus cause a further two week delay until such time as tides and moon were again favorable. Furthermore, the Admiral stressed, the decision would have to be made in the next few hours. Montgomery again urged that the operation proceed as planned.

So, there it was. The ball was now in Eisenhower's court. He and he alone must decide the fate of thousands of men and perhaps the entire war. As Supreme Commander, his was the order that counted. The 'loneliness of command' was never greater than at that moment. Rising from his chair, he moved to the window and stared out at the torrential rain. A few minutes later he turned and said, "Alright, we go."[23] Overlord was on.

Sure enough, a few hours later the rain ceased and the skies began to clear. Eisenhower spent the fifth trying to relax. He visited troop assembly areas, met with the press, spent time with Butcher, and tried to appear as nonchalant as humanly possible. During the afternoon he sat down at his desk and drafted a statement.

Our landings in the Cherbourg-Havre area have failed to gain a satisfactory foothold and I have withdrawn the troops. My decision to attack at this time and place was based upon the best information available. The troops, the air and the navy did all that bravery and devotion to duty could do. If any blame or fault attaches to the attempt it is mine alone.[24]

Although he refused to believe that the effort would fail, it would have been unusual for him to feel anything but anxiety over the enormous undertaking. Thus, he prepared himself for any contingency.

That evening, he visited the base where the 101st Airborne was preparing to take off for their drop zone near Carenten. The tough paratroopers greeted him enthusiastically and were genuinely proud that their Commander in Chief took the time to visit them. Eisenhower remained until the last plane took off. Then, he turned with tears in his eyes and ordered Miss Summersby to drive him back to headquarters. That night would be one of the longest of his life.

On the morning of June 6, 1944, the greatest amphibious undertaking in the history of warfare waded ashore at Normandy. The Germans were caught totally by surprise. Thanks to the inclement weather, they took it for granted that no invasion was possible. Unfortunately for them, German meteorologists had failed to detect the clearing trend that Stagg had noticed. Consequently, their guard was relaxed. The German Army group commander, Rommel, was away on leave and other senior generals were either involved in exercises or relaxing.

On all beaches except Omaha, Allied troops surged ashore and met with light resistance. On the latter, however, the 1st American division ran smack into the fresh German 352nd Infantry division and clung tenaciously to their foothold. Casualties mounted as the enemy poured a withering fire into the American ranks. Only the sheer bravery of the troops and the inspired leadership of General Norman Cota prevented a disaster. Eventually, the Americans established a firmer position. It was soon evident that they had come to stay and would not be dislodged.

Eisenhower spent June 6 nervously awaiting dispatches from the front. News that the landings went forcefully on was received with joy at headquarters, but later, the disturbing news from Omaha Beach cast a pall of gloom over the communications area. Late in the day, however, the situation improved and a sense of euphoria prevailed since it was clear that Overlord was a huge success.

Eisenhower had no need for his earlier statement. Instead, the following message was released to the press and for broadcast.

Under the command of General Eisenhower, Allied naval forces, supported by strong air forces, began landing Allied armies this morning on the northern coast of France.[25]

The democratic nations of the West reveled in jubilation. People stopped work, celebrated, bells pealed and groups gathered to sing their national anthems.

For the next few days, other than a quick trip by destroyer to visit the beachead, Eisenhower took little active part in the battle preferring to leave the tactical struggle to his subordinates, Montgomery and Bradley. Both commanders pushed inland, but the going was difficult and by the end of the third day, the objectives of D-Day + 1 had not been reached.

On his trip to Normandy, Eisenhower met with both men. The British objective, Caen, remained firmly in German hands while Montgomery continued his buildup. A half-hearted attempt to capture the city had resulted in a bloody repulse, thanks to the efforts of Rommel who had returned quickly to the front.

Meanwhile, on Bradley's side, the troops made slow but steady progress inland. Concerned lest the Germans counterattack and split the American forces, Eisenhower directed Bradley to turn his spearheads inward so that they could link up and form a massive block. Other than that, Ike would not interfere in the conduct of the battle.

Since World War II, some historians have criticized what they feel was an Allied obsession with the capture of ports. However, as events proved themselves, Eisenhower was absolutely justified in establishing the capture of ports as one of the immediate prime objectives of Overlord. Lack of port facilities large enough to accommodate enormous quantities of men and supplies meant that the Allies would be reduced to supplying their armies over open beaches. If a quick buildup was to be accomplished, this method would never do. Artificial floating docks were anchored off the Normandy beaches to facilitate the immediate buildup, but these were not intended as permanent installations and their capacity was inadequate. Consequently, the port of Cherbourg at the tip of the Cotentin Peninsula was one of the prime objectives of Bradley's First Army. As soon as adequate forces were available, the attack began in earnest. The battle for Cherbourg is examined at length in the chapter on Bradley. At the other end of the front, Montgomery's failure to deliver Caen became a source of irritation to the Americans.

One June 10, Eisenhower greeted Marshall and the

other members of the Joint Chiefs of Staff who arrived in London en route to the beachhead. Two days later, the group visited Bradley's headquarters and expressed satisfaction with the progress thus far. Still, Eisenhower was beginning to have reservations.

It appeared that little progress was being made toward breaking into metropolitan France. Bradley's terrain included the dreaded hedgerows which slowed the advance considerably.

At Caen, Montgomery was having his own difficulties. The Germans had concentrated the bulk of their available forces on his front, including most of their panzer divisions. The enemy continued to cling to the port. Eisenhower was disturbed by Montgomery's apparent failure. He expected the breakout to occur on the British front, but after two weeks, the D + 1 objectives were still in German hands. Instead, Montgomery continued to build up his beachhead.

On the American front, Bradley was having trouble, too. The *bocage* country reduced the rate of advance to yards at a time. By the twelfth, Collins' VII Corps was also short of its D-Day objectives. The Germans were determined to stand and fight.

Added to the problem of the sluggish advance was the arrival of the first V-1 bombs on June 13. The V-1 flying bombs were actually rocket-propelled, unmanned weapons carrying almost two thousand pounds of explosives. From their launching sites on the coast, the bombs could climb to a height of three thousand feet and attain a speed of three hundred seventy-five miles per hour before plunging to earth on English soil. Although the first day's effort was relatively light, the quantity of bombings increased daily until England found itself involved in another blitz.

Eisenhower decided to reinforce Bradley with

another corps and on June 14, the XIX Corps moved into line between V and VII Corps. This was followed a few days later by Middleton's VIII Corps. Even so, Bradley could make little headway. Until the breakout from Normandy occurred, Eisenhower planned to remain in England since there was little he could achieve at an advance headquarters.

On June 17, Collins finally managed to cut the Cotentin Peninsula. Two days later, he began the final thrust on Cherbourg, but the city held out for ten more days. When the Americans finally broke in, most of the dockyard facilities were found to have been destroyed by the Germans. It was many more weeks before Cherbourg became functional.

Still, the buildup continued. The Germans bitterly contested every foot with a grim determination and made excellent use of the natural terrain. Repeated attacks by Montgomery at Caen failed to dent the enemy front while Bradley remained bogged down in Normandy. Eisenhower was unhappy with the situation. His objective was to liberate Europe, not capture a small part of Normandy and sit still. Were it not for the huge success of Fortitude, the enemy's Fifteenth Army would also have joined the fray and made events even worse. For this at least Eisenhower was grateful.

Finally, Montgomery came forward with a plan. He would launch a full-scale attack (Operation Goodwood) in the vicinity of Caen and draw most of the enemy formations to his front. This would enable Bradley to launch his own attack (Operation Cobra), consolidate his gains, and prepare for a final breakout. Afterward, Montgomery insisted that this had been his plan all along, but there is little evidence to support this. It was, though, a wise move and whether it was conceived in England or during the heat of battle is academic. The fact is it served its purpose.

On the fifteenth of the month the weather again took a turn. The worst storm in over twenty years ravaged the English Channel, lashed the beachhead, destroyed shipping, wrecked the artificial harbors, grounded the air forces, ultimately halting all military operations. Since this was supposedly the only other period during the month when tidal and lunar conditions were favorable, the only consolation Eisenhower could draw from the storm was that it justified his gamble of June 4 when he made the decision to launch the invasion. In the face of this raging storm, it would have been impossible to proceed.

Upset with the lack of any significant progress, Eisenhower set out for the front on July 1 to spend a few days with Bradley and see for himself what the trouble was. After observing the front line for 5 days, Eisenhower returned to England satisfied that Bradley was giving his all. Bradley was a highly competent commander and so were the corps commanders. Yet, the offensive could not gather momentum.

While at the front, Eisenhower did a rather fool-hardy thing. Bradley's fighter commander, General Pete Quesada, told Eisenhower that he was flying towards Paris in search of action. Ike asked to come along and Quesada eagerly consented. Thus, the Supreme Commander of the entire Allied effort hitched a ride aboard Quesada's Mustang and flew off over enemy lines spoiling for a fight. Fortunately, no enemy aircraft was encountered and both generals landed safely. Eisenhower's staff was stunned. To them, the episode showed a lack of responsibility.

Returning to England, Eisenhower decided to breathe some new life into the stalemate. George Patton was released from command of Fortitude's fake army and allowed to head for France. Although his Third Army was not scheduled to be activated until

August 1, Eisenhower felt that George might just provide the needed spark.

Montgomery's effort at Caen still failed to gain new ground. Eisenhower was visibly upset with what he considered over-cautiousness on the part of the British commander, but in the interest of unity and teamwork refused to get involved directly. The Deputy Supreme Commander, Tedder, who had little use for his countryman was not so generous and was all for sacking him once and for all. Eisenhower would not hear of it since an incident of this nature was politically out of the question.

Conscious of the fact that the critics were clamoring for his scalp, the day after the conclusion of Goodwood, Montgomery invited Eisenhower to visit his headquarters alone. The British general was sure he could smooth things over and reason with Eisenhower, but knew that his sales pitch would fall on deaf ears if Tedder, Smith, or Bradley came along. Ike also knew that negative feelings towards Montgomery ran deep at headquarters, so he accepted the invitation.

On July 20, the two generals met at Montgomery's headquarters where the latter's persuasive manner managed to excuse the failure of Goodwood. However, upon returning to his own headquarters, Eisenhower dashed off a memo stating,

A few days ago when armored divisions of Second Army assisted by tremendous air attack broke through the enemy's forward lines I was extremely hopeful and optimistically I thought that at last we had him and were going to roll him up. That did not come about.[26]

The letter failed to express the depth of Eisenhower's disgust accurately, but he would not yield to Montgomery's critics. Ike had no intention of either sacking or antagonizing his British commander. Montgomery was a showman, a superb salesman, and held a high opinion of himself. Many fell victim to the almost mystical spell he was able to cast when presenting his position; Eisenhower was one of those taken in by Montgomery's charisma. Therefore, except to urge a more intensified effort, Eisenhower was content to let the matter stand even though, deep down, he was acutely disturbed.

Montgomery's effort had accomplished something, however. It drew the bulk of the enemy armor onto his front. Now was the time to take advantage of the situation. Eisenhower had just the men to exploit it; Bradley, Lightning Joe Collins, and George Patton. Exploit it they did, in a truly magnificent fashion. During the last week in July, Collins' VII Corps succeeded in breaking through the enemy defenses near St. Lo. On the twenty-eighth, Middleton's VIII Corps under Patton's guidance blew a gap in the German front near Avranches with a strong armored attack. The stalemate was over.

On August 1, Eisenhower moved Bradley up to army group command and officially sanctioned the activation of Patton's Third Army. Courtney Hodges succeeded Bradley in command of First Army. Montgomery retained overall ground command to the dismay of the American commanders.

With Brooke's approval, Montgomery began to intensify his effort to retain overall ground command permanently. The two British generals never had agreed with Eisenhower's strategic plan. Instead of having a group of armies advance into Germany shoulder to shoulder presenting a powerful phalanx of power, they proposed a strong thrust along a single front into the heartland of Germany via the industrialized Ruhr. And who better to command this thrust than the hero of Alamein himself, Bernard L. Montgomery. The American armies were to support this thrust, placing them in a secondary role.

This proposal was rejected by Eisenhower out of hand. Although he was reluctant to antagonize Montgomery, the Supreme Commander did not share Brooke's estimate of Monty's military ability. Furthermore, he knew that Marshall would flatly refuse to sanction such an arrangement. The feelings of the American commanders also deserved consideration. Eisenhower knew that Patton and Montgomery were bitter antagonists, but even more significant, Bradley made no secret of his unwillingness to serve under his British counterpart. Above all other Allied commanders, Eisenhower valued Bradley. Although Eisenhower considered the matter closed, Montgomery would persist in broaching the subject at every opportunity. Eventually, this led to an irreconcilable difference between the two.

While the British continued to hack away at the shackles around Caen, Patton, in grand fashion, moved to exploit the breakthrough. With four corps, he left Normandy in his wake and fanned out into the French countryside. (See Map 5).

Eisenhower was overjoyed at the prospect of finally being able to boast some progress.

If the intercepts are right, we are to hell and gone in Brittany and slicing them up in Normandy.[27]

Now that the race for Germany was on in earnest, he began preparations for moving his headquarters to the continent permanently. According to Miss Summersby and Commander Butcher, the chief seemed to be more relaxed and at ease. During the stalemate in Normandy, he had begun to show evidence of high blood pressure, but the symptoms seemed to subside as the offensive moved forward. With his headquarters closer to the fighting front, Eisenhower began to take the reins more firmly in his own hands. As it would continue to do, the question of obtaining port facilities to allow for adequate supply of the Allied forces dominated strategy.

Meanwhile, Patton was loose in France and running wild. By the first week in August, it was obvious that the Germans had blundered seriously when they counterattacked against Bradley's army group in the area of Mortain. Thanks to Ultra intercepts, Allied headquarters anticipated the German move and Hitler's refusal to call it off when failure was obvious. Thus, while First Army dealt with the enemy counterattack, Third Army maneuvered into the rear of the German Seventh Army.

Between August 12 and the 20, the Germans suffered a disastrous defeat at Falaise, thanks to Patton's rapid advance. Unfortunately, the victory was incomplete, thanks to Montgomery's inability to close the trap. Eisenhower's responsibility for the escape of the German army was in the failure to assume overall command himself, Bradley took this as a vote of confidence in the British commander and refused to appeal the latter's decision to halt Patton at Argentan while his own forces attempted to close the trap. When Patton appealed the decision to Eisenhower over Bradley's head, Ike refused to overrule the previous order. Consequently, one of the great opportunities of the war was missed.

Not only did Eisenhower have to deal with the friction between his subordinates, he was plagued by the presence of Charles DeGaulle. After the fiasco in

North Africa, the Allies decided to recognize DeGaulle and his Free French movement. Like Giraud earlier, this French leader began to make impossible demands on the Supreme Commander. DeGaulle was easily offended and considered himself the true voice of France. All attempts to enlist French aid had to be approved by him. He was an Anglophobe and made life miserable for Eisenhower.

On the eve of the invasion, DeGaulle had threatened to withhold his support unless his demands were met and it was only Eisenhower's persuasive manner which finally won over 'le grand Charles.' Nevertheless, DeGaulle insisted on the liberation of Paris as one of the early objectives of the campaign. In addition, he would have the Allies recognize him as the head of the French government. Not only was Paris to be freed, but this must be accomplished by French troops. Such was the state of affairs staring Eisenhower in the face. With a huge military problem sitting on his shoulders, the Supreme Commander certainly did not need the added burden of an ugly political situation.

Eisenhower had not planned on moving into Paris early. Recapturing the city meant that the Allies would be bound to supply food, clothing, and other essentials for the citizens of the French capital. With the port facilities barely able to provide for the military needs, additional demands would be a great hardship.

Despite Eisenhower's attempts to reason with DeGaulle, the French leader continued to press his demands and was not adverse to the use of threats and outright blackmail. Finally, Eisenhower was forced to concede; he needed French cooperation. Then he demonstrated a trait which tarnished the image of an easy-going, generous leader.

After the debacle at Falaise, Patton's Third Army swung eastward and continued to thrust deeper into France. Leonard Gerow's V Corps was approaching Paris during the third week in August when suddenly, without prior notification, it was transferred from Third to First Army. At first, Patton was furious, but this soon subsided and he resigned himself to his fate. Eisenhower had not completely forgiven Patton for his prior indiscretions. Although Ike respected Patton's fighting ability and felt a need for him in the campaign, their personal relationship had cooled. Consequently, Patton was denied the glorious opportunity of liberating the first city of France. The honor went to Hodges.

Fortunately for Eisenhower, General LeClerc's 2nd French Armored Division was close at hand and to this formation went the honor of freeing the French capital, thanks to DeGaulle's intercession.

In August of 1944, events were proceeding at a mind-boggling pace. Falaise, Paris, and the breakout were enough to tax the brain of any man charged with the overall coordination. To this burden was added the unleashing of Anvil (renamed Dragoon) on the fifteen of the month. The Allies finally managed to bring off landings in southern France. It was a cause that had long been championed by Eisenhower and Marshall and the two American generals were highly pleased that their determination had finally born fruit. The American Seventh Army under General Alexander Patch, bolstered later by the addition of the French First Army under General De Lattre, both part of Jacob Devers' Sixth Army Group, made rapid progress up the Rhone valley and completely justified Eisenhower's refusal to abandon the project in the face of determined resistance from Churchill, Brooke, and Montgomery. Right up until the eve of the invasion, the British maintained pressure on Eisenhower to cancel Dragoon. Fortunately for the Allied cause, the Supreme Commander refused to be swayed.

But, Dragoon was not the only new concern thrust upon the shoulders of the Supreme Commander. A choice had to be made between Patton and Montgomery. This time, personal feelings did not affect objective reasoning despite what the critics might say. The critical shortage of gasoline due to the inability of the Allies to stockpile adequate supplies necessitated a temporary abandonment of the broad front approach. A week earlier, Eisenhower had hoped to cross the Seine in strength. The Germans were on the run and he wanted to retain the initiative and deny them the opportunity of concentrating their forces. At the time, he chose to ignore the increasingly critical supply situation while clinging to the hope that the Germans could be defeated before the shortage became acute. It was a futile dream.

On August 22, Montgomery's chief of staff, De-Guingand, hand-carried a proposal to Eisenhower suggesting a rapid drive on Antwerp. The prospect appealed to Ike since the urgent need for another deep water port was paramount. Only one strong offensive could be supported and the obvious thing was to support the British drive. Not only was Europe's finest port, Antwerp, in the path of Montgomery's advance, so too were the V-1 launching sites. Naturally, this meant that Patton would have to bite the bullet since any stocks left over from the British would have to go to Hodges whose First Army covered the inboard flank of Montgomery's armies.

As mentioned, Antwerp was not the only objective. Daily, the diabolical V weapons rained death and destruction on a helpless England. The outcry for some sort of action against these sites could not be ignored. Therefore, as far as Eisenhower was concerned, there was little other choice. Unfortunately, he continued to have faith in Montgomery's ability to move rapidly despite an outcry by the American generals and Tedder. Bradley and Patton also protested vehemently, but to no avail. The former felt that since First Army was directed to support the British advance, he was in effect relinquishing command to Montgomery. For his part, Patton believed that he was being deliberately shut out in favor of the British general. Since he did not share Ike's opinion of the Englishman, all was not harmonious in the Allied camp.

The day after DeGuingand's visit, Eisenhower paid a call at the Twenty First Army Group headquarters where Montgomery sold him a bill of goods. He convinced Ike that a solid thrust into the Ruhr was essential for victory. The Supreme Commander decided to agree with Montgomery's proposition, but when the subject of an overall ground commander was again broached, Ike refused to consider it. Nevertheless, Patton would have to halt.

Being forced to decide between Montgomery and Patton was not the only bitter pill Eisenhower had to swallow. On September 1, when he officially assumed direct command, Churchill degraded the move by promoting Montgomery to the rank of Field Marshal; the subordinate outranked the commander in chief. It was a deliberate slap in the face by the British hierarchy. The American generals were furious. In an unusual outburst Bradley said:

> Montgomery is a third-rate general and he never did anything or won any battle that any other general could not have won as well or better.[28]

For once, Patton was at a loss for words. His simple comment was, "That field marshal thing made us sick."[29]

On August 26, Montgomery's forces crossed the Seine and set out on their drive along the Channel coast towards Antwerp. The Germans fell back reluctantly in the face of superior opposition and British progress was unusually fast, unlike their previous efforts.

Although he might have, Eisenhower did not adopt an 'I told you so' attitude. On September 2, he met with Patton, Bradley, and Hodges. The unified voice of the three American generals caused Eisenhower to change his mind once more. The previous day Third Army had captured the famous World War I battlefield of Verdun, despite the critical shortage of gasoline. Patton continued to advance at will, so did First Army, and Hodges was moving up the Belgium border. Consequently, Eisenhower allocated additional fuel to Patton and altered First Army's support role by returning it to Bradley's operational command.

Two days later, he again traveled to Montgomery's headquarters to inform the British commander that plans had been changed once more. A few weeks earlier, while returning to his own headquarters, Eisenhower's small plane had been forced down near the coast. The pilot selected a suitable beach and set the plane safely down near the water. When he and his illustrious passenger attempted to move the aircraft safely from the water's edge, Eisenhower slipped in the sand and wrenched his knee. Though not serious, the injury was nonetheless painful and his doctor ordered the leg placed in a cast. Therefore, when he showed up at 21st Army Group headquarters, the cumbersome cast prevented him from leaving the plane. The meeting was held aboard the aircraft.

When Montgomery heard the latest plan, he began rudely to harangue Eisenhower and denounce the strategy, returning repeatedly to the single thrust theory as opposed to the broad front strategy. At the height of the argument, Eisenhower cut the disagreement short by placing his hand on Montgomery's knee and stating, "Steady, Monty. You can't speak to me like that. I'm your boss."[30]

Montgomery apologized and set forth an alternative plan. Although it was a desperate gamble designed to retain the key role in the offensive, Eisenhower saw merit in it and thought the plan bold and imaginative. He quickly gave his consent. Thus was born operation 'Market Garden,' the ill-fated airborne attack on Arnhem.

The approval of Market Garden meant once more shifting emphasis to the British sector. Thanks to Eisenhower's agreement, Montgomery assumed that the drive to the Ruhr was on once more. The highly touted attack began on September 17 and ended dismally eight days later with the loss of all but a handful of the 1st British Airborne Division. Still, Montgomery would not relent and continued to insist that a narrow front thrust under one commander was the proper course of action. Unfortunately, Eisenhower had little option but to continue his support of Montgomery's drive. As the end of September approached, Patton was bogged down in front of Metz. When Montgomery did reach Antwerp, he allowed German General von Zangen to remain between his forces and the sea. The German Fifteenth Army controlled both banks of the Scheldt Estuary, the approach route to the port. Thus, the area was useless to the Allied cause. Because Antwerp sat in the

British zone, emphasis had to remain in their sector.

Eisenhower was not happy with the prospect of being forced to support Montgomery. During a conversation with a visiting American general, Everett Hughes, he said, "I want Antwerp but I have to depend on Monty."[31]

When Hughes suggested that Eisenhower offer Montgomery an incentive for success such as a promotion Eisenhower replied,

> To what? When the King was in North Africa he said he was delighted to discover that Monty wasn't after his job."[32]

Throughout October, the stalemate continued. Only First Army was able to register significant gains. The British paused to regroup and concentrate their efforts on clearing the Scheldt Estuary and opening up Antwerp while Patton remained bogged down, out of gas, out of ammunition, and out of patience.

As November approached, the entire Allied effort rolled inexorably forward. The invigorating days of chewing off huge chunks of enemy territory were past. The fall of 1944 was marked by bloody static battles. Metz, Aachen, the Scheldt, and the Huertgen Forrest saw some of the most bitter fighting of the entire European war. On Devers' front, the Germans held on in the Colmar Pocket despite all efforts to reduce the salient. The onset of winter boded ill and brought the days of great campaigning to a halt.

The Germans, though, were far from finished. On December 16, the greatest crisis of Eisenhower's military career threatened the Allies with the prospect of a disastrous defeat. Erupting out of the Ardennes on First Army's front, two German Panzer armies supported by two additional flanking armies suddenly counterattacked and rolled over the Allied formations in their path. Allied headquarters was taken totally unawares. (See Map 8).

Eisenhower hadn't dismissed the possibility of a German counterattack, but never in his wildest dreams did he think the enemy was capable of launching such a powerful stroke. The Allied offensive thus far had been so successful that it lulled the commanders into a false sense of security which caused them to neglect defensive dispositions. With the possible exception of Patton, the entire Allied command felt this way. The Allies were caught napping, probably because Allied intelligence groups had come to place too much reliance on Ultra. Since the enemy forbade the use of wireless during the buildup for the Ardennes offensive, Allied intelligence had little information on which to base their assessments of German intentions. Eisenhower had repeatedly cautioned against this very thing. From the time he first learned of the existence of Ultra, he could see how such a marvelous weapon might be abused by over-reliance on it. At every opportunity, Ike emphasized that he preferred to have Ultra's information confirmed by more traditional intelligence-gathering methods, such as the use of spies, aerial photographs, and reports from resistance groups.

The situation was so critical that Eisenhower himself took a direct hand in planning countermeasures. As each hour passed, the German steamroller gathered momentum and pushed First Army units aside or smashed them where they stood. The first thing Eisenhower sensed when looking at a map of the area was that Bastogne was a pivot point. It was a key road junction, lying directly in the path of the German advance of which the enemy had to gain possession if his offensive was to be successful. All American forces in the area were immediately rushed into Bastogne and ordered to hold on at all cost. He then contacted his key commanders and ordered them to meet with him on the nineteenth.

In the interim, Eisenhower made every effort to scrape all available man power together and rush them to the front. Pardons were offered to prisoners in stockades throughout France if they were willing to fight. The rear areas were combed and stripped of all unessential noncombatants. These troops too were issued weapons and sent forward. Despite these efforts, the situation deteriorated with each passing hour.

When Eisenhower reached Verdun on the nineteenth, Patton, Bradley, and Devers awaited him. Ike made no bones about who was in charge. Patton was ordered to pull much of Third Army out of line, swing it around, and head for Bastogne. Devers was directed to backfill the vacated sector with units from his army group. The meeting adjourned with all participants united in one goal—defeat of the German attack.

The following morning, Eisenhower went one step further. This battle had no room for consideration of personal feelings. The northern side of the Bulge consisting of the bulk of Hodges' command was placed under Montgomery's leadership. Bradley retained control of the southern half, but this consisted of only Patton's Third Army.

Two days before Christmas, St. Vith, on the northern side of the Bulge, fell after an heroic struggle. This marked the high point of the German offensive in that sector. On Christmas day, Patton made contact with the defenders of Bastogne. Third Army had accomplished the incredible. It had pulled out of line, swung around ninety degrees and conducted a flank march through blinding snow and slippery roads. Patton drove into the southern flank of the German attack and began to drive the enemy back from whence he had come.

In the north, the enemy attack ran out of steam because of insufficient fuel and a determined American defense. Monty asked for a fighting American general to command a counterattack. Eisenhower and Hodges sent him one of the finest, 'Lightning Joe' Collins. When Montgomery hesitated in launching the attack, Collins became impatient and attacked on his own initiative. Between Patton and Collins, the enemy advance was brought to an abrupt halt.

Eisenhower then ordered a counterattack all along the front for January 1. When the date arrived, Bradley dutifully launched his, but Montgomery's was not forthcoming. Ike was furious. His patience with the British commander finally wore thin enough to snap. Montgomery insisted that he had not agreed to a counterattack, but Eisenhower knew better. It was the final straw. Ike began to contemplate seriously relieving Montgomery once and for all. DeGuingand got wind of the idea and forewarned his boss who hastily swallowed his pride and apologized.

In the interim, the British chiefs had gotten involved. They wired Marshall their opinion that the Bulge was the result of Eisenhower's refusal to adopt Montgomery's single thrust theory. In a strongly worded reply, Marshall reminded the British that America was making the greatest effort in Europe and reported that an American general would remain in charge. After Brooke informed Monty of this reply, the field marshal abandoned his pursuit of overall ground command once and for all. He knew now that he was expendable.

Bolstered by Marshall's vote of confidence,

Eisenhower took a firmer stand. Nevertheless, the British drive into the Ruhr remained the dominant Allied strategy.

After a brief pause following the Battle of the Bulge, the entire Allied line surged forward. First Army was returned to Bradley's command, but Simpson's Ninth U.S. Army which had been activated the previous fall remained under Montgomery's direction.

By the end of the first week in March, all Allied armies stood ready to cross the Rhine. The great undertaking was to be in the north where the British crossing was scheduled for the twenty-third. However, on the 7th, elements of First Army captured an intacted bridge over the river near the town of Remagen. Bradley and Hodges ordered the capture exploited, but Eisenhower directed that the bridgehead be consolidated only. Montgomery would make the supreme effort. (See Map 13).

Patton, too, crossed ahead of the British. On March 22, near Oppenheim, the 5th Division using boats established a bridgehead on the opposite bank. Patton and Bradley saw to it that the news was made public. Montgomery's crossing on March 23 was anticlimatic.

Since landing in Normandy, all the Allied field commanders had set their sights on reaching Berlin and took it for granted that the German capital was the final objective. Now, Eisenhower began to have reservations. His wartime correspondence proves that until the spring of 1945, he had contemplated a drive to Berlin by whichever army was closest when the opportunity arose.

Increasing rumors of a last ditch German stand in the Hartz mountains could not be ignored. From this so-called National Redoubt, the Germans could hold out indefinitely. Then, there was the prospect of heavy casualties if the enemy elected to stand and fight for Berlin. Therefore, it was decided that Berlin was not a military target worthy of the effort and the strategic objectives were revised.

Patton was directed to slice through southern Germany to prevent the Germans from securing the fortification. Simpson was removed from Montgomery's command and, in conjunction with Hodges, was ordered to encircle and reduce enemy resistance in the Ruhr. The British were told to drive for the Baltic. Berlin was to be ignored.

When the decision to ignore Berlin was made, Eisenhower wired Stalin on his own recognizance and informed the Russian leader that it was the Allies' intention to halt on the Elbe River and await the linkup with Soviet forces advancing westward. It was a foolish attempt to meddle in politics which were beyond the sphere of his responsibility. Churchill was livid when he found that Eisenhower had contacted Stalin without clearing it first. Fortunately, the war was almost at an end and Eisenhower survived the crisis. On the other hand, post-war opinions are still debated to this day.

Near the end of April, the last remaining German army in the west surrendered when First and Ninth Armies linked up at the eastern edge of the Ruhr. The Allies were harried more by refugees and troops eager to surrender before being overrun by the Russians than they were from enemy resistance. An attempt to surrender portions of the German Army to Montgomery failed when the British commander refused to consider anything but total surrender in the west. He was a team player at last. Finally, on May 7, at Eisenhower's headquarters near Rheims, the unconditional surrender of all German forces to both the Allies and the Russians was signed by General Alfred

Jodl. Bedell Smith signed for the Allies.

Eisenhower remained in Germany before returning home to a jubilant and grateful nation. One of his final acts before leaving Europe was to relieve Patton of command of Third Army. Patton had incurred Eisenhower's wrath again with his liberal interpretations of orders governing fraternization with the defeated enemy and his public statements denouncing the Russians. Now that there was no need for his military talent, Eisenhower could afford to part with Patton. The Third Army commander was transferred to Berlin and charged with writing the history of the war.

Eisenhower remained on active duty until 1951. After returning home, he succeeded his mentor Marshall as Chief of Staff. He then returned to the scene of his wartime triumph as commander of the NATO forces in Europe. In 1951, he attained the ultimate, Commander in Chief, when he was elected to the Presidency of the United States. Ironically, his election took place during a period when America was involved in another war, the Korean conflict. Just as they had turned to him ten years earlier, the citizens of the United States looked to their beloved Ike to lead them through another war.

Post-war criticism of Eisenhower's wartime record could fill volumes. As expected, much of this reproof comes from British sources. A feud between Ike and Montgomery continued unabated until their respective deaths, with both parties taking occasional sarcastic jabs at each other's competence. The British never had considered Eisenhower a brilliant general and post-war assessments clearly prove their opinions remain unchanged. Brooke was particularly critical.

Neither have American historians been any kinder. Among the less flattering things Eisenhower has been called are, 'a top rate clerk,' 'Marshall's mouthpiece,' and 'a mediocre commander.' With few exceptions history has treated the man roughly.

The irrefutable fact remains that Eisenhower accomplished the job he set out to do. Could the great ones—Marshall, Bradley, Montgomery, Brooke, Patton, or MacArthur—have achieved the same level of success in the European theater? The answer is no. Eisenhower's assignment was to mold an Anglo-American force into a formidable war machine and lead it to victory over Nazi Germany and he succeeded brilliantly. Eisenhower was not expected to lead an army on the field of battle. For this purpose, he had highly competent subordinates, commanders who he hand-picked. That he could manage such a diverse group of personalities was an achievement in itself. Though it frequently appeared that he favored Montgomery over the American commanders, this can be attributed to his exposure to Fox Connor during the twenties. Connor's words about coalition warfare being the most difficult type were never forgotten. Thus, Eisenhower may have gone overboard to appease Montgomery just because he was British. Eisenhower took these diverse soldiers, put together a team, went out, and won a war.

Eisenhower's greatest assets were his warm, engaging manner, the ever-present 'Ike smile,' and his ability to charm and persuade. When he became President, an entire new generation of Americans succumbed to his down home, humble manner. His eight-year term of office was one of the most peaceful and prosperous of this century for the United States. Eisenhower's success in his dealings with people came from his ability to make them feel an important part of the team, not because he was unwilling to make a decision himself, as so many detractors are wont to accuse him of. In the end, even Montgomery acknowledged Ike's great achievement.

> I owe much to your wise guidance and kindly forbearance. I know my own faults very well and I do not suppose I am an easy subordinate; I like to go my own way. But you have kept me on the rails in difficult and stormy times, and have taught me much.[33]

The magnificent wartime career of General of the Army, Dwight D. Eisenhower, ended with the appropriate words.

> The mission of this Allied force was fulfilled at 0241 local time, May 7, 1945.[34]

Chapter 6

Who was this man, General of the Army Douglas MacArthur? Military genius? Fighter? Politician? Military Governor and would-be Emperor? In truth, he was all that and more. In a sense, Douglas MacArthur is indescribable. He was certainly a man of extremes. His political views were ultra-right wing and yet, as military leader of post-war Japan, he proved to be an enlightened liberal. During the first World War, he was a front line soldier even though he held the rank of General, but at Bataan during World War II his men tagged him with the nickname 'Dugout Doug' as his appearances on the battlefield were infrequent at best. Yet, he was the most highly praised military strategist of the war. Churchill called him a 'glorious commander.' Lord Alanbrooke, British Chief of the Imperial General Staff also proclaimed him the greatest general and finest strategist of the war. Even General George C. Marshall, no friend of MacArthur's, said that he was America's most brilliant commander. Brilliant, yes, but at times his brilliance seemed to desert him and he made some rather serious errors.

Nine hours after Pearl Harbor, his B-17s at Clark Field in the Philippines were destroyed while still on the ground parked wing tip to wing tip. He then neglected to stock enough food in Bataan, despite the knowledge that his last stand would be at that particular place. In addition, MacArthur drastically under valued the ability of the Japanese before the war, just as he later underestimated the movement of the Chinese Communist forces in Korea. Nevertheless, in spite of these errors in judgment, his record of victories is unmatched. His economic use of men was nothing short of remarkable. There were fewer casualties in his entire theater of operations from the beginning of the struggle in Australia to the Japanese surrender than America suffered in the Battle of the Bulge alone. His mastery of the use of combined operations (air, sea, and land) is without parallel in military history. During the course of his career, he launched no fewer than eighty-seven amphibious landings in all. Sir Basil Liddell-Hart has said,

> MacArthur was supreme among the Generals. His combination of strong personality, strategic grasp, tactical skill, operative mobility and vision put him in a class above other Allied commanders in any theater.[1]

His bravery cannot be doubted. He earned twenty-two medals for heroism, including the Congressional Medal of Honor, the Distinguished Service Cross, and the Silver Star. During the First World War, he came to believe that a commander should lead from the front. One night, while on reconnaissance, he heard the rumbling of vehicles on the move. When he saw that they were German, he immediately sensed that the enemy was pulling back. This then was the time to hit them before they could re-establish their lines. Lacking sufficient time to consult higher authority, he took it upon himself to gather up his battalion and ordered them to advance. The attack proved a huge success and for his audacity he was awarded a fourth Silver Star. On many occasions during the Second

World War, he took chances that some people said were suicidal.

There are many appropriate adjectives available to describe this enigma in a soldier's uniform: pompous, blustery, imperious, egotistical, and showy. The latter was perhaps the most obvious. As a Brigadier General in the First World War, he disdained the use of a helmet, would not carry a gas mask, went about unarmed, carried a riding crop in his hand, and could usually be found in the trenches instead of at headquarters. In the Philippines, he had a special gold braided cap designed and this, along with his famous corn cob pipe, added to the mystique.

Where did this magnificent soldier come from?

My first recollection is that of a bugle call.[2]

Musketry, pounding hooves, trumpet blasts, the boom of field guns, Indian war cries, all formed the backdrop, sights, and sounds for young Douglas MacArthur who was born on January 26, 1880. His formative pre-school years were spent in the forts of the Old West. To a young boy, the life was idyllic. Douglas and his older brother Arthur III learned to ride and shoot even before mastering reading and writing. Their days were spent in riding, hunting, and the observance of their idol, Arthur MacArthur, Jr., the Civil War hero of Missionary Ridge. His father was Douglas' boyhood ideal, a man to whom he constantly looked for approval and who he would later use as a measuring rod for his own life's accomplishments. Young Douglas grew up amidst stories of great Indian battles and the even more famous battles of the Civil War. Though his father was his idol, it was his mother who had the greatest influence. She would remain his constant companion until he was in his fifties and even accompanied him up the Hudson River to the United States Military Academy where she was so close that she was able to observe him in his room. This remarkable woman instilled in her son from his early days his attitudes on life and especially the importance of duty.

When they finally left the wilderness, the MacArthurs went first to Fort Leavenworth then to Washington, D.C. To the youthful Douglas, life in civilization seemed dull compared to that on the Great American Desert. In Washington, he was enrolled in public school for the first time. His father was heard to have remarked at the time, "I think there is the material of a soldier in that boy." Douglas never forgot that, though only thirteen, his course was set straight towards that goal.

After four years in the nation's capital, Arthur was assigned to Fort Sam Houston in San Antonio, Texas. There, Douglas entered the academy which later became known as the Texas Military Institute. He excelled in both academics and athletics and achieved an academic average of 97.3, earning for himself the Institute's Gold Medal in addition to the distinction of Class Valedictorian of 1897.

An appointment to West Point was then enthusiastically sought by the MacArthurs. For over a year, both his father and grandfather had been soliciting letters of recommendation and political endorsements. Unfortunately, Douglas was not rewarded with an appointment. Even the preliminary physical was unfavorable and revealed a curvature of the spine. Not to be outdone, MacArthur's forceful mother moved her residency to the district of a Congressman who was a friend of Douglas' grandfather and sought out a doctor who could correct the spinal problem. Since the Congressman was beseiged with more candidates than he had appointments for, in order to be fair, he authorized a competitive exam to be given to the prospective nominees. MacArthur scored the highest and was given the coveted appointment. Thanks to the indomitable will of his mother, Douglas' military career commenced.

At West Point, Cadet MacArthur earned honor after honor, finishing first in his class with an accumulative average of 98.14, one that had been surpassed only twice before. As a graduate of the Class of '03, Second Lt. MacArthur would have preferred an assignment to the cavalry, but instead, he went into the Corps of Engineers where, it was reasoned, chances for advancement were more promising.

While Douglas attended West Point, his father's career took an uphill turn when he was assigned the command of the American contingent and became Governor General of the Philippines. Just as quickly, however, his fortunes skidded backward after political problems with William Howard Taft necessitated the General's recall.

After graduation, the young lieutenant was assigned to the Philippines. En route to take up his first command, he stopped off in San Francisco where he managed to spend some time with his father before boarding ship. His first contact with the Philippines deeply impressed the young shave-tail.

Already he had fallen in love with the 7,083 island Philippine archipelago.[3]

He was initially posted to Iboilo on Panay, then to Tacloban on Leyte where he supervised construction of a dock and led patrols into the interior. During one of these patrols, hostile tribesmen fired on him, ripping a hole in the top of his campaign hat. Like a lawman of the Old West, he quickly drew his revolver and felled the would-be assassins. Shortly thereafter, he was posted to Manila where he took and passed his examination for advancement to First Lt. From there he was sent on a surveying detail of the Bataan Peninsula. He quickly recognized the great defensive potential of the area. In fact, the Philippine Nationalist hero, Emilio Aquinaldo, had only recently made his last stand there and at the time MacArthur was overheard to say that it had been a very wise move.

In October 1904, he found himself back in San Francisco. The following July, he was appointed acting Chief Engineer of the Division of the Pacific which necessitated his proceeding to Tokyo and reporting to none other than Major General Arthur MacArthur as aide-de-camp. Arthur was scheduled to leave on an inspection tour of the Orient and was desirous of having his wife and son accompany him. They first toured Japan, then Shanghai, Hong Kong, and Java. From there, they traveled to Singapore, Burma, and India. After leaving India, the return journey took them to Japan via Thailand, Indo-China, and the Chinese mainland. The trip affected Douglas profoundly. In his reminiscences, he said of the trip,

It was without doubt the most important factor of preparation in my entire life. . . . It was crystal clear to me that the future and, indeed the very existence of America, was irrevocably entwined with Asia and its island outposts. It was to be sixteen years before I returned to the Far East, but always was its mystic hold upon me.[4]

In the autumn of 1906, MacArthur was back in the United States where he attended the Engineering School at Washington Barracks. He graduated the following August and was assigned to construction duty in Milwaukee, Wisconsin. Two years of frustration followed for the young man who was torn between duty and family responsibility. Since he lived with his parents, their never ceasing demands kept him preoccupied to the point of neglecting his engineering duties. His commanding officer scathingly struck out at MacArthur with poor efficiency reports. Not until his transfer to Fort Leavenworth did he finally find his true vocation, command of troops. He reveled in this duty and shaped his company to A-1 efficiency. He remained at this post for four years and thoroughly enjoyed the experience.

On February 11, 1911, MacArthur was finally promoted to Captain. After a few brief tours of routine duty, he was assigned to Washington following the death of his father. Thanks to influential friends of the now deceased parent, Douglas and his mother, to whose care she was now entrusted, found themselves once more in the District of Columbia.

In May 1913, he was appointed Superintendent of the Old State, War and Navy Building and the following September was named a member of the General Staff. But, would the young officer have the opportunity to outshine his illustrious father? As Europe plunged towards war, the United States found itself involved in its own foreign problem with its neighbor to the south, Mexico. As the situation drifted slowly towards war, the U.S. Chief of Staff, General Leonard Wood, desired information on Mexico badly. MacArthur was sent to Vera Cruz on May 1, 1914. An epic story followed as the thirty-five year old captain penetrated the Mexican interior. Danger marked the path as his group was ambushed a number of times. General Wood subsequently recommended MacArthur for the Medal of Honor, but the awards board turned it down to the young man's chagrin. One thing, however, was certain; Captain MacArthur had demonstrated initiative, enterprise, and an abundance of courage.

On his return from Mexico, he was reappointed to the General Staff and received his promotion to Major in December of the following year. As America became irrevocably drawn towards the debacle in Europe, Major MacArthur prepared himself for the inevitable. He became the champion of National Guard units. There was a question as to whether these units should fight. A departmental study recommended they be bypassed; MacArthur disagreed and advocated their use. There were, unfortunately, political implications to overcome. Since the National Guard was formed by states, there was an inherent danger that one state would complain that their boys were being used more than those of other states. This problem was solved when MacArthur suggested forming divisions of units drawn from several states. Thus, the 42nd Division, the famous Rainbow Division, was born. It was given its name because "it will stretch over the whole country like a rainbow."[5]

MacArthur was appointed Colonel and given the post of Chief of Staff to General William Mann, the Divisional Commander.

Douglas MacArthur's career during the First World War could make a book of its own and therefore only the briefest outline can be covered here in order to focus more on his World War II exploits. The troops of the 42nd idolized him. He shared their discomforts and dangers. His reputation grew as his exploits became legendary. MacArthur was cited many times for valor and the Doughboys called him "The D'Artagnan of the AEF . . . the fighting dude."[6]

Though wounded twice, by and large he seemed to

lead a charmed life.

During the summer of 1918, MacArthur received his first star designating him Brigadier General. Even as a general, however, he remained at the front. His divisional commander at the time said of him,

> MacArthur is the bloodiest fighting man in the army. I'm afraid we're going to lose him sometime, for there's no risk of battle that any soldier is called to take that he is not liable to look up and see MacArthur at his side.[7]

He quickly became the best known man in the A.E.F. His reputation, his distinctive dress, his ability as a fighter, and daredevil feats became renowned. After all, when had a general ever crawled into no-man's-land to reconnoiter? MacArthur was cited twelve times for valor. One of these citations stated,

> On a field where courage was the rule, his courage was the dominant factor.[8]

Just prior to the end of the war, he was named commander of the Rainbow Division becoming, at the age of 38, the youngest divisional commander of the war. On October 17, 1918, General John (Black Jack) Pershing informed MacArthur that he had recommended him for the rank of Major General. But the Armistice intervened, ended hostilities, and froze all promotions. Thus, the coveted rank was denied him.

At war's end, MacArthur had earned a great reputation. In addition to the twelve decorations, he had received nineteen honors from the Allied nations. The one decoration he yearned for was, unfortunately, denied him again. The awards board considered him ineligible for the Medal of Honor. Inwardly, he fumed.

Brigadier General MacArthur returned home in April of 1919. A new challenge loomed on the horizon. West Point was in dire need of revitalization. General Peyton March, Army Chief of Staff, desired that hazing be suppressed, courses updated, and military instruction modernized to include the valuable lessons learned during the recently concluded conflict. To accomplish this, he said, the academy needed a new superintendent with a measure of brilliance combined with a great deal of charisma, a man who could relate to the modern world and understand the needs of the present day cadet. The man chosen by March was, of course, Douglas MacArthur, the most decorated general officer of the Great War.

MacArthur was hesitant, but March persisted and on June 19, 1919, West Point received its first postwar superintendent. The assignment was not only a great challenge but a prestigious plum as well. Furthermore, it served to confirm MacArthur in his brevet rank of Brigadier General rather than having that rank reduced to the pre-war level of Major.

West Point badly needed some sort of reform. Coming as he did so recently from the battlefield, MacArthur was able to recognize that modern wars would be fought by nations in arms and not merely by small professional armies. These conditions would thus require officers with a broad, liberal education rather than simply an education dealing with the art of warfare. Consequently, the new superintendent immediately introduced an updated program which called for a broader curriculum, brought in university lecturers, and sent members of the teaching staff to visit other colleges and universities. Hazing was severely curtailed and other aspects of cadet life were brought into line with the changing times. As an example, each cadet was required to read two newspapers a day and be prepared to discuss current events. Censorship of mail was eliminated, cadets were granted the right to an allowance, and could be issued weekend passes. Finally, MacArthur officially recognized the academy's honor system.

These changes were not accepted overwhelmingly by the academic staff. While the cadets admired their new superintendent, the staff resisted change. Some of them still remembered their new superior as one of their students and resented this young non-faculty member dictating academic changes they wouldn't agree with. Another source of irritation to the instructors was MacArthur's unannounced classroom visits and his habit of returning salutes with a casual flick of his riding crop. This latter habit the staff considered a mockery and totally unmilitary. The staff also felt that his proposals for academic change would threaten the close-knit camaraderie between them and the corps of cadets and turn the latter's attention away from the job at hand, that of becoming soldiers. Powerful forces conspired against MacArthur as many former influential alumni sided with the academic community.

On Valentine's Day in 1922, Douglas MacArthur married Louise Cromwell Brooks, a wealthy divorcée. It was a complete mismatch and the groom's mother was visibly upset. This event, however, not only disturbed his mother, but it also alienated the new Chief of Staff, General Pershing who had his own designs on the bride. With the academic staff infuriated by his reforms and the powerful Pershing jealous of the marriage, MacArthur found himself abruptly relieved of his post and transferred along with his newly acquired wife to Manila. In many corners, this was viewed as an exile, but Pershing vehemently denied the charges and said it was time MacArthur experienced a little foreign service.

MacArthur was delighted with the turn of events since he was truly fond of the Philippines. Initially assigned to command the military district of Manila, he shortly assumed command of the Philippine Scout Brigade. One of his assignments was to survey the Bataan Peninsula, an unusual task for a Brigadier General. It was this job and the conclusions reached during it that helped the Washington strategists develop War Plan Orange which stated that, in the eventuality of an invasion of the Philippines by the forces of Imperial Japan, the defenders should withdraw to Bataan and hold out there until the arrival of a relief expedition.

Unlike her husband, MacArthur's wife did not readily adapt to life in Manila and quickly became restless and disenchanted. Thus were planted the first seeds of domestic discord.

On January 17, 1925, MacArthur received his second star, designating him Major General. Attaining this rank made him over-qualified for the Philippine command and so, to his wife's delight, he received a posting to Baltimore, Maryland.

Isolation and pacifist sentiments now gripped the nation and caused America's military preparedness to slip and the careers of those in its armed services to stagnate. One of MacArthur's most distasteful duties was serving on the board convened for the court martial proceedings against General Billy Mitchell, the air power advocate. Not only was Mitchell a friend of MacArthur's, but the latter believed much of what he said. However, Mitchell was placed on trial for conduct prejudicial to good order and military discipline which was said to bring discredit upon the military. The defendant was found guilty, and MacArthur's vote has remained a secret. However, it is the opinion of many historical scholars that MacArthur dissented.

Whatever he did, Mitchell shied away from him because of his participation in his humiliation.

In 1928, after serving briefly as president of the American Olympic Committee, MacArthur received orders to return to the Philippines and assume command of all the forces in that area. Once more, he was delighted, but his wife not only refused to accompany him but sued for a divorce which was finalized the following year.

The next two years were crucial for the general as he cemented two very important friendships. The first was with the then Governor-General of the Philippines who later became Secretary of State under Hoover and Secretary of War under Roosevelt, Henry L. Stimson. The other close bond formed was with the Filipino patriot and future President, Manuel Quezon. When President Hoover brought Stimson home to join his cabinet, MacArthur watched the Washington scene with keen interest since he aspired to the post of Chief of Staff.

On August 6, 1930, Hoover confirmed MacArthur's appointment to command the army. After his return from the Philippines in November, MacArthur was sworn in as the eighth Chief of Staff. The position called for the rank of Full General so MacArthur's shoulders were adorned with four bright stars. His mother commented, "If only your father could see you now! Douglas, you're everything he wanted to be."[9]

MacArthur assumed his new position just as the Great Depression was making itself felt throughout the country and the world and at a point when the army was at its lowest point since before the Spanish American War. With disarmament in vogue, the U.S. Army was miniscule; in fact, the Portuguese and Greeks possessed larger armies than the United States. The great power had only the sixteenth largest army in the world. In addition to the reduced man power, its equipment was pitifully obsolete. During his tenure as Chief of Staff, MacArthur became a voice crying out in the wilderness, fighting budget cuts and further reductions in man power as well as cautioning about future political dangers. During his first two years in office, he visited Europe twice and witnessed first-hand the military preparedness of the continental countries.

Impressed by French mechanization, MacArthur backed the development of an American tank force and attempted to develop a modern air force. But time and again, his efforts were thwarted by an uncertain budget. The Depression was taking its toll.

Probably the greatest blemish on his term as Chief of Staff was the one that occurred over the problem of the bonus marchers. These World War I veterans were promised bonuses soon after the end of the war. Instead, they were compensated in the form of insurance policies. Now, in the depth of the Depression, they desired to cash in the policies and receive their long awaited bonuses. MacArthur was firmly convinced that ninety percent of the many thousands that marched on Washington and pitched their tents there were not really veterans but Communist agitators. In reality, just the opposite was true and two thirds of the marchers had served overseas. When given the order to evict the marchers, he responded with relish. His aide, Major Dwight Eisenhower, vainly attempted to mitigate the harm to his boss, but MacArthur was adamant and led the eviction forces in person. He ordered tanks, infantry, and cavalry under Major George Patton to break the back of the bonus marchers.

The outcome of this action has left many questions unanswered while it served to both enhance and damage the general's reputation. He took a severe beating from the national press for his involvement and found himself a symbol of the right wing.

> MacArthur, in the eyes of many, was a symbol of repression and right wing fanaticism which he was unable to shake off throughout his career.[10]

Whatever the overall effect of the incident, MacArthur, after all, was simply following the orders of his Commander in Chief.

1932 saw Franklin Roosevelt win an overwhelming victory in the presidential election. In Roosevelt, MacArthur finally found his match. His encounters with the President always left the general with a sense of frustration. Although he continued to work for military preparedness, his warnings were continually ignored. Congress kept right on rejecting his appeals and the army's appropriations hit rock bottom.

Like other unheeded voices of the 1930s, MacArthur prophesized the horrors of the following decade, the *blitzkrieg*, the devastation caused by heavy bombardment. Liddell-Hart made this observation of the contemporary MacArthur.

> In the war he made his reputation as a commander in the historic tradition, one who pushed right forward himself in order to keep his finger on the pulse of battle and seize opportunities. General MacArthur's present report shows that in the field of military theory he is no less forward in ideas. No more progressive summary of modern military conditions and the changes now developing has appeared from the authoritative quarters of any army.[11]

At the expiration of MacArthur's term as Chief of Staff, Roosevelt ordered it extended for an additional year. However, by the end of 1934, Manual Quezon had already approached the general with the proposition of returning to the Philippines in order to aid them on their road to independence. The island nation was slated for complete independence in 1946, but before this freedom could become a reality, it had to be made self-sufficient and able to defend itself. This is what Quezon had in mind for MacArthur. Accordingly, Roosevelt responded by appointing MacArthur Philippine High Commissioner and in the fall of 1935 he and his staff, which included Eisenhower and James Ord, set sail for the Philippines.

MacArthur immediately began to tackle the objective, that of making the islands militarily capable of defending itself from any agressor. He advocated formation of a flotilla of swift hard-hitting P.T. boats, an air fleet of some 250 planes, and a rather large conscript army of forty divisions built around a force of professional career officers and enlisted men.

The Filipino people came to love and revere the general, but the Americans resented his loftiness. Nevertheless, he and his chief of staff, Eisenhower, worked relentlessly, finding their main obstacle the same as it had been back in the states, money. The Philippine Government simply lacked the funds to provide the forces needed. Monetary obstacles were not the only problem. The conscripted troops spoke eight distinct languages and no less than eighty-seven various dialects. In addition, virtually one quarter of them were illiterate which hampered their ability to work together.

Yet another problem was naval defense. Any serious attempt to defend the islands would have to rely on the aid of the U.S. Navy. The drawback here was the tremendous distance of the country from America as opposed to its relative nearness to Japan who, it was estimated, would probably in the event of hostilities seize the Philippines because of the country's strategic location astride the passage way to the rich Dutch East Indies. Unfortunately, in America's pre-war plan, the islands were yielded to the Japanese by default. MacArthur thus faced a monumental task, chief of which was America's decision to concede the Philippines in the event of an attack.

MacArthur, however, was insistent that any attack against the country could be met at the water's edge and thrown back into the sea. He approached the defense problem with an air of optimism, secure in the knowledge that U.S. air power could easily turn the enemy back and that American superiority was capable of dealing with Japanese inferiority.

In August of 1936, President Quezon gave MacArthur a title never held by an American soldier before or since. The First Lady of the Commonwealth presented the General with a gold baton signifying his elevation to the rank of Field Marshal. For the occasion, he outfitted himself with the braided cap later to become his trademark.

On his return to the Philippines, MacArthur had met Jean Marie Faircloth. After his divorce in 1929, it was not known if he ever intended again to make the plunge into matrimony. His mother had passed away in Manila in 1935 and Jean Faircloth was like her in many ways, at least as far as heritage went, both had grown up in the south. On April 30, 1937, at the age of fifty-seven, MacArthur married Jean. Within a year, a son was born to the ecstatic general and his wife and was naturally named Arthur MacArthur IV.

The general accompanied Quezon on a tour of the U.S. in 1937 where he attempted once more to convince the government of the necessity for additional military aid for the Philippines. Again, finances were the determining factor. Returning to the islands, he settled down again to the task at hand. On July 7 of that year, at the Marco Polo Bridge near Peking, Japanese and Chinese troops clashed, precipitating war. As the conflict spread rapidly through China, the urgency of the situation prompted MacArthur to greater lengths to insure the security of the Philippines.

On the final day of the year, General MacArthur formally resigned from the U.S. Army's active list. His letter of resignation stated that he was blocking the promotion of junior officers. In fact, there was a much deeper reason for his action. Many in Washington disagreed with his Philippine policy and there was a move afoot to have him brought home. When he got wind of this, he resigned before action could be initiated.

With the termination of his affiliation with the U.S. Army, MacArthur's status with the Philippine President began to decline as he was now simply another government employee. Quezon had second thoughts about the general's war plans. He saw how rapidly the Japanese were destroying the reputedly strong Chinese Army. This frightening turn of events caused him to propose to Roosevelt that the Philippines be granted their independence in 1939 instead of 1946. Knowing that in any conflict between Japan and America the Philippine Islands would become a battle zone, Quezon reasoned that by becoming an independent nation he could declare neutrality and possibly save his country. Naturally, Roosevelt was cool to the suggestion. Quezon's opinion, however, was on a collision course with that of his field marshal. In the meantime, the budget for the country's armed forced dwindled and the prospect of independence appeared dim as 1939 dawned on the horizon.

During these last few years of peace, MacArthur gathered around himself the men who would form the core of his staff or court, as detractors later commented. Sidney Huff, Hugh Casey, Charles Willoughby and, of course, the most ruthless but efficient chief of staff, Richard Sutherland, formed the heart of this group.

The Asian situation continued to deteriorate. The Japanese had seized the whole of the Chinese coast and were making menacing gestures against French Indo-China. With the rapid fall of France to the German *blitzkrieg* in June of 1940, Japan viewed the French colony as a piece of fruit ripe for the picking. So they simply occupied the northern portion of the country. In addition to their aggression in Asia, the Japanese also signed the Tripartite Pact in September of the same year, linking the destiny of the Sons of Nippon to that of Nazi Germany and Fascist Italy.

As Japan continued to creep southward, MacArthur prepared against strong odds. As he prepared, so too did the Washington strategists who, along with the British, were even then conducting secret talks and drawing up future strategy for the time when America finally entered the war. In June 1941, a joint war plan was adopted known as the 'Rainbow Five' plan which stated that in the event of a two-ocean war the European enemy would be defeated first, leaving the forces in the Pacific to stand on the defensive until that was accomplished. This plan wrote *finis* to any Philippine relief expedition which formed the heart of War Plan Orange. In short, the Philippines were being abandoned even before a shot was fired.

Meanwhile, MacArthur sought complete command of all American and Filipino forces. This maneuver became possible when he was officially recalled to active duty on July 26, 1941. General Marshall wrote MacArthur,

> Stimson and I have decided that your outstanding qualifications and vast experience in the Philippines make you the logical selection for the Army in the Far East should the situation approach a crisis.[12]

The situation was indeed reaching a critical point. That same month, Japan occupied all of Indo-China. Roosevelt reacted by freezing all Japanese assets in the United States and embargoing all shipments of supplies, particularly oil, to the Japanese on the very day that MacArthur was recalled to active duty.

The action taken by the American President, especially the oil embargo, made war between the United States and Japan inevitable. The Japanese had little choice but to withdraw from Indo-China and the Chinese mainland (which was unlikely) or invade Malaya and the Dutch East Indies and garner their own resources (which was more liable to happen).

American codebreakers followed the belligerent tone of messages as they flowed from the Japanese Prime Minister, Hideki Tojo, and the foreign embassies around the world. The Japanese felt justified in their anger since both Britain and Holland declared similar embargoes. Consequently, Japan felt strangled and held the U.S. responsible.

MacArthur was faced with a great challenge. He had twenty-two thousand U.S. troops and Philippine scouts together with a commonwealth army of about eighty thousand Filipinos of dubious quality. It was highly possible that this force would be asked to face a Japanese army of at least six million men. At best, it was an eleventh hour struggle, but in many ways it was already too late. MacArthur knew he had to accomplish all he could with the little time and money available. However, he did not know as yet of the existence of the Rainbow Five Plan. Ironically, Marshall announced that it was the policy of the U.S. to defend the Philippines so he did dispatch some token aid, but it was pitifully slow in arriving. From July through December, only six thousand eighty-three American regulars arrived even though thousands more had been promised.

Not until October, did the War Department finally decide that MacArthur should see the Rainbow Five Plan. Predictably, he did not approve of it. The general was optimistic that he could successfully keep the Japanese out of the Philippines altogether. Then the islands could be used as a base from which enemy ships could be bombed. Some revisions to the plan were made and Marshall and Stimson approved many of MacArthur's defense ideas. It appeared that some of the latter's hope had rubbed off. He was convinced he could stop the Japanese on the shores and proceeded to plan in that vein by storing supplies in strategic places throughout the islands. The only drawback to that plan was that, if the Japanese managed to land successfully, the defenders would be forced to retreat to Bataan just as every feasibility study of Philippine defenses since 1909 had emphasized. However, the islanders would then be left short of supplies, particularly food. The plan was not surprising since MacArthur was never one to prefer a purely defensive posture. Even though he might find himself pushed back into Bataan, it was his original intention to fight on the beaches. He completely underestimated the ability of the Japanese and overestimated the ability of his own forces.

America also reinforced the Philippines with B-17 bombers and P-40 fighters. It was wrongly believed that the Japanese would not dare attack if they knew the islands were defended by such an array of war planes. In fact, there were only two hundred and seven planes available in the islands and seventy-six more in Hawaii. The presence of these aircraft gave an euphoric sense of false security. Even General Marshall felt secure enough about the Philippines.

> He felt the U.S. position in the Philippines was highly favorable. Our strength in the islands, he said, was far larger than the Japanese imagined. We were preparing not only to defend the Philippines but to conduct an aerial offensive from these islands against Japan. . . . If war did start, the B-17's would immediately attack the enemy's naval bases and would set the 'paper cities' of Japan on fire.[13]

This comment was made three weeks before Pearl Harbor. The false confidence and the underestimation of the ability of the Japanese would later exact a heavy toll of the Americans and their command.

Last minute negotiations between the Japanese and American diplomats in Washington were proving futile. All the while, Admiral Yamamoto was preparing his forces for a surprise raid on the great U.S. Naval Base at Pearl Harbor. While MacArthur pontificated in late November that no attack could possibly come before spring, General Homma was ordered to conquer the islands within sixty days of the opening of hostilities. A powerful Imperial Navy task force was cutting a path through the stormy Pacific heading for Hawaii. (see map 18)

369

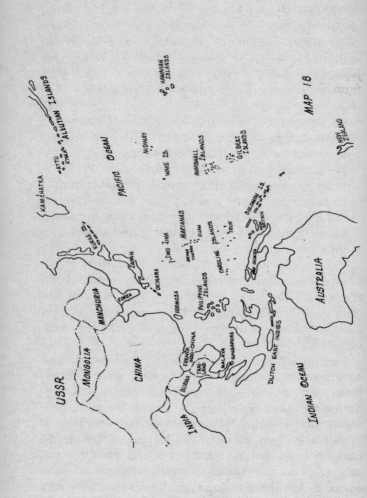

As the first days of December rolled around, the American codebreakers intercepted ominous messages indicating the approach of war. All Pacific outposts were alerted.

"Air raid Pearl Harbor! This is no drill!" Admiral Hart, naval commander in the Philippines was the first U.S. commander to hear the shocking news of the Japanese attack. However, he neglected to pass this information along to MacArthur who heard the news from his chief of staff, Sutherland, who received word from the duty officer listening to a California radio station. In this way, the general received the word at 3:40 A.M. Soon after, he received a call from Washington. The caller was General Leonard Gerow, chief of the army's War Plans Division, confirming the news bulletin.

What transpired next is in many ways a puzzle. Why was MacArthur's air force destroyed on the ground a full nine hours after receipt of the news about Pearl Harbor? A great deal of confusion cloaks this disaster. The Japanese pilots could hardly believe their eyes when they flew over Clark Field and saw their prey bunched together simply waiting to be destroyed. What had happened? Who was to blame? General Lewis Brereton, MacArthur's airman, had earlier proposed that the B-17s be sent into the air at once to strike at Japanese bases on Formosa. Three times that fateful morning, Brereton approached Sutherland and each time the latter dismissed him. Meanwhile, the bombers were in the air, but without any bombs. Finally, MacArthur himself ordered an attack on Formosa, but he scheduled it for the afternoon. Thus, at half past eleven, the bombers were back on the ground at Clark being rearmed and refueled. The P-40s were also down, leaving the field completely unprotected. Just at this point, Japanese aircraft, delayed by fog from taking off from Formosa earlier, arrived overhead and proceeded to destroy the air base. If the bombers had been sent earlier, as Brereton had suggested, the outcome might have been entirely different. But, MacArthur later denied ever hearing of Brereton's proposals and shifted the blame to Sutherland. Nevertheless, MacArthur was the overall commander and his lack of aggressive action condemned the air fleet. He should have reached the decision on his own to have the planes up and out against the Formosan air bases. If this was unfeasible at the time, he should at least have ordered them out of the range of the Japanese. For all his apparent brilliance, this costly error proved that the general was not infallible. Some historians have argued extenuating circumstances. MacArthur had unquestionably underestimated the Japanese, in fact, he initially thought the enemy had suffered a serious reverse at Pearl Harbor. When the truth became know, it was already too late. It has also been stated that MacArthur was under strict orders not to initiate any action until the Japanese opened fire. But, could not the attack on Hawaii be interpreted as the opening act of war? Luckily, he completely redeemed himself later, but he would first have to suffer the consequences of this fatal lapse. To say that this mistake lost the Philippines is too broad a statement. The final outcome would probably have been the same, but the Japanese conquest might have been made more painful for them. Now, with his air arm destroyed, MacArthur was forced to face defeat.

The general now turned to the Navy for support, but Admiral Hart was decidedly worried. The U.S. Naval base at Cavite was in flames and two days later came news of the destruction of the mighty British battleship *Prince of Wales* and the battle cruiser

Repulse off Malaya. The Admiral justifiably feared for his fleet and was determined to bring his ships to a safe port. MacArthur was startled by the naval commander's attitude since he had counted on Hart to keep the sea lanes open for the support vessels bringing in troops and supplies from America.

Hart informed MacArthur that the Japanese had the Philippines completely blockaded. The indomitable general, now in control of his senses stated that it was merely a paper blockade. Hart disagreed. MacArthur then cabled Washington, stressing the absolute necessity of the U.S. putting every effort into defending the Philippines. Victory or defeat, he emphasized, would be decided there. If the Philippine people thought for one moment that they were being abandoned, the political and social institutions would collapse. Naval support, he went on, was crucial to the defense. Unfortunately, the Chief of Naval Operations, Admiral Harold Stark, had already written off the islands. Consequently, MacArthur found himself confronted by a most difficult situation, one he would be very bitter about in years to follow. With its air power rendered useless and the navy about to abandon it, the Philippines faced a grim future.

Undaunted, MacArthur simply refused to believe that the situation was as bad as Washington painted it. Typically, he went about his work unmindful of the inherent danger. He was observed smoking a cigarette and swinging a cane while watching Japanese aircraft overhead. Never once was he seen diving for a shelter. News reporters faithfully reported the courage and defiance of the general.

Four days after Pearl Harbor, Germany and Italy declared war on the United States. To the Philippines this was a death sentence because of the Rainbow Five Plan. MacArthur never would concede this strategy.

MacArthur showed a complete lack of understanding of America's capabilities at this time, and disagreed violently with her 'Europe first' policy.[16]

The general set about preparing for the next Japanese move. Since the enemy controlled the sea and the sky, an invasion was expected soon. Already MacArthur's opponent, General Homma, commander of the Japanese Fourteenth Army, had made minor unopposed landings at Legaspi in southeast Luzon and at Aparri and Vigan in the northern and western portions of the island, respectively. MacArthur sensed that these landings did not constitute the main invasion but were instead diversions. Correctly, he decided that the main assault would come at Lingayen. (see map 19)

Though conscious that War Plan Orange called for a retreat into Bataan where the defenders would hold on until rescued, MacArthur was determined to contest the enemy on the beaches. A number of strategists maintain that his great misjudgment lay in not withdrawing earlier and that his decision to oppose the Lingayen landings was a decisive error. He encouraged the Filipinos to fight where they stood. In lieu of stockpiling food supplies in Bataan, preparations were made to repulse the foe. At Cabanatuan alone, fifty million bushels of rice were left unused. MacArthur scorned defeatism and would not initiate a withdrawal into Bataan. Possibly it was his vanity which caused him to decide as he did. Certainly, he underestimated the enemy, but be that what it may, he was resolved to stop the Japanese at the beaches.

Finally, on December 22, the Japanese blow in Lingayen Gulf fell. The defenders made a pitiful showing and were quickly overwhelmed by Homma's

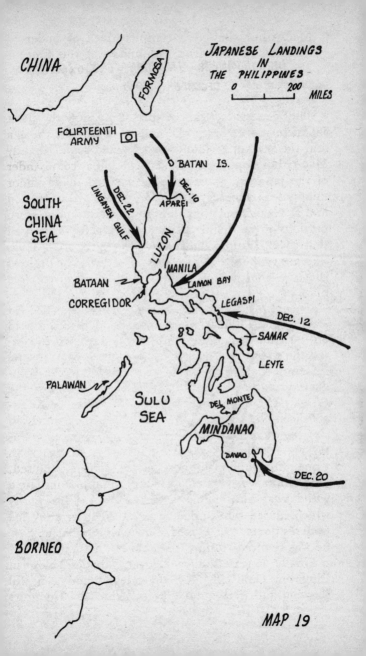

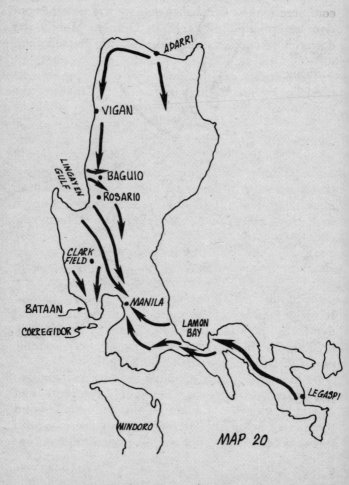

THE JAPANESE INVASION OF LUZON
DECEMBER 1941

0   50
MILES

APARRI

VIGAN

LINGAYEN GULF

BAGUIO

ROSARIO

CLARK FIELD

BATAAN

CORREGIDOR

MANILA

LAMON BAY

LEGASPI

MINDORO

MAP 20

veterans of the Chinese war. By afternoon, the attackers were firmly ashore and heading for Manila. Soon afterward, another Japanese force waded ashore at Lamon Bay, sixty miles southeast of the capital. The driving pincers converged, sweeping toward Manila with the joint objective of capturing the city and destroying the American-Filipino defense. MacArthur continued to waver. Finally, after lengthy consideration, he decided that there was no other option but to initiate War Plan Orange. Manila was declared an open city and the exodus to Bataan commenced. (see map 20)

The sideslip into Bataan was a masterpiece, even the Japanese marveled at its execution. To them, the move was unexpected they were certain they would be required to fight a decisive battle near Manila. The actual withdrawal was not easily accomplished by any means. In fact, under normal circumstances it would be considered difficult. Under the existing circumstances, with the enemy closing in, it seemed an impossible task. Thanks to MacArthur's superb strategic mind, this maneuver proved an eminent success.

Taking a map, the general drew five delaying lines. He then pointed out the vital bridges which were either to be held or blown up. When to abandon these delaying lines had to be timed with expert precision. It was a strategy of "stand and fight, fall back and dynamite. It was savage and bloody, but it won time."[17] He placed this effort in the very capable hands of General Jonathan Wainwright.

By January 6, eighty thousand fighting men and approximately twenty-six thousand refugees had streamed into the Bataan Peninsula. What saved them from being cut off was not only the masterful tactics of MacArthur, but also the enemy's misconception of the move. Homma was sure the main battle would take place near Manila and, instead of pressing on towards Bataan, sent the bulk of his forces toward the city and only a regimental combat group onto the peninsula. This allowed the American and Filipino forces to slip away.

Although MacArthur may have saved the army to fight again another day, feeding it was another story. The food supply was totally inadequate and there was only enough on hand to support one hundred thousand men for thirty days. MacArthur himself was to blame for this and the defenders had to pay dearly for his inadequate preparation.

From his headquarters on the island of Corregidor, MacArthur organized and directed the evacuation and defense of Bataan. He also dispatched urgent messages to Washington inquiring about the 'relief forces.' Quezon would later write: "Douglas MacArthur was a rock of strength and a source of inspiration for all who fought by his side."[18]

During air raids he calmly strolled without a helmet while others darted for protection. The same front line bravado shown during the First World War was still in evidence twenty-four years later. Unfortunately, only a few managed to observe it. MacArthur spoke with pride about this defense, yet a very negative response was observed among the defenders. Although he was obviously not lacking in individual courage, only once, on January 10, did he visit Bataan even though the peninsula was a mere five minutes away by P.T. boat. Unquestionably, this was out of character for the man. Why he remained closeted on Corregidor instead of visiting the fighting men is a mystery. The troops began to call him 'Dugout Doug.' One critic has gone so far as to say,

If MacArthur's motto had been to lead from the front in the First World War, his reputation was that of one who led from the rear and deserted in the face of the enemy when the chips were down at Bataan.[19]

The 'Dugout Doug' tag would remain with him all the way to Korea. A derogatory song originated there on Bataan and lasted for many years. The lyrics were sung to the tune of "The Battle Hymn of the Republic."

Dougout Doug MacArthur lies ashakin' on the
rock
Safe from all the bombers and from any sudden
shock
Dugout Doug is eating of the best food on
Bataan
And his troops go starving on.[20]

Some historians have speculated that it was his acute embarrassment at having promised reinforcements then been unable to deliver that caused MacArthur to shun the front lines. Whatever the reasons, this action was unquestionably an error. It demonstrated a marked lack of respect for the caliber of men doggedly fighting under him. How could they blame him if help was not forthcoming? In fact, they probably would have felt a closer bond with the man had he shown himself to them, convincing them he shared their plight. He could still have continued to cling to hope of reinforcement in order to maintain morale, but his presence would have given the men even more a leader who they felt cared. If only they knew just how much he really did care it might have prevented the defamation of his character and ended the 'Dugout Doug' statements.

Meanwhile, the soldiers, starving and ill, managed to put up a determined defense. The Japanese juggernaut was all-conquering everywhere. Within a few months, they had seized an empire covering a seventh of the globe. Hong Kong, Malaya, Singapore, Java, Sumatra, Borneo, The Bismarks, The Gilberts, Wake, Guam, The Solomons, and more than half of New Guinea fell to the relentless soldiers of Nippon. Burma was under assault and China's supply line would soon be severed. Australia and New Zealand were threatened. All forms of defense seemed to melt before the Emperor's warriors. Only in the Philippines where they faced the forces of General MacArthur was their war machine halted. Homma was given a February 8 deadline, but that date passed and still the battlements held.

Bataan Peninsula is shaped like a miniature Florida. It measures twenty-five miles long and twenty miles wide at the neck. It is dominated by a spiny back of extinct volcanoes rising nearly five thousand feet. Its thick vegetation includes huge mahogany, eucalyptus, and banyan trees which form impenetrable screens. The wild life contained there includes the deadly python. Malaria was endemic, but the troops also suffered from dengue fever, beriberi, hookworm, and pellagra. Food, of course, was an obsession. They ate anything that could be found, roots, leaves, papaya, breadfruit, monkeys, chickens, and wild pigs. On top of all this was the heat, the murderous tropical heat which drove malaria patients to distraction. This was compounded by the relentless enemy who were determined to conquer the staunch defenders.

MacArthur did everything possible to induce Washington to send reinforcements to the beleaguered islands. So much seemed to be promised yet nothing arrived to the intense anger of the general. As long as he believed in Washington's promises of help, MacArthur's optimism was infectious and he shared it with the troops. But, when the aid failed to appear, this hope turned to despair. In reality, he should have remembered the Rainbow Five Plan which wrote the Philippines off in no uncertain terms.

Nevertheless, plans were being made in Washington for the reconquest of the Pacific. These plans, however, did not include reinforcing a garrison considered lost as early as December 14. On that Sunday, one week after Pearl Harbor, General Marshall ordered the newly promoted Brigadier General and former MacArthur chief of staff, Dwight D. Eisenhower, to assume the position of Deputy Chief of the War Plans Division. Marshall asked Eisenhower about the possibility of the Philippines holding out. Thinking it over, Ike responded:

General, . . . it will be a long time before major reinforcements can go to the Philippines, longer than the garrison can hold out with any driblet assistance, if the enemy commits major forces to their reduction. . . . Our base must be Australia, and we must start at once to expand it and to secure our communications to it.[21]

Marshall agreed. Though he would have preferred to rescue the garrison, deep down he know it simply could not be done. Still, he clung to the hope that something more could be accomplished. Under the auspices of the Administration, steamers were chartered to attempt to run the Japanese blockade. Although these attempts were heroic, the end result was a foregone failure.

By mid-February, it was obvious to both MacArthur

and Quezon that they had been abandoned. Quezon was livid, he was aware of the fact that the United States was going out of its way to aid Britain and Russia while doing nothing for the Philippines. The President was finally evacuated, but MacArthur was ordered to fight as long as he could. The general was bent on fighting to the end, to die if necessary. He would not surrender.

General Marshall, however, was having grave doubts about the prospect of losing his Far East commander. MacArthur was much too experienced an officer to be sacrificed. Not only had he proved that he knew how to fight the Japanese, he had become America's national hero. To lose him, therefore, would cause serious repercussions. In addition, it would give the Japanese a great psychological victory if they managed to capture or kill him. MacArthur had to be saved and the President agreed. For many weeks previous, Roosevelt had been under pressure from various groups and influential people clamoring for the general's safe return. The press, the Republican Party, even Sir Winston Churchill, to name but a few, begged for MacArthur's evacuation to Australia where he could mollify the frightened Australians. She had sent most of her fighting men to the Western Desert to fight against Rommel. The Prime Minister of Australia was applying pressure for their return and Churchill hoped that MacArthur's presence in Australia would pacify the government.

MacArthur was visibly shaken when he received the Presidential message ordering his evacuation. He did not care to leave his men, but then again, as a soldier he had no wish to disobey a Presidential order. He threatened to resign his commission, enlist as a volunteer, and return to Bataan. His staff, however, persuaded him that the reason he was being sent to

Australia was to lead a relief expedition back to the Philippines. After considering this, MacArthur concluded that his staff's arguments made sense. From every indication, it did seem like Australia was being built up as a base for a great counteroffensive. MacArthur agreed to the order and cabled Roosevelt his conditions. The message informed the President that he would go, but he must be allowed to select the right psychological moment to leave lest a collapse occur. Marshall and the President concurred.

As the days passed and MacArthur showed no inclination of leaving, the President sent another message on March 6, urging his swift departure. Three days later, yet another nudge was sent. In truth, MacArthur had made up his mind to leave. The problem was how to accomplish this in light of the Japanese blockade. Naval offices on Corregidor gave him a one-in-five chance of successfully evading the Japanese patrols. As a vehicle of escape, MacArthur finally chose a flotilla of P.T. boats and set March 11 as his last day.

As this date drew nearer, MacArthur summoned General Wainwright to his office and invested the latter with command of all forces on Luzon until his return. Then he said:

> Jonathan, I want you to understand my problem very plainly. I'm leaving for Australia pursuant to repeated orders of the President. Things have gotten to such a point that I must comply with these orders or get out of the army. I want you to make it known throughout all elements of your command that I'm leaving over my repeated protests.[22]

MacArthur then ordered Wainwright to hold out and

the latter responded, "I told him that holding Bataan was our aim in life."[23]

Actually, MacArthur intended to coordinate the defense of the Philippines from Australia. He made it clear that Wainwright was to command only on Luzon and only under MacArthur's direction. By doing this, MacArthur felt that, even if Bataan and Corregidor fell, the rest of the country could continue fighting. However, he never communicated that command structure to Washington. Ignorant of this fact, Marshall invested Wainwright with command of all Philippine forces and gave him a third star. Both Washington, and later the Japanese, assumed Wainwright was the overall commander with power to surrender all the islands, if it came to that. This was in contrast to MacArthur's express wishes.

The story of MacArthur's escape is an epic. John Buckeley, the commander of the P.T. flotilla, was a swashbuckling sort of commander, just the type needed for so daring an escape.

Danger lurked over every horizon. On more than one occasion, they were almost discovered by Japanese destroyers. They were nearly spotted by Japanese coastal artillery whose huge guns had the ability to blast the general, his wife, child, and staff to bits. Finally, on Friday, March 13, they reached Cagayan on Mindanao, thirty five hours and five hundred sixty miles from Corregidor. On shore, the MacArthurs were escorted to Cagayan Village where they remained for four days until B-17s took them to Australia.

The general was anxious to reach that country. He was under the distinct impression that huge forces were being accumulated there which could be used to begin an immediate counteroffensive in the Philippines. He had believed the many communiqués from Washington emphasizing the huge build up in Australia. His disappointment was soon in evidence.

After landing in Australia following a touch-and-go flight, MacArthur asked an American officer how the buildup for the reconquest of the Philippines was progressing. The officer seemed bewildered. MacArthur's first reaction was one of shock as he began to piece together the truth. Yes, he was now the Supreme Commander of all Allied Forces in the Southwest Pacific, but the command at the time was comprised of 'ghost divisions.' In fact, there were only thirty-two thousand Allied troops in the country, the majority of which were non-combatants. Ironically, MacArthur had left more troops behind than he found waiting for him. Learning of this "was my greatest shock and surprise of the whole war."[24] Upon debarking the train which brought his party across much of Australia's wastelands, he made his now famous speech which included World War II's most memorable phrase, "I came through and I shall return."[25] Unfortunately, he now realized that the return would not be as rapid as he had hoped. He felt betrayed by Washington.

To offset negative propaganda and show the world that America believed in the general, Marshall recommended him for the Congressional Medal of Honor. Roosevelt agreed immediately and, on March 26, MacArthur was awarded the decoration. He became the second man in his family to receive this coveted award.

He was now faced with a monumental task. His theater of operations was vast and the rough equivalent of the distance from the English Channel to the Persian Gulf. The first duty facing him, however, was not, as he anticipated, the return to the Philippines. Instead, his prime concern was for the defense of Australia. While awaiting instructions from Washington which were a long time in coming, the Japanese colossus continued to roll forward. The Admiralty Islands fell, followed by portions of the Solomons, including Buka, Bougainville, and New Georgia, then the north coast of New Guinea with Lae and Salamaua.

Finally, on April 18, the Joint Chiefs hammered out an agreement. In effect, this treaty struck a compromise between Nimitz and MacArthur. Both were to share command in the Pacific, MacArthur the Southwest Pacific Area (SWPA) and Nimitz the South Central and North Pacific. Their joint commands would form giant dual pincers with MacArthur fighting along the large land masses in the southwest while the Admiral's forces cut a swath along the small islands of the Central Pacific. Before that could transpire, however, the Japanese spearheads had to be blunted. Then, of course, there was still Coregidor. By this time, Bataan had fallen.

Preparing to take the offensive was no simple task since MacArthur's theater was low on the priority list. Only Burma was lower. To MacArthur's everlasting disgust, when the Allies later invaded Italy, more supplies were sent to Italian civilians in a few months than to the Southwest Pacific in an entire year. Justifiably, he was upset with Washington, and would tell his staff he was a "victim of shoestring logistics."[26]

Meanwhile, the fate of Corregidor was irrevocably sealed. MacArthur cabled Wainwright and ordered him not to surrender, but the latter faced an impossible situation. On May 6, the guns on 'The Rock' fell silent and white flags flew where only the day before Old Glory had waved. When Wainwright attempted to surrender, Homma would accept nothing less than the total capitulation of the entire Philippines. The American commander informed his Japanese counterpart that he only commanded the forces on Corregidor and that MacArthur was the only one with authority to surrender the balance. Homma stated that his information was contrary and that, as far as he knew, Wainwright was empowered to surrender everything. Should this fail to take place, Homma went on, the Japanese would resume attacks against Corregidor. Wainwright was left with little option. Though MacArthur fumed, Wainwright accepted Homma's terms.

For the Japanese, their victory occurred much sooner than they had anticipated and presented them with a dilemma. Where would they go from here? Admiral Yamamoto, the architect of the Pearl Harbor operation, advocated an attack against *Midway* with the objective of destroying the American aircraft carriers in a decisive naval engagement. Other commanders favored an advance towards Port Moresby, a city on the southern shore of Papua, New Guinea. The capture of Port Moresby, they said, could bring Japan within bombing range of Australia in addition to providing the Imperial Navy with an excellent anchorage.

Though reluctant about the *Midway* operation, the Japanese soon became convinced of its importance after a daring bombing raid on Tokyo, led by General 'Jimmy' Doolittle flying B-25 bombers from the carrier *Hornet*. The Japanese hierarchy then decided that only when the American fleet rested on the bottom of the ocean, could the Land of the Rising Sun be completely safe. Before assulting *Midway*, however, they elected to concentrate on Port Moresby.

Thanks to the efforts of American codebreakers, the U.S. was made aware of the Japanese movement into the Coral Sea. The advance towards Port Moresby reached a climax on May 8 when two American carriers encountered the Japanese fleet. Though the enemy managed to seize Tulagi and Guadalcanal and sink the American carrier *Lexington* and damage the *Yorktown*, they failed in their primary objective of capturing the port. For that reason alone, the U.S. considered the Battle of the Coral Sea a victory. One month later, again thanks to the codebreakers, the Battle of *Midway* sealed the fate of the Imperial Japanese Navy when they lost four carriers of their own.

Though halted at *Midway*, the Japanese remained confident that they could sever the life line to Australia and isolate MacArthur in the sub-continent. With that very purpose in mind, airfields were constructed in the Solomons. In June, U.S. codebreakers discovered that a new airfield was under construction on the island of Guadalcanal. MacArthur was convinced that the enemy would try again for Port Moresby, reasoning that it was much too valuable for them to ignore.

After capturing Buna and Gona on Papua's north coast, the Japanese prepared for an advance on Port Moresby, just as MacArthur predicted. Anticipating that the enemy would attempt an end run around Milne Bay, the Supreme Commander ordered the veteran desert warriors, the 7th Australian Division, to Milne Bay where they fought an epic battle and heroically defeated a Japanese force. This marked the first time in the war that a Japanese amphibious attack had been turned back after establishing a beachhead. Still, they were determined to gain control of Port Moresby and revised their strategy. This time they would try to take the city by land.

Glancing at a map of the Papua section of New Guinea, one notes that Port Moresby is situated a mere ninety miles from Buna. That ninety miles, however, encompasses some of the world's most forbidding terrain. The Owen Stanley Mountains form the back bone of Papua. These jungle-clad mountains rise to over ten thousand feet in places. One jungle tract, the Kokoda Trail, winds its way precariously over the spiny back of the mountains. In places, the jungle completely covers the trail. This requires difficult cutting which, after an hour, might reward the hackers with a net gain of a few yards. The heat is intense, the wildlife dangerous, including such horrors as fire ants, fleas, poisonous spiders, and other insects which land on a sleeping man and, like vampires, suck out his body fluids. Rain in Papua is incessant, making the trails as slippery as ice, causing many to fall thousands of feet into uncharted gorges. If the intense heat, the wildlife, or the many and varied diseases failed to kill a person, the razor-sharp blades of grass standing seven feet high, capable of cutting a man open as easy as a bayonet, could. Quicksand and swamps comprise the balance of the jungle. Often, the trail was covered waist deep with scum. The air in this jungle is stifling and the stench of rotting undergrowth pervades the entire area. Little light penetrates the thick canopy during the few times the rain ceases and when the sun appears, the area turns into a vast suffocating sea of steam which rots the clothes right off a man's back.

This then was the Green War, the battle MacArthur's forces would wage over the next three years. Entering this hell, the Japanese soldiers moved on Port Morseby. (See map 21) MacArthur was forced to react quickly. The Australian government was frozen in fear. They wanted to fall back to a line called the 'Brisbane Line' and make a stand in defense of their country at that point. The idea was rejected by MacArthur. Pointing to a map he said, "We'll defend Australia in New Guinea. We must attack, attack, attack."[27]

AS FAR AS THE JAPANESE WERE CONCERNED, THE GENERAL'S DECISION TOOK THEM TOTALLY BY SURPRISE.

The Japanese did not think that General Mac-Arthur would establish himself in New Guinea and defend Australia from that position. They also did not believe that he would be able to use New Guinea as a base for offensive operations against them. The Japanese felt that General MacArthur could not establish himself in Port Moresby because he did not have sufficient forces to maintain himself there.[28]

MacArthur was hell-bent on preventing the Japanese from reaching their goal.

While he made preparations for this, on August 7, U.S. Marines invaded Guadalcanal and Tulagi. Fierce fighting lay ahead for the Leathernecks.

A most important person was added to MacArthur's staff at this point and would contribute significantly to subsequent victory, General George Kenney. He became the new air commander for the Southwest Pacific area. His superb knowledge of air strategy would later go a long way toward reducing the effectiveness of Japanese air power in the Pacific by crippling the major enemy base at Rabaul and establishing Allied control of the air.

By now it was mid-September. The marines on Guadalcanal staunchly held a defensive perimeter around the captured airfield, renamed Henderson Field. In Papua, the Japanese were only forty miles from Port Moresby when, on September 20, their commander, General Horri, issued an order stating that he had decided to withdraw back across the Owen Stanleys. Incredible as this decision may sound, there were a number of credible reasons for Horri's order. The fact that the Australians had managed to stop the Japanese drive at Ioribaiwa was a significant deterrent. More reinforcements were required to

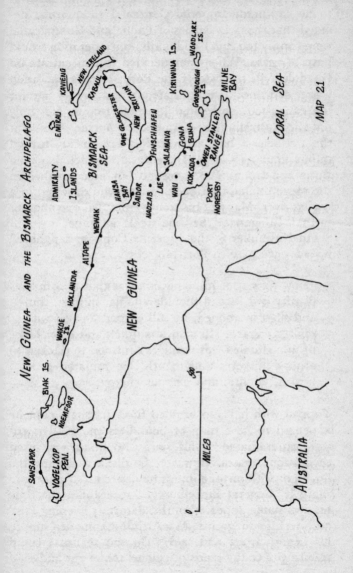

NEW GUINEA AND THE BISMARCK ARCHIPELAGO

BIAK IS.
NOEMFOOR
SANSAPOR
VOGELKOP PEN.

WAKDE IS.
HOLLANDIA
AITAPE
WEWAK

NEW GUINEA

HANSA BAY
SAIDOR
NADZAB
LAE
WAU
KOKODA
PORT MORESBY
OWEN STANLEY RANGE
BUNA
GONA
SALAMAUA
FINSCHHAFEN

ADMIRALTY ISLANDS

BISMARCK SEA

EMIRAU
KAVIENG
NEW IRELAND
RABAUL
NEW BRITAIN
CAPE GLOUCESTER

KIRIWINA IS.
GOODENOUGH IS.
WOODLARK IS.
MILNE BAY

CORAL SEA

MAP 21

MILES
0   50

AUSTRALIA

break the stout Australian defense if Port Moresby was to be captured. Imperial General Headquarters decided that the twin battles of Papua and Guadalcanal were simply too much to handle; one operation would have to cease. When they decided to concentrate on Guadalcanal, the fate of the Port Moresby operation was sealed until a future date. It was a cruel fate for the exhausted, emaciated Japanese troops. Not only did the Australians and Americans pursue them, but the wet season had arrived. Retreat quickly turned into a rout as the Japanese feverishly fell back on Buna and Gona. Ten thousand Japanese perished in the move, including General Horri who drowned in a raging river. Many of his troops trampled one another in their hunger for the food stocks at Buna.

On November 6, the Supreme Commander moved his advance base to Port Moresby.

"Now sixty-two, his condition was that of a man of fifty-two. Broad-shouldered, flat hipped, slim and slightly stooped, he still carried himself with soldierly grace. His step was quick and sure, his profile chiseled, his wrinkles confined to puckers around his eyes and mouth. He radiated good health, vitality, and nervous energy."[29]

Topped with his gold-braided field marshal's cap, he appeared to be a man of boundless energy. His enthusiasm radiated to his staff who in turn sparked their subordinates. However, he disliked sharing the limelight with anyone unless he desired that person to share it. General Eichelberger wrote about the time his own name appeared in the 'Saturday Evening Post' and in 'Life' magazine. MacArthur summoned him to his headquarters and said, "Do you realize I could reduce you to the grade of colonel tomorrow and send you home?"[30] He didn't, of course, but this incident gives a good idea of MacArthur's attitude toward anyone trying to eclipse his fame. One thing everyone was painfully aware of; the Southwest Pacific Theater was MacArthur's and no one else's.

As the Japanese fell back on the north coast, MacArthur decided to assault their position frontally. Once the north coast of Papua was captured, the general knew that the entire Southwest Pacific Theater would be exposed for exploitation.

The American GI and Australian 'Digger' hacked their way through the dense jungles, scaling the towering peaks, fording the deep rivers and swamps, pursuing the retreating enemy. Still, they were wary of the Japanese whom they knew would be waiting when they reached the plantations and villages of Gona, Buna, and Sanananda Point. The Japanese fell back to prepared defenses of coconut log bunkers positioned in such a way that each were mutually supportive of the other. As the Allies approached, enemy planes from Rabaul dropped heavy loads of explosive on the wet, exhausted pursuers. A stalemate resulted at Buna.

To MacArthur's dismay, an Australian officer proposed that more of his countrymen be sent as reserves since it appeared they were outfighting the GIs. This criticism infuriated the Supreme Commander who summoned Eichelberger to his headquarters. He spelled out the stalemate before Buna and the lack of aggressive drive in the American assault. Eichelberger was ordered to go to the front and relieve the divisional commander of the 32nd. Then, in a pontifical tone, he added", If you capture Buna, I'll give you a Distinguished Service Cross and recommend you for a high British decoration. Also . . . I'll release your name for newspaper publication."[31] He also said, "Bob, take Buna or don't come back alive."[32] The real

MacArthur is exposed in these accounts.

The fighting was intense, but in a few weeks time the Japanese collapsed, resulting in an Allied victory in Papua. MacArthur's attitude continued to puzzle the front line soldier. Not once did he visit Buna, yet the newspapers made constant reference to MacArthur leading his forces. Instead, he remained in Port Moresby. What had happened to the soldier who during the First World War detested armchair commanders? Were the 'Dugout Doug' stories true?

By January 1943, the Japanese had been defeated both on Guadalcanal and in Papua. Whatever forces remained in Papua traveled westward overland while those at Guadalcanal were evacuated to New Georgia. MacArthur announced to the world that a great victory had been won in Papua with minimal loss of life. Actually, the report was in error. The mortality report showed three thousand three hundred killed and five thousand five hundred wounded.

It was now 1943 and everywhere the Allies were on the move. The great Southwest Pacific Japanese air and Naval base at Rabaul became an obsession with the Americans. They realized that no movement beyond Papua was possible without the elimination of that bastion. The Japanese also realized this and prepared themselves accordingly. The New Guinea ports of Lae and Salamaua were obvious targets since they were ideally situated for use as jumping off points for Cape Gloucester on the island of New Britain where Rabaul is located. MacArthur thus planned his next move.

After the fall of Guadalcanal, MacArthur had received command of Admiral Halsey's forces in the Solomons. These forces would form a strong right wing. Halsey's objective for 1943 was to climb the Solomon's ladder, clearing the jungle for air bases, moving ever closer to Rabaul. As Halsey proceeded up the Solomons, MacArthur intended to move westward along the north coast of New Guinea towards Lae and Salamaua. The Japanese, alert to the danger, sent reinforcements. Three thousand troops were dispatched to seize an airstrip at Wau, just south of Lae and about thirty-two miles southwest of Salamaua. MacArthur expected this move and airlifted in a brigade of Australians who decimated the enemy a mere four hundred yards from the field. The Japanese also ordered naval forces, originally intended as reinforcements for Rabaul, diverted to Lae. Again MacArthur was waiting to intercept them with a force of B-17s. Using the tactic of skip bombing (like skipping a flat stone over the water), the B-17s sank eight transports and four escorts, effectively thwarting the enemy attempt to reinforce Lae. When MacArthur received word of the victory, he was ecstatic.

Meanwhile as plans continued for a campaign again Rabaul, the Combined Chiefs of Staff met in 1943 for a series of very important conferences, first in Casablanca, then Washington, Quebec, Cairo, and finally Tehran. Each conference found the Allies closer to victory, but resulted in additional frustration for MacArthur. The Pacific was still low on the priority list behind the European theater. Then, when the strategy for the Pacific was finally discussed, MacArthur found himself blocked by other concerns. The Joint Chiefs were divided on which approach towards Japan was best, a central Pacific approach using the Marshall and Mariana Islands as stepping stones, or the southwest Pacific approach advocated by MacArthur. Both approaches offered certain advantages. In the central Pacific thrust, the navy would be able to utilize its new large fleet of fast aircraft carriers to the greatest advantage while a southwest Pacific approach would deprive the enemy of his raw materials. Obviously, MacArthur pushed for the latter. It was, he said, the shortest route to the Philippines. Besides, he further emphasized, an assault of the fortified central Pacific islands would prove a bloody task. How perceptive he truly was would soon become evident. The Joint Chiefs finally resolved the issue by sanctioning a dual drive with each area supporting each other by diverting sea power and totally confusing the Japanese.

Even though the strategy was adopted by mid-year, the problem of supplies continued to exist. MacArthur found himself receiving even less than Nimitz. His anger mounted. He knew that he would have to rely on whatever he could obtain and make do with what he had. Rabaul was his first priority, but he knew that once it was eliminated the rest of New Guinea would have to be seized. As he perceived it, his war was one fought over trackless jungle. It was a battle protected by air. Victory, he emphasized, depended on the advancement of the bomber line. Thus, airfields received priority. Take an area, develop an airfield, and move on.

What of Rabaul? It contained four airfields, a great naval anchorage, and a garrison of one hundred thousand Japanese infantry. It held the key to the entire 'Bismark Barrier.' To conquer Rabaul, MacArthur realized that he would have to take the Huon Peninsula in New Guinea, then jump to Cape Gloucester on New Britain.

Meanwhile, on April 15, Halsey flew to Brisbane to see the Supreme Commander and seek his approval for an invasion of New Georgia which, Halsey reasoned, would become the springboard for a jump to Bougainville further north. MacArthur agreed. He held Halsey in high regard. In his reminiscences, he said this about the aggressive admiral,

He was of the same aggressive type as John Paul Jones, David Farragut and George Dewey. His one thought was to close with the enemy and fight him to the death. The bugaboo of many sailors, the fear of losing ships, was completely alien to his conception of sea action. I liked him from the moment we met, and my respect and admiration increased with time. . . . No name rates higher in the annals of our country's naval history.[33]

Late in June, MacArthur unleashed three operations. Halsey invaded New Georgia, General Krueger, recently arrived in the theater, occupied Kiriwina and Woodlark Islands northeast of Papua, and the Australians landed at New Guinea's Nassau Bay. Early in September, a division landed on the Huon Peninsula followed the next day by an airborne assault at Nadzab, northeast of Lae. MacArthur himself flew in a B-17 to observe the airdrop. When these areas were captured, fighters and bombers could easily raid Rabaul. The noose around the target was tightening.

On September 12, Salamaua fell, followed by Lae four days later. Finschafen, on the tip of the Huon Peninsula fell on October 2. Now MacArthur was ready to jump to New Britain. In November, Krueger landed at Arawe, a village on New Britain's southwest coast. The Allies had now reached the home island of Rabaul. The enemy reacted swiftly to the Arawe landings, but that assault was simply a diversion, cloaking a December 26 landing by the 1st Marine Division on Cape Gloucester. Within four weeks, the area was in Allied hands and, following the successful assault on Bougainville the previous month, Rabaul was bracketed. Bombers from both areas proceeded to fire on the area incessantly. The Japanese at Rabaul prepared for the anticipated American landings. In addition to the one hundred thousand men, they had one thousand artillery pieces expertly dug in and sighted, along with hundreds of miles of underground caves. But these preparations went for nought. What had caused the warriors of Dai Nippon to languish until war's end in Rabaul?

MacArthur credits himself in his reminiscences with the strategy that called for isolation rather than assaulting the heavily fortified position.

> To push back the Japanese perimeter of conquest by direct pressure against the mass of enemy-occupied islands would be a long and costly effort. My staff worried about Rabaul and other strong-points. . . . I intended to envelop them, incapacitate them, apply the hit 'em where they ain't — let 'em die on the vine.[34]

Some historians, however, credit the Joint Chiefs with this idea. Whether MacArthur invented it or not is beside the point, the fact remains that he used it most successfully. The tactic of bypassing strong points and hitting them where they weren't not only reduces casualties, it allows one the ability to weaken the enemy where it hurts; in the stomach. Once an enemy strongpoint is bypassed, they would find themselves cut off and left to starve or forced to attempt a costly evacuation. MacArthur learned from the bloodletting at Buna that costly frontal assaults only serve to lengthen the war by years and push casualties into the hundreds of thousands.

Though MacArthur credits himself for the bypassing effort at Rabaul, actually it was at the Quadrant Conference in Quebec that Rabaul's neutralization was guaranteed as a compromise in order to speed things up in the Pacific. MacArthur used the tactic superbly and it became the key to victory. After the war, during an interrogation, Japanese colonel Matsuichi Juio stated, "The type of strategy we hated most were the swooping envelopments."[36]

As 1943 became 1944, MacArthur found he needed one more base to seal the fate of Rabaul, the Admiralty Islands. Intelligence sources informed him that the largest of the islands, Los Negros, was manned by many enemy troops. Air reconnaissance, however, failed to confirm this. Gambling that the intelligence appreciation was an exaggeration, MacArthur ordered the operation to proceed despite the stern protests of his staff. To cover himself, he called the operation a reconnaissance in force. To confirm his faith in the operation, MacArthur decided to accompany the 1st Cavalry Division on the venture in the event an evacuation order was required. When the Supreme Commander told Krueger that he would accompany the men ashore, the latter was appalled and said so in no uncertain terms. But MacArthur had made up his mind.

On February 29, 1944, in a pouring rain, MacArthur went ashore with the attackers. Strolling casually amid gunfire, the general paced through the twisted debris of blasted jungle growth. Bullets ricocheted around him, but appearing invincible, he hardly gave it a thought. Two hours later, he was back aboard ship satisfied that no evacuation order would be necessary. Three days later, Los Negros and Manus, with its excellent anchorage, were in American hands. MacArthur had a victory despite the vehement protests of his staff. Actually, there were four thousand Japanese on Los Negros, but MacArthur's bold stroke combined with poor strategy on the enemy's part sealed the fate of the Admiralties. With the capture of

Emirau Island in March, Rabaul was no ringed and bombed into destruction. When the Emperor issued his Imperial Receipt ending the war, thousands of emaciated Japanese surrendered, never having fulfilled their promise to stop the American invader.

Now MacArthur cast his sights westward along New Guinea's northern coast. Hollandia, more than four hundred miles from his nearest base, was the next target. Manchester said this about the operation.

> It looms as a military classic, comparable to Hannibal's maneuvering at Cannae and Napoleon's at Austerlitz.[36]

Once more, his staff was reticent about the operation because, they argued, they would be unable to provide air cover for Hollandia since it was beyond fighter range. The staff proposed Wewak as the next target. MacArthur, however, stuck to the Hollandia landing judging that the Japanese probably expect a landing at Wewak. Hollandia would therefore be a tactical surprise, a hitting where they aren't. As anticipated, the Japanese were in force at Wewak and the Hollandia landings came as a complete surprise. Thousands of enemy troops were bypassed and had to work their way back to their own lines with disastrous results. The landings were a true MacArthur production, feints at Wewak, landings on both sides of Hollandia, and a landing at Aitape, midway between the two areas. The Japanese were dazed as their bases were seized or bypassed and put to use by the Americans for their own westward movement. The total cost of the Hollandia operation was one hundred and fifty American lives.

Hollandia became the new advance headquarters for the Supreme Commander. Consequently, a building fit for a man of his exalted rank was erected there. Unfortunately, it gave rise to some nasty stories about how the Supreme Commander was living in great luxury while the foot soldier slogged it out in the trackless jungle. The building was derogatorily called 'Dugout Doug's White House.' In fact, MacArthur hardly used it, spending only four nights there. Responsibility for the construction of this building rests with his staff, but MacArthur was the butt of the bad press.

The advance continued westward. Hansa Bay, which was bypassed, fell on June 15 and late in July, Sansapor on the western tip of the Vogelkop Peninsula fell. Biak proved to be more difficult and the enemy there was not eliminated until early in August. Since arriving in Australia early in 1942, MacArthur had traveled two thousand miles. The Philippines loomed on the horizon.

Before proceeding with the military picture, mention must be made of MacArthur's political aspirations. From 1943 onward, in some conservative Republican circles, his name began to crop up as a possible G.O.P. candidate for 1944. He was popular, a hero, and to some the bulwark of all that is right with America. The far political Right, former isolationists, the America First group, and that irrepressible lunatic fringe which haunts every generation, backed the general. The other side also jumped on the bandwagon, but against him, branding him a fascist and ultra-racist. After a year of outward denials but inward desires, the politcally naive MacArthur renounced any desire to run for the presidency. In reality, he did want to run, but a badly mishandled campaign ended his chances.

After MacArthur dropped out of the Presidential race, Roosevelt decided to meet with him in Hawaii. There was a more important issue at stake than politics. Admiral King, the Chief of Naval Operations and member of the Joint Chiefs of Staff, had boldly proclaimed that the Philippines should be bypassed in favor of Formosa. At first, MacArthur was not aware of what the topic of the conference was to be but once he found out, he knew he had to prevent King's proposal from becoming a reality. In July, MacArthur left Brisbane in his B-17 for the twenty-six-hour flight to Hawaii's Hickam Field, ready to debate.

Why did King advocate bypassing the Philippine Islands? He reasoned that there was no purpose for tying down U.S. troops in a land battle through the jungles of the massive island complex. It would be, he claimed, too costly and time-consuming. Formosa, on the other hand, would present an easier target and one closer to Japan, able to provide B-29 bases. The Joint Chiefs were divided. General Henry 'Hap' Arnold of the Army Air Forces naturally cast his lot with King because of his desire for the B-29 bases. Initially, General Marshall favored the proposal, but later changed his mind. Roosevelt was rapidly losing patience with the ambivalence among his chiefs and thus decided to have a face-to-face meeting with the two commanders involved, MacArthur and Nimitz, the latter representing King's viewpoint.

On July 26, the principals assembled. MacArthur, in typical bravado style, was the last to arrive aboard the cruiser where the official greetings were held.

After an uneasy delay the President and his party were about to disembark when an automobile siren wailed, a huge open car rolled onto the dock, circled, and drew up at the gangplank—and out stepped MacArthur.[37]

The general made his grand entrance, dashed up the

gangplank amid a loud ovation, then greeted the President.

Following two days of touring the base installations, the participants got down to the main order of business. After a delightful dinner in a beautiful mansion overlooking Waikiki Beach, Roosevelt pointed to a map of the Pacific and said to the general, "Well, Douglas, where do we go from here?" MacArthur replied, "Mindanao, then Leyte and Luzon." Nimitz then proceeded to argue his case which was not presented as forcefully as MacArthur's. MacArthur then expounded on the political ramifications if the Philippines were bypassed. The Filipinos already felt betrayed, to overlook them now would constitute yet another betrayal and subject them to Japanese brutality. The reputation of the United States was at stake. Roosevelt felt empathy for that line of reasoning, but was fearful there would be a heavy toll of lives during a campaign on Luzon. MacArthur answered,

> Mr. President, my losses would not be heavy, any more than they have been in the past. The days of frontal attack should be over. Modern infantry weapons are too deadly, and frontal assault is only for mediocre commanders. Good commanders do not turn in heavy losses.[38]

Roosevelt accepted MacArthur's appraisals. The Philippines would be next. The plan originally conceived called for a landing on Morotai on September 15 followed by another on Leyte on December 20.

In early September, however, Halsey conducted a series of carrier raids in the central Philippines and found them to be a hollow shell. Very little opposition was met from the ground-based aircraft. In his own words, the admiral said,

I began to wonder whether I dared recommend that MacArthur shift to Leyte the invasion which he had planned for Mindanao, and advance the date well ahead of the scheduled November 15.[39]

After mulling it over, he radioed Nimitz in Pearl Harbor, recommending the cancellation of the preliminary assaults on the Talauds, Mindanao, and the Palaus. As an alternative, Halsey urged that Leyte be attacked quickly. Unfortunately, it was already September 13 by the time he contacted Nimitz, too late to cancel the Palaus operation. This invasion subsequently cost the United States almost ten thousand lives, losses incurred for an unnecessary objective. As for Leyte, the Joint Chiefs agreed to advance the date.

On September 15, MacArthur stepped ashore at Moratai Island, accomplishing yet another successful unopposed landing. He was now a mere three hundred miles from the Philippines and elated over the prospect of returning ahead of schedule.

The Japanese were well aware of the importance of the Philippines to their empire. If this area were lost, they would no longer have access to the oil and other vital resources of the East Indies. Imperial General headquarters had thus drawn up a do-or-die plan called 'Sho-Go' or 'Operation Victory.' They were planning to throw in everything they had left to prevent the Americans from securing a successful lodgement in the islands. As Japanese Admiral Toyoda put it,

Should we lose in the Philippine operations even though the fleet should be left the shipping lane to the south would be completely cut off so that the fleet, if it should come back to Japanese waters, could not obtain its fuel supply. If it should remain in southern waters, it could not receive supplies of ammunition and arms. There would be no sense in saving the fleet at the expense of the loss of the Philippines.[40]

Holding the Philippines was therefore essential and the Japanese were perfectly willing to risk all in order to accomplish this.

When the Japanese finally realized that the main invasion area was Leyte, they were elated at the prospect of finally encountering the Americans in an all-out battle. Lt. General Tomoyuki Yamashita, the 'Tiger of Malaya' and conqueror of Singapore, was named to command the Philippine defense. This move inspired the Japanese and provided encouragement.

MacArthur arrived at Leyte, accompanied by an awesome naval force consisting of Halsey's Third Fleet and the Seventh Fleet under Admiral Kinkaid. To the Supreme Commander, Leyte represented an essential target. It would form, he said, the springboard from which he would be able to bound for Luzon.

At daybreak of October 20, 1944, from the deck of his flagship, the cruiser *USS Nashville*, MacArthur watched the massive volume of fire from the battleships as they pounded the invasion beaches of Leyte. Forty-one years before, he had stood near this same spot gazing at these very same beaches. Now, as Supreme Commander, he watched with anticipation as the amphibious vehicles transported Krueger's army towards Red, White, Violet and Yellow beaches. (See map 22) After lunch, the general made ready for his triumphant return. An array of correspondents and dignitaries accompanied him on this historic occasion. Sergio Osmena, President of the Philippines since the death of Quezon the previous July, and Carlos Rom-

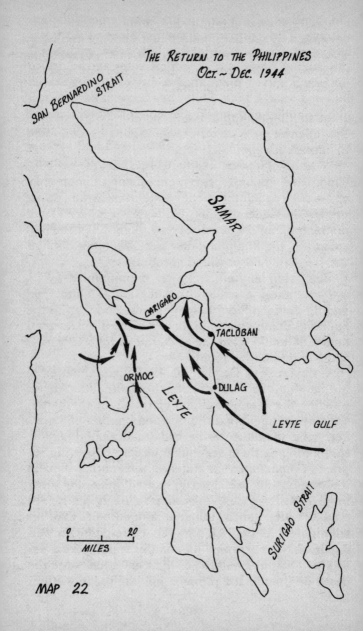

THE RETURN TO THE PHILIPPINES
OCT. ~ DEC. 1944

SAN BERNARDINO STRAIT

SAMAR

CARIGARO

TACLOBAN

ORMOC

DULAG

LEYTE

LEYTE GULF

SURIGAO STRAIT

0   20
MILES

MAP 22

ulo, a personal aide and writer, were among the entourage. The return was dramatic. Since no dock was left intact, the general, used to histrionics, stepped off the landing barge into knee-high water and waded to the beach. His staff and the accompanying dignitaries followed suit. All the while, newspaper and newsreel photographers excitedly documented the event. Amid the wreckage, with Japanese snipers still firing near the beach, MacArthur took pen in hand and wrote a letter to the President, explaining the tactical importance of Leyte.

> Strategically, it would sever the enemy's defensive line extending along the coast of Asia from the Japanese homeland to the tip of Singapore.[41]

He then made his famous speech to the people he had saved.

> People of the Philippines, I have returned. . . .
> Rise and strike. . . . Let every arm be steeled.[42]

He then proceeded to inform the islanders that their hour of redemption was at hand and that now was the time to strike. He then returned to the *Nashville*. No Hollywood producer could have staged it better.

Meanwhile, the land and sea battles in and around Leyte were intense. The Japanese decision to oppose the landings with everything available led to the largest naval battle in history, the Battle of Leyte Gulf. That battle was actually four distinct separate engagements, and the outcome was the final destruction of the Imperial Japanese Navy. Though they managed to provide the Americans with a nasty little surprise, U.S. naval might and the indecisive actions of Admiral Kurita sealed the fate of the once proud and powerful Japanese Navy. The land battle, however, proved to be a long, drawn-out campaign. The cause of this was the Japanese order to reinforce Leyte. Originally, Yamashita had intended to fight the decisive land battle on Luzon, but following the American landings on Leyte, he was ordered to fight the battle there. As a result, reinforcements poured into the island.

From the American viewpoint, one of the prime objectives of the campaign was again the establishment of air bases. To MacArthur's dismay, however, the ground at Leyte, thanks to the incessant rain, proved unsuitable for airfield construction. He had designated Leyte a springboard but, unfortunately, it proved to be a very soggy one indeed. Since airfield development proved to be prohibited, the Americans were forced to struggle without the expected support of land-based planes. Happily, Halsey's carriers remained in the area a month longer than originally planned. Otherwise, the Americans would have found themselves totally exposed from the air. Finally, a new airstrip was built at Tanuan which afforded the American troops P-38 support, but on the whole, Leyte never lived up to expectations.

Through November into December, the fighting continued as the 'Tiger of Malaya' locked horns with the Supreme Commander. Little by little, Yamashita's doubts began to mount about the feasibility of continuing the fight on Leyte, especially after the U.S. 77th Division made an end run at Ormoc on the island's west coast on December 7. The Japanese now found themselves caught in a vice between two American forces. Yamashita decided that his troops should be evacuated to Luzon, but Field Marshal Terauchi, his superior, ordered him to continue resisting at Leyte. By Christmas, however, Leyte was as good as captured. It had become a nightmare for the enemy soldiers. Yamashita was proved correct in his assessment; the battle had been a catastrophe. The Japanese had lost over sixty-five thousand troops, the major portion of their fleet, and virtually all of their air forces with the exception of a new and lethal weapon which, for the first time in the Pacific War, became part of the Japanese strategy, the *kamikaze*.

In December, MacArthur was promoted to five star rank and given the title General of the Army. To commemorate the promotion, a native Filipino melted down American, Philippine, Dutch, and Australian coins to form two circlets of five stars.

Prior to the final capture but with its fall imminent, MacArthur ordered an invasion of Mindoro, an island two hundred miles southwest of Manila and about three hundred miles from Leyte. With its seizure on December 15, he was now ready to strike Luzon. To both his and General Kenney's delight, the ground on Mindoro proved to be excellent for airfield construction. Now the general had all the air cover necessary to insure a successful landing on Luzon.

As the new year dawned, MacArthur eagerly awaited the climax of his long trek from Australia, an assault on Luzon. Under his command were nearly a thousand ships, over three thousand landing craft, and two hundred and eighty thousand men. Yamashita, however, had managed to amass two hundred and seventy-five thousand men, the largest ground army yet faced by the Americans in the Pacific War. General Yamashita knew that, in the face of superior American fire power, resistance at the beach was useless. Therefore, he moved his forces into Luzon's interior. This 'defense in depth' was adopted by the Japanese here and utilized again at Okinawa later on, proving extremely costly to the attackers.

MacArthur selected the very same beach Homma had chosen more than three years before, Lingayen. This second return of MacArthur commenced on January 9, 1945. Shortly after the Sixth Army established its beachhead, the Supreme Commander waded ashore. His order to his commanders was to capture Manila quickly. While the American forces moved on the capital, Yamashita massed his strength in the mountains to the east. Krueger worried about the Japanese move for fear that the enemy might swing behind him during his drive on Manila. MacArthur, however, was not concerned. All he could see was Manila and the prisons where the survivors of the Bataan garrison were being held. Although Krueger disagreed vehemently with his chief, MacArthur stood his ground.

Yamashita, meanwhile, was made impotent by the intensity of the American attack. While Krueger assaulted Clark Field, MacArthur struck elsewhere, a Subic Bay, on the west coast above Bataan, at Mariveles, and paratroopers were dropped on Nasugbu forty miles south of Manila. Bataan was captured in seven days and Manila was virtually surrounded. It was a brilliant piece of strategy which condemned Yamashita to parcel out his men piecemeal in an attempt to plug the many leaks in his defense. Even Corregidor was retaken by a combined airborne and sea assault. In the short span of ten days, 'The Rock' was subdued with the commander of the Japanese garrison committing suicide in a huge explosion. Only two hundred and ten Americans lost their lives retaking Corregidor.

MacArthur was like a man in his thirties, darting here and there. At the front line, his élan was unbounded. His care for his own life was, to say the least, reckless. Manchester notes,

In late January he was inspecting the 161st Infantry when the regiment was struck by a tank-led counterattack. The American lines buckled and MacArthur personally rallied the men. When Stimson heard about it, the general was awarded his third Distinguished Service Cross.[43]

So much for the 'Dugout Doug' criticism.

On February 3, the first American patrols entered Manila. The victory, however, was no easy one. When the city was finally secured, seventy percent of the utilities, seventy-five percent of the factories, eighty percent of the southern residential district, and one hundred percent of the business district were found destroyed. Hospitals were set on fire after patients had been strapped to their beds, bodies were mutilated, women of all ages were raped before being slain, babies were slaughtered and their eyeballs gouged out and smeared on walls like jelly. Nearly one hundred thousand Filipinos were cruelly murdered. MacArthur placed the blame squarely on the shoulders of Yamashita who, after the war, paid for this atrocity with his life. The responsibility, however, was not his. In fact, Yamashita had declared Manila an open city but somehow, one or two Japanese admirals either failed to receive the order or elected to disregard it and ordered the garrison of thirty thousand to defend the city to the last man. As the battle raged, so did the torture. This was not, however, the first time Japanese troops practiced marked bestiality on a conquered foe. One can easily recall the rape of Nanking in 1937.

The battle for Manila gave the jungle-trained Americans a unique experience, fighting in paved streets. The fighting was exceptionally fierce, at times devolving into hand-to-hand combat. It raged throughout the entire city, from the baseball stadium to the old walled section of Spanish days known as Intramuros. There the Japanese made their final stand. MacArthur was particularly distraught at the carnage in the city he had come to regard as home.

As the fighting continued, he visited the P.O.W. camps. The prisoners rallied around him, crying repeatedly, "You're back." In turn, the general would answer in a voice obviously cracking from emotion, "I'm a little late, but we finally came."[44] On the last day of February, while the fighting continued to rage in Intramuros, MacArthur attended a ceremony at the Presidential Palace during which he formally restored the Capital to Sergio Osmena. By early March, calm had descended on the city and the work of rebuilding had begun. On the sixth of the month Jean and his seven-year-old son returned to a Manila scarcely recognizable.

Meanwhile, the systematic reduction of the Japanese in the hills continued, as it would until the end of the war. In addition to clearing Luzon, he proceeded to plan and execute nearly a dozen major amphibious landings in the central and southern Philippines. These operations were ordered without prior approval of the Joint Chiefs. In a sense, MacArthur exerted an independent command. However, the Joint Chiefs saw fit not to interfere. As Manchester says:

> The general's real motives were personal, political, and humanitarian. He wanted to become the liberator of all the Philippines.[45]

Formal announcement of the liberation of the Philippines came on July 5, 1945. During the previous months, the Eighth Army did an outstanding job of routing the Japanese in the outlining islands. At the same time, the Australians under MacArthur's command did a magnificent job of reconquering the East Indies.

While MacArthur's forces went about the business of clearing the Philippines and East Indies, all through the spring Japan itself was feeling the effects of the war thanks to firebombing raids conducted by B-29s stationed in the Marianas. With Iwo Jima captured in March and Okinawa assaulted on April 1, the United States' forces found themselves in Japan's backyard. On June 21, after two and a half months of deadly warfare highlighted by the largest *kamikaze* attacks to date, Okinawa was finally subdued. Now it was Japan's turn.

Back in late March, it was decided by the dying Roosevelt that MacArthur should lead the final assault on Japan. On April 3, the Pentagon made it official, Nimitz would command the naval units and Mac-Arthur all the ground forces.

As June turned into July, the general made his preparations. He knew that the Japanese were doomed, but also realized that they would fight to the death unless the Emperor himself called for an armistice. The Emporor was the key and MacArthur knew it. Understandably, he was piqued when the delegates at the Potsdam Conference demanded that Japan surrender unconditionally. Many people in America called for the outright abdication of the Emperor. MacArthur realized, however, that the Japanese would never renounce their leader. How right he was. Unfortunately, only after the unleashing of the nuclear nightmare did Japan consent to surrender, but ironically, the surrender was conditional.

Unaware of the secret 'Manhattan Project' developing the atom bomb, MacArthur continued to plan for the proposed invasion. The first stage of the move called 'Operation Olympic' was scheduled to land on

Kyushu on November 1, 1945. The main assault 'Operation Coronet,' was planned for Honshu on March 1 of the following year. Then the atom bomb was dropped on Hiroshima on August 6, followed three days later by another on Nagasaki. On August 14, Emperor Hirohito went on the radio and ended hostilities. The war was over.

With the approval of the other Allied leaders, the new American President, Harry S. Truman appointed MacArthur Supreme Commander for the Allied Powers (SCAP). The first order of business was to arrange and organize the formal surrender ceremony. Once more, the MacArthur bravado surfaced as he landed unarmed at Atsugi Airport amid millions of Japanese who not more than two weeks previously had been living for the sole purpose of annihilating him. Winston Churchill and MacArthur's own staff felt that the general was taking an unnecessary risk and cautioned against it. There was, they felt, a strong possibility that some fanatic might make an assasination attempt. The warnings failed to stop him. Propellers were removed from all Japanese aircraft and he arrived safely on August 30. He took two steps down from the plane, puffed on his famous corncob pipe, posed for the assembled cameramen, then descended.

His first encounter with the Japanese was a huge success. Within a very short time, he gained their trust and soon became the second most revered man in the country, next to the Emperor. Right from the beginning, he was determined to have a benign occupation. He recalled the punitive occupation of Germany after the First World War and he wanted to avoid the same pitfalls.

MacArthur established his official residency at the New Grand Hotel. On the evening of August 31, Lt. General Jonathan Wainwright, recently liberated by the Russians from a Manchurian prison, was brought to the hotel. The emaciated Wainwright was embraced by MacArthur with great emotion.

The surrender ceremony took place on the morning of September 2 aboard the battleship *Missouri* anchored in Tokyo Bay. MacArthur was placed center stage, Wainwright, and General Percival, the British defender of Singapore, were given places of honor behind him. After the playing of the 'Star Spangled Banner,' MacArthur walked briskly between Admirals Nimitz and Halsey to his place. Ranks of dignitaries from all the Allied powers were present, bedecked with all their ribbons of honor. In contrast, MacArthur wore none. He had received no official instructions for the occasion and was completely on his own. Holding a sheet of paper before him, he said,

We are gathered here, representatives of the major warring powers, to conclude a solemn agreement whereby peace may be restored.[46]

He went on to say that he hoped a better world would emerge from the ashes of war, one dedicated to the dignity of man.

Listening to the oration were four rows of Japanese dignitaries. Their feelings of uncomfort must have been obvious as thousands of eyes peered down at them. MacArthur's words rang well to his former enemies. One representative felt relieved at the lack of harshness. "I was thrilled beyond words, spellbound, thunderstruck."[47] After the speech, the formal signing of the Instrument of Surrender took place. First the Japanese signed, followed by the representatives of each Allied Nation, finally the Supreme Commander. For the signing, five fountain pens were used. One MacArthur gave to Wainwright, the second to Perci-

415

val, the third to West Point, the fourth to Annapolis, and the final one he gave to his wife. MacArthur's final words were "These proceedings are now closed."

The primary intent of this chapter has now been fulfilled. The general's career, however, continued beyond the war with six more active, vibrant years of public service, first as SCAP in Japan and later as U.N. Commander during the initial stages of the Korean War. Let it be noted that his remaining six years deserve special consideration. What he accomplished for Japan was nothing less than monumental and the effects of his efforts are still felt in that country today. His later actions and decisions in Korea, culminating in his dismissal by Truman, exposed a very sensitive issue, military versus civilian control.

MacArthur made an enormous impression on the Japanese people. His fertile mind conceived many original plans for the recently vanquished country. Being a subscriber to Clausewitz's theory that your former enemy could become your strongest ally if treated fairly, he treated the Japanese with respect. Above all, he wished to make life more democratic for them. Women were given the right to vote, he pushed for free elections, the formation of labor unions, the elimination of military indoctrination in education, and the demilitarization of the Japanese way of life and the abolition of emperor worship.

From the outset, MacArthur was determined to be conciliatory. He was above gloating over a vanquished foe. Any policy decisions had to go through him. Although technically he was subordinate to the politicians in Washington, in reality he made his own policy. His word was absolute. Never before or since in American history had such power been placed in the hands of a single individual. In many ways, he assumed the role of a legendary figure from Japan's past, the Shogun. Even such controversial decisions as the punishment of Japan's military leaders, including Tojo, Homma, and Yamashita failed to raise the ire of the people and diminish his stature, so deep was their respect for the general. MacArthur's biggest problems during the post-war years came not from within Japan, but from detractors and critics outside the country.

The Constitution which he helped frame became one of the most liberal documents in history. The Emperor was reduced to a symbolic status, the Diet or Parliament was empowered to make laws, feudal aristocracy was abolished, popular liberties were guaranteed as was collective bargaining, and the equality of the sexes was established. While the Diet contained the legislative powers, executive power was invested in the hands of a Prime Minister whose term of office was four years. The Constitution included a most unique clause, Article XI. It was called the 'no war' clause and basically stated that the Japanese people forever renounced war as a sovereign right of the nation. This Constitution, 'The MacArthur Constitution,' is still in effect today and remains one of his enduring achievements.

As the years passed and MacArthur continued his benign lordship and guidance over Japan, international situations in the Orient became ominous. Nationalist China, long an ally of the U.S., lost out in a power struggle to Mao Tse-tung's Communists and the Red Star flew over China. The repercussions of this were shortly felt. Once more, Japan's position became one of prominence. At home in America, the communization of China reverberated strongly and accusing fingers were pointed at Communist sympathizers in Washington. This led to one of the most shameful eras of American history, the regrettable 'McCarthy era' of denounciations.

MacArthur was of the impression that the U.S. should increase its military presence in Japan in light of events in the Far East. Thus, he requested additional ships, planes, and men. He advocated increased military aid for Chiang Kai-shek on Formosa, but Truman responded negatively saying that the U.S. would not establish military bases on Formosa at that particular time.

The subsequent conflict known as the Korean War, led by the U.S. against North Korea, who was bolstered by Chinese and Russian support, is a long and complicated story. To MacArthur, it was an old soldier's fondest desire, another war. Space precludes dwelling at length on the conflict, so the reader must be satisfied with the fact that MacArthur demonstrated the same bravado which had characterized him in the past. His amphibious landing at Inchon, leading to the liberation of Seoul, can only be considered a work of genius. MacArthur's miscalculation of the intent of the Chinese, however, was a grave error. The conflict between him and Truman finally sealed his fate. The issue of civilian versus military rule was decided once and for all by Truman's act of recalling MacArthur in 1951. Though this raised a storm of controversy that probably caused the Democrats to lose the White House in 1952, most historians agree that what Truman was fighting for was vitally important. MacArthur's desire to move against the Chinese, though militarily correct, was politically fraught with danger. The controversy ran deep. To MacArthur, a military man, the objective of any nation at war was ultimate victory, total, immediate, and complete. If wars are to be fought, then they should be placed in the hands of the professional soldier and brought to a successful conclusion.

If a nation wasn't willing to make that total military commitment, it shouldn't fight at all.[48]

This then was the heart of the Truman-MacArthur conflict.

His recall from command ended MacArthur's active military career. Returning to the United States for the first time since 1937, he received a tumultuous welcome. Although he desired the homecoming to be a quiet one, feeling that it would be difficult to return under the circumstances of his relief, his wishes were not publicly known. Arriving in San Francisco late at night, he found a large reception waiting. The governor of California, Mayor of San Francisco, and thousands of cheering citizens welcomed the returning hero home. Everywhere he traveled, the reaction was the same. MacArthur was the man of the hour. On April 19, he was in Washington where he spoke before a joint session of Congress. The speech showed MacArthur at his best. The dangerous international situation and America's role in the contemporary world were expertly summed up. The speech was interspaced with ornamental rhetoric typical of the general. In closing, he made a universally acclaimed statement and, even today, excerpts from it are used.

I am closing my 52 years of military service. When I joined the Army, even before the turn of the century, it was the fulfillment of all my boyish hopes and dreams. The world has turned over many times since I took the oath on the Plain at West Point, and the hopes and dreams have long since vanished. But I still remember the refrain of one of the most popular barracks ballads of that day, which proclaimed, most proudly, that 'Old soldiers never die. They just fade away.' And like the old soldier of that ballad, I now close my military career and just fade away—an old soldier who tried to do his duty as God gave him the light to see that duty. Goodbye."[49]

MacArthur took up residency at the Waldorf Astoria in New York City and called this home till his death in 1964. Before settling down, however, he, his wife, and son traveled to scores of American cities where huge crowds turned out to welcome the hero. From May 3 until June 25, he met with a congressional committee and discussed at length the events leading up to his abrupt recall.

Not counting his family, Douglas MacArthur had two great love affairs during his lifetime. One, of course, was with the Philippines to whom he returned in 1961 to help that nation celebrate the fifteenth anniversary of its independence. The other great love affair was with West Point. At the academy's commencement exercises in 1962, he was invited to address the corps of cadets. For a man accustomed to inspirational oration and whose phrases became everyday expressions, the final sentences of this commencement at West Point were perhaps the most memorable, and certainly the most moving, he ever uttered.

Today marks my final roll call with you. But I want you to know that when I cross the river my last conscious thoughts will be of The Corps, and The Corps, and The Corps. I bid you farewell."[50]

On April 5, 1964, at the ripe age of 84, General of the Army Douglas MacArthur crossed that river. Truly, he had led a full life. Without doubt, history will prove that Douglas MacArthur was unquestionably one of the greatest commanders of World War II or any era. His strategy and brilliant use of tactics were superb. He was unsurpassed in his use of combined operations, his many amphibious landings during the war and the Inchon landing in Korea are testimony to his mastery of these plans. His economic use of man power is probably his greatest credit and his decision to bypass many strongholds and leave them to wither on the vine are proof.

However, before canonizing him, his faults and errors must be reviewed. The B-17s at Clark Field, the failure to store adequate food on Bataan, and the miscalculation of the Chinese Communist's true intent. His arrogance, ego, and vanity speak against him. MacArthur was self righteous and usually saw only his side of things. Although he made errors, he had the resiliency to overcome them. However, there was no bouncing back from his inexcusable challenge to the authority of the President of the United States, Mr. Truman. This fatal error finally brought about his downfall.

Yet, there can be no question of his patriotism and ability to inspire. The Australians loved him and looked upon him as their protector. The Filipinos sanctified him and looked to him as their savior. The Japanese, the former enemy, revered him second only to the Emperor. Finally, the American public adored him.

General MacArthur touched the lives of millions, more so than any other person during this century. Traditionally, historians fail to draw the distinction between a great commander and a great leader. Of all the outstanding military personages of World War II, a mere handful were able to bridge this gap and combine both talents in one personality. Unquestionably, history will reserve an important place for General of the Army, Douglas MacArthur.

Notes to Chapter Introduction

1. Kent Roberts Greenfields, ed. *Command Decisions*, p. 175.
2. *Ibid*, p. 178.
3. Maurice Matloff and Edwin Snell, *Strategic Planning for Coalition Warfare 1941-1942*, p. 267.
4. *Ibid*, p. 278.
5. Henry L. Stimson and McGeorge Bundy, *On Active Service In Peace and War*, p. 436.
6. Winston Churchill, *Closing The Ring*, pp. 332-333.

Notes to Chapter One

1. Francis D. Cronin, *Under the Southern Cross*, p. 12.
2. J. Lawton Collins, *Lightning Joe*, p. 147.
3. W. Halsey & J. Bryann, *Admiral Halsey's Story*, p. 148.
4. *Ibid*, p. 148.
5. Russell Weigley, *Eisenhower's Lieutenants*, p. 713.
6. Wilfried Strik-Strikfeldt, *Against Stalin and Hitler*, p. 235.
7. Guy Salisbury-Jones, *So Full a Glory*, p. 144.
8. Charles MacDonald, *The Mighty Endeavor*, p. 407.

Notes to Chapter Two

1. Ladislas Farago, *Patton: Ordeal and Triumph*. p. 70.
2. Charles Whiting, *Patton*. p. 8.
3. H. Essame, *Patton—A Study in Command*. p. 84.
4. Farago, *op cit*, p. 273.
5. Albert Garland and Howard M. Smyth, *Sicily and the Surrender of Italy*, pp. 417-418.
6. Whiting, *op cit*, pp. 43-44.
7. Martin Blumenson, *The Patton Papers 1940-1945*, p. 452.
8. Frederick Winterbotham, *The Ultra Secret*, p. 151.
9. Farago, *op cit*, p. 469.
10. Essame, *op cit*, p. 172.
11. *Ibid*, p. 172.
12. Blumenson, *op cit*, p. 528.
13. Whiting, *op cit*, p. 90.
14. Omar Bradley, *A Soldier's Story*, p. 473.
15. Col. Robert S. Allen, *Lucky Forward*, p. 54.
16. Russell Weigley, *Eisenhower's Lieutenants*, p. 696.
17. Ladislas Farago, *The Last Days of Patton*, p. 305.

Notes to Chapter Three

1. M. Blumenson & J. Stokesbury, *Masters of the Art of Command*, p. 295.
2. Michael Carver, ed., *The War Lords*, p. 538.
3. Charles Whiting, *Bradley*, p. 14.
4. Omar Bradley, *A Soldier's Story*, p. 31.
5. Whiting, *op cit*, p. 14.
6. Bradley, *op cit*, p. 45.
7. *Ibid*, p. 87.
8. *Ibid*, p. 87.
9. *Ibid*, p. 130.
10. *Ibid*, p. 135.
11. *Ibid*, p. 318.

12. Whiting, *op cit*, p. 23.
13. *Ibid*, p. 26.
14. Bradley, *op cit*, p. 350.
15. Charles B. MacDonald, *The Mighty Endeavor*, p. 305.
16. Whiting, *op cit*, p. 32.
17. Stephen F. Ambrose, *Ike's Spies*, p. 114.
18. Whiting, *op cit*, p. 33.
19. *Ibid*, p. 33.
20. Ambrose, *op cit*, p. 119.
21. Ladislas Farago, *Patton: Ordeal and Triumph*, p. 519.
22. Bradley, *op cit*, p. 339.
23. *Ibid*, p. 57.
24. David Irving, *The War Between the Generals*, p. 336.
25. Whiting, *op cit*, p. 65.
26. *Ibid*, p. 65.
27. Bradley, *op cit*, p. 459.
28. *Ibid*, p. 462.
29. Whiting, *op cit*, pp. 70-71.
30. *Ibid*, p. 75.
31. *Ibid*, p. 97.
32. Farago, *op cit*, p. 730.
33. Bradley, *op cit*, p. 536.
34. Farago, *op cit*, p. 753.
35. Carver, *op cit*, pp. 542-543.
36. *Ibid*, p. 550.

Notes to Chapter Four

1. General Joseph W. Stilwell, *The Stilwell Papers*, p. 106.
2. Michael Carver, ed. *The War Lords*, p. 356.
3. Barbara W. Tuchman, *Stilwell and the American Experience in China, 1911-1945*, p. 21.
4. *Ibid*, p. 38.
5. *Ibid*, p. 57.
6. *Ibid*, p. 91.
7. *Ibid*, p. 114.
8. Tuchman, *op cit*, p. 153.
9. *Ibid*, p. 168.
10. Stilwell's Report Summarizing the War: G-2 No. 6, 900, 25 Sept. 38.
11. G-2 Report on Chiang Kai-Shek: No. 9716, 24 Jan 39, Carmel A-17.
12. Tuchman, *op cit*, p. 216.
13. Stilwell, *op cit*, p. 11.
14. Tuchman, *op cit*, p. 237.
15. Henry Stimson & McGeorge Bundy, *On Active Service in Peace and War*, p. 530.
16. Stilwell, *op cit*, p. 30.
17. Tuchman, *op cit*, p. 270.
18. Stilwell, *op cit*, p. 60.
19. Field Marshal Slim, *Defeat into Victory*, pp. 35-36.
20. D.D. Rooney, *Stilwell*, p. 34.
21. Tuchman, *op cit*, p. 281.
22. Stilwell, *op cit*, p. 86.

23. *Ibid*, p. 79.

24. W.G.F. Jackson, *Alexander of Tunis*, p. 174.

25. Frank Dorn, *Walkout with Stilwell in Burma*, p. 159.

26. Tuchman, *op cit*, pp. 302-03.

27. *Ibid*, p. 338.

28. *Ibid*, p. 343.

29. *Ibid*, p. 347.

30. Stilwell, *op cit*, p. 186.

31. Tuchman, *op cit*, p. 368.

32. *Ibid*, p. 392.

33. Stilwell, *op cit*, p. 231.

34. *Ibid*, p. 231.

35. Charles F. Romanus and Riley Sunderland, *Stilwell's Command Problems*, p. 65.

36. Stilwell, *op cit*, p. 266.

37. Tuchman, *op cit*, p. 418.

38. *Ibid*, p. 424.

39. *Ibid*, p. 451.

40. Romanus and Sunderland, *op cit*, p. 383.

41. Stilwell, *op cit*, p. 324.

42. *Ibid*, p. 333.

43. *Ibid*, p. 334.

44. Romanus and Sunderland, *op cit*, p. 447.

45. *Ibid*, p. 462.

46. Tuchman, *op cit*, p. 506.

47. *Ibid*, p. 512.

48. Carver, *op cit*, p. 356.

Notes to Chapter Five

1. Kay Summersby Morgan, *Past Forgetting*, p. 115.

2. Stephen Ambrose, *The Supreme Commander*, p. 7.

3. Dwight D. Eisenhower, *Crusade in Europe*, p. 14.

4. Ambrose, *op. cit*, p. 21.

5. *Ibid*, pp. 21-22.

6. Robert Ferrell, ed., *The Eisenhower Diaries*, pp. 50-51.

7. *Ibid*, p. 49.

8. Mark Clark, *Calculated Risk*, p. 9.

9. Ambrose, *op. cit*, pp. 47-48.

10. Eisenhower, *op. cit*, pp. 54-55.

11. *Ibid*, p. 83.

12. Ambrose, *op. cit*, p. 141.

13. Eisenhower, *op. cit*, p. 89.

14. Ambrose, *op. cit*, p. 138.

15. Ladislas Farago, *Ordeal and Triumph*, p. 279.

16. Ambrose, *op. cit*, p. 215.

17. *Ibid*, p. 223.

18. *Ibid*, p. 265.

19. *Ibid*, p. 232.

20. *Ibid*, p. 232.

21. *Ibid*, p. 309.

22. *Ibid*, p. 345.

23. *Ibid*, p. 417.
24. *Ibid*, p. 418.
25. Charles MacDonald, *The Mighty Endeavor*, p. 279.
26. David Irving, *The War Between the Generals*, p. 217.
27. Harry Butcher, *My Three Years With Eisenhower*, p. 630.
28. Irving, *op. cit*, p. 268.
29. *Ibid*, p. 267.
30. *Ibid*, p. 278.
31. *Ibid*, p. 286.
32. *Ibid*, p. 286.
33. *Ibid*, p. 415.
34. National Archives.

Notes to Chapter Six

1. William Manchester, *American Caesar*, p. 280.
2. *Ibid*, p. 39.
3. *Ibid*, p. 64.
4. Douglas MacArthur, *Reminiscences*, p. 32.
5. *Ibid*, p. 46.
6. Manchester, *op cit*, p. 89.
7. *Ibid*, p. 97.
8. *Ibid*, p. 107.
9. *Ibid*, p. 144.
10. Sydney L. Mayer, *MacArthur*, p. 46.
11. Manchester, *op cit*, p. 159.
12. *Ibid*, p. 189.
13. Hanson W. Baldwin, *Battles Lost and Won*, p. 117.
14. Mayer, *op cit*, p. 74.
15. Manchester, *op cit*, p. 219.
16. *Ibid*, p. 232.
17. Mayer, *op cit*, p. 89.
18. Gavin Long, *MacArthur as Military Commander*, p. 82.
19. Dwight D. Eisenhower, *Crusade in Europe*, pp. 21-22.
20. Jonathan M. Wainwright, *General Wainwright's Story*, pp. 3-4.
21. *Ibid*, p. 4.
22. Manchester, *op cit*, p. 270.
23. *Ibid*, p. 271.
24. *Ibid*, p. 285.
25. *Ibid*, p. 298.
26. Charles A. Willoughby and John Chamberlain, *MacArthur 1941-1951*, p. 77.
27. Manchester, *op cit*, p. 320.
28. *Ibid*, p. 322.
29. Robert L. Eichelberger, *Our Jungle Road To Tokyo*, p. 22.
30. Manchester, *op cit*, p. 325.
31. MacArthur, *op cit*, pp. 173-174.
32. *Ibid*, pp. 168-169.
33. Manchester, *op cit*, p. 338.
34. *Ibid*, p. 344.
35. James M. Burns, *Roosevelt: The Soldier of Freedom 1940-1945*, p. 488.

36. Mayer, *op cit*, p. 131.
37. William F. Halsey, *Admiral Halsey's Story*, p. 199.
38. Manchester, *op cit*, p. 381.
39. *Ibid*, p. 388.
40. Gavin Long, *MacArthur As Military Commander*, p. 152.
41. Manchester, *op cit*, p. 412.
42. *Ibid*, p. 415.
43. *Ibid*, p. 429.
44. *Ibid*, p. 452.
45. *Ibid*, p. 452.
46. *Ibid*, p. 630.
47. Long, *op cit*, p. 224.
48. Clay Blair, Jr., *MacArthur*, p. 330.

Bibliography to Introduction

Ambrose, Stephen, *The Supreme Commander*, Doubleday & Co., New York, 1970.

Bryant, Arthur, *The Turn of the Tide 1939-43*, Doubleday & Co., New York, 1957.

Churchill, Winston S., *The Grand Alliance*, Houghton Mifflin Co., Boston, 1950.

Churchill, Winston S., *Closing the Ring*, Houghton Mifflin Co., Boston, 1951.

Cline, Ray S., *Washington Command Post, The Operation Division*, Office of the Chief of Military History, Washington, 1951.

Coakley, Robert & Leighton, Richard, *Global Logistics and Strategy*, Office of the Chief of Military History, Washington, 1968.

Grigg, John, *1943 The Victory That Never Was*, Hill and Wang, New York, 1980.

Greenfield, Kent R., ed., *Command Decisions*, Office of the Chief of Military History, Washington, 1960.

Loewenheim, Francis L. et al. ed., *Roosevelt and Churchill Their Secret Wartime Correspondence*, E.P. Dutton & Co., New York, 1975.

Matloff, Maurice & Snell, Edwin, *Strategic Planning for Coalition Warfare 1941-1942*, Office of the Chief of Military History, Washington, 1953.

Matloff, Maurice, *Strategic Planning for Coalition Warfare 1943-1944*, Office of the Chief of Military History, Washington, 1959.

Pfannes, Charles & Salamone, Victor, *The Great Commanders of World War II, Volume II—The British*, Zebra Books, New York, 1981.

Pitt, Barrie, *Churchill and The Generals*, A Bantam Book, New York, 1981.

Pogue, Forrest C., *George C. Marshall. Ordeal and Hope 1939-1942*, The Viking Press, New York, 1966.

Pogue, Forrest C., *George C. Marshall. Organizer of Victory 1943-1945*, The Viking Press, New York, 1973.

Sherwood, Robert F., *Roosevelt and Hopkins: An Intimate History*, Harper Bros., New York, 1948.

Stimson, Henry L. & Bundy, McGeorge, *On Active Service In Peace And War*, Harper Bros., New York, 1947.

Watson, Mark S., *Chief of Staff: Prewar Plans and Preparations*, Historical Division, United States Army, Washington, 1950.

Bibliography to Chapter One

Adelman, R. & Walton, G., *The Champagne Campaign*, Walker & Co., New York, 1962.

Ambrose, Stephen, *The Supreme Commander*, Doubleday & Co., New York, 1969.

Codman, Charles, *Drive*, Little Brown & Co., Boston, 1957.

Coggins, Jack, *The Struggle for Guadalcanal*, Doubleday & Co., New York, 1972.

Collier, Basil, *The War in the Far East*, William Morrow & Co., New York, 1969.

Collins, J. Lawton, *Lightning Joe*, L.S.U. Press, Baton Rouge, 1979.

Cronin, Francis D., *Under the Southern Cross—Saga of the Americal Division*.

Farago, Ladislas, *Patton—.Ordeal and Triumph*, Ivan Obolensky, New York, 1963.

Farago, Ladislas, *The Last Days of Patton*, McGraw Hill, New York, 1980.

Halsey, W. & Bryann, J., *Admiral Halsey's Story*, Curtis Publishing Co., New York, 1947.

Irving, David, *The War Between the Generals*, Congdon & Lattes, New York, 1981.

Kent, Graeme, *Guadalcanal—Island Ordeal*, Ballantine Books, New York, 1971.

MacDonald, Charles, *The Mighty Endeavor*, Oxford University Press, New York, 1969.

Pogue, Forrest, *George C. Marshall—Organizer of Victory*, Viking, New York, 1973.

Pogue, Forrest, *George C. Marshall—Ordeal & Hope*, Viking, New York, 1965.

Robichon, Jacques, *The Second D-Day*, Walker & Co., New York, 1962.

Salisbury-Jones, Guy, *So Full a Glory—A Life of Marshall De Lattre De Tassigny*, Weidenfeld & Nicolson, London, 1954.

Salmaggi, C. & Pallavisini, A., *2,194 Days of War*, Windward, New York, 1977.

Strik-Strikfeldt, Wilfried, *Against Stalin & Hitler*, The John Day Co., New York, 1973.

Weigley, Russell, *Eisenhower's Lieutenants*, Indiana University, Bloomington, 1981.

Bibliography to Chapter Two

Allen, Col. Robert S., *Lucky Forward*, The Vanguard Press, Inc., New York, 1947.

Ayer, Fred Jr., *Before the Colors Fade*, Houghton Mifflin Corp, Boston, 1964.

Baron, R., Baum, A., Goldhurst, R., *Raid*, G.P. Putnams Son, New York, 1981.

Blumenson, Martin, *Breakout and Pursuit*, Historical Div., U.S. Army, Washington, D.C., 1961.

Blumenson, Martin, *Sicily—Whose Victory*, Ballantine Books, New York, 1968.

Blumenson, Martin, *Eisenhower*, Ballantine Books, New York, 1972.

Blumenson, Martin, *The Patton Papers*, Houghton Mifflin Co., Boston, 1974.

Bradley, Omar, *A Soldier's Story*, Henry Holt, New York, 1951.

Cave Brown, Anthony, *Bodyguard of Lies*, Harper and Row, New York 1975.

Codman, Charles, *Drive*, Little Brown & Co., Boston, 1957.

Cole, Hugh M., *The Lorraine Campaign*, Historical Div., U.S. Army Washington, D.C., 1950.

Cole, Hugh M., *The Ardennes—Battle of the Bulge*, Historical Div., U.S Army, Washington, D.C., 1965.

Elstob, Peter, *Bastogne: The Road Block*, Ballantine Books, New York, 1968.

Elstob, Peter, *Hitler's Last Offensive*, Macmillan, New York, 1971.

Essame, H., *Patton—A Study in Command*, Charles Scribner's Sons, New York, 1974.

Farago, Ladislas, *The Last Days of Patton*, McGraw Hill, New York, 1981

Farago, Ladislas, *Patton: Ordeal and Triumph*, Ivan Obolensky, New York, 1963.

Florentin, Eddy, *The Battle of the Falaise Gap*, Hawthorn, New York, 1967.

Frankel, Nat & Smith, Larry, *Patton's Best*, Hawthorn, New York, 1978.

Garland, Albert & Smyth, Howard, *Sicily and the Surrender of Italy*, Historical Div., U.S. Army, Washington, D.C., 1965.

Irving, David, *The War Between the Generals*, Congdon & Lattes, New York, 1981.

Jackson, W.G.F., *The Battle for Italy*, Harper & Row, New York, 1967.

Mason, David, *Breakout—Drive to the Seine*, Ballantine Books, New York, 1968.

MacDonald, Charles, *The Last Offensive*, Historical Div., U.S. Army Washington, D.C., 1973.

Patton, George S., *War as I knew It*, Houghton Mifflin Co., Boston, 1947.

Pfannes, C., & Salamone, V., *The Great Commanders of WW II Volume I—The Germans*, Zebra Books, New York, 1980.

Pfannes, C. & Salamone, V., *The Great Commanders of WW II Volume II—The British*, Zebra Books, New York, 1981.

Price, Frank, *Troy Middleton, A Biography*, L.S.U. Press, Baton Rouge, 1974.

Semmes, Harry, *Portrait of Patton*, Paperback Library, New York, 1955.

Weigley, Russell, *Eisenhower's Lieutenants*, Indiana University, Bloomington, 1981.

Wilmot, Chester, *The Struggle for Europe*, Harper & Row, New York, 1952.

Whiting, Charles, *Bradley*, Ballantine Books, New York, 1970.

Winterbotham, Frederick, *The Ultra Secret*, Harper & Row, New York, 1974.

Bibliography to Chapter Three

Ambrose, Stephen, *The Supreme Commander*, Doubleday & Co., New York, 1970.

Ambrose, Stephen, *Ike's Spies*, Doubleday & Co., New York, 1981.

Belfield, E. & Essame, H., *The Battle for Normandy*, Dufour Editions, 1965.

Blumenson, Martin, *Breakout and Pursuit*, Office of the Chief of Military History, Washington, 1961.

Blumenson, Martin, *The Duel for France*, Houghton Mifflin Co., Boston, 1963.

Blumenson, Martin, *The Patton Papers*, Houghton Mifflin Co., Boston, 1974.

Blumenson, M., & Stokesbury, J., *Masters of the Art of Command*, Houghton Mifflin Co., Boston, 1975.

Bradley, Omar N., *A Soldier's Story*, Henry Holt and Co., New York, 1951.

Cave Brown, Anthony, *Bodyguard of Lies*, Harper & Row, New York, 1975.

Carver, Sir Michael, ed., *The War Lords*, Little, Brown and Co., Boston, 1976.

Collins, J. Lawton, *Lightning Joe*, L.S.U. Press, Baton Rouge, 1979.

Farago, Ladislas, *Patton: Ordeal and Triumph*, Ivan Obolensky Inc., New York, 1963.

Farago, Ladislas, *The Last Days of Patton*, McGraw Hill Book Co., New York, 1981.

Florentin, Eddy, *The Battle of the Falaise Gap*, Hawthorn Books, New York, 1967.

Howe, George F., *Northwest Africa: Seizing the Initiative in the West*, Office of the Chief of Military History, Washington, 1957.

Irving, David, *The War Between the Generals*, Congdon & Lattes Inc., New York, 1981.

Lewin, Ronald, *Ultra Goes To War*, McGraw-Hill Book Co., New York, 1978.

MacDonald, Charles B. *The Siegfried Line Campaign*, Office of the Chief of Military History, Washington, 1963.

MacDonald, Charles B., *The Mighty Endeavor*, Oxford University Press, New York, 1969.

MacDonald, Charles B., *The Last Offensive*, Office of the Chief of Military History, Washington, 1973.

Merriam, Robert, *Dark December*, Ziff-Davis, 1947.

Middleton, Troy, *Troy Middleton, A Biography*, L.S.U. Press, Baton Rouge, 1974.

Montgomery, B.L., *Memoirs*, Collins St. James Place, London, 1958.

Pfannes, C.E. & Salamone, V.A., *The Great Commanders of World War II Volume I: The Germans*, Zebra Books, New York, 1980.

Pfannes, C.E. & Salamone, V.A., *The Great Commanders of World War II Volume II: The British*, Zebra Books, New York, 1981.

Pogue, Forrest C., *The Supreme Command*, Office of the Chief of Military History, Washington, 1954.

Pogue, Forrest C., *George C. Marshall: Organizer of Victory 1943-1945*, The Viking Press, New York, 1973.

Ryan, Cornelius, *The Longest Day*, Simon and Schuster, New York, 1959.

Weigley, Russell F., *Eisenhower's Lieutenants*, Indiania University Press, Bloomington, 1981.

Whiting, Charles, *Patton*, Ballantine Books, New York, 1970.

Whiting, Charles, *Bradley*, Ballantine Books, New York, 1971.

Wilmot, Chester, *The Struggle For Europe*, Harper and Row, New York, 1952.

Winterbotham, F.W., *The Ultra Secret*, Harper and Row, New York, 1974.

Bibliography to Chapter Four

Baker, Alan, *Merrill's Marauders*, Ballantine Books, New York, 1972.

Belden, Jack, *Retreat With Stilwell*, Alfred A. Knopf, New York, 1943.

Bidwell, Shelford, *The Chindit War*, Macmillan Publishing Co., New York, 1979.

Calvert, Michael, *Chindits—Long Range Penetration*, Ballantine Books, New York, 1973.

Carver, Michael, ed., *The War Lords*, Little, Brown and Co., Boston, 1976.

Dorn, Frank, *Walkout With Stilwell In Burma*, Thomas Y. Crowell Co., New York, 1971.

Eldridge, Fred, *Wrath in Burma*, Doubleday & Co., New York, 1946.

Heiferman, Ron, *Flying Tigers: Chennault in China*, Ballantine Books, New York, 1971.

Koenig, William, *Over the Hump: Airlift to China*, Ballantine Books, New York, 1972.

Ogburn, Charlton Jr., *The Marauders*, Harper Bros. Publishers, New York, 1956.

Pfannes, Charles & Salamone, Victor, *The Great Commanders of World War II, Volume II—The British*, Zebra Books, New York, 1981.

Pogue, Forrest C., *George C. Marshall. Education of a General 1880-1939*, The Viking Press, New York, 1963.

Pogue, Forrest C., *George C. Marshall. Ordeal and Hope*, The Viking Press, New York, 1965.

Pogue, Forrest C., *George C. Marshall. Organizor of Victory*, The Viking Press, New York, 1973.

Rooney, D.D., *Stilwell*, Ballantine Books, New York, 1971.

Romanus, Charles & Sunderland, Riley, *Stilwell's Misson to China*, Office of the Chief of Military History, Washington, 1953.

Romanus, Charles & Sunderland, Riley, *Stilwell's Command Problems*, Office of the Chief of Military History, Washington, 1956.

Romanus, Charles & Sunderland, Riley, *Time Runs Out In CBI*, Office of the Chief of Military History, Washington, 1959.

Schaller, Michael, *The U.S. Crusade in China 1938-1945*, Columbia University Press, New York, 1979.

Seagrave, Gordon S., M.D., *Burma Surgeon*, W.W. Norton & Co. Inc., New York, 1943.

Slim, General Sir William, *Defeat Into Victory*, David McKay Co. Inc., New York, 1961.

Smith, E.D., *Battle for Burma*, B.T. Batsford Ltd., London, 1979.

Stilwell, General Joseph, *The Stilwell Papers*, William Sloane Associates, New York, 1948.

Stimson, Henry L. & Bundy, McGeorge, *On Active Service In Peace and War*, Harper & Bros., New York, 1947.

Tuchman, Barbara, *Stilwell and the American Experience in China 1911-1945*, The MacMillan Co., New York, 1970.

United States War Department, *Merrill's Marauders*, American Forces in Action Series, Washington, 1945.

Wedemeyer, Albert C., *Wedemeyer Reports*, Henry Holt & Co., New York, 1958.

White, Theodore & Jacoby, Annalee, *Thunder Out of China*, William Sloane Associates, New York, 1946.

Bibliography to Chapter Five

Ambrose, Stephen, *The Supreme Commander*, Doubleday Inc., New York, 1969.

Bennett, Ralph, *Ultra in the West*, Charles Scribner's Sons, New York, 1970.

Blaxland, Gregory, *The Plain Cook and the Great Showman*, William Kimber, London, 1977.

Blumenson, Martin, *Eisenhower*, Ballantine Books, New York, 1972.

Blumenson, M. & Stokesbury, J., *Masters of the Art of Command*, Houghton Mifflin Co., New York, 1975..

Bradley, Omar, *A Soldier's Story*, Rand McNally, Chicago, 1978.

Butcher, Harry, *My Three Years With Eisenhower*, Simon & Schuster, New York, 1946.

Clark, Mark, *Calculated Risk*, Harper & Bros., New York, 1950.

Eisenhower, Dwight, *Crusade in Europe*, Doubleday, New York, 1948.

Farago, Ladislas, *The Last Days of Patton*, McGraw Hill, New York, 1981.

Farago, Ladislas, *Patton—Ordeal and Triumph*, Simon & Schuster, New York, 1968.

Ferrell, Robert, ed., *The Eisenhower Diaries*, W.W. Norton, New York, 1981.

Grigg, James, *1943—The Victory That Never Was*, Hill & Wang, New York, 1980.

Irving, David, *The War Between The Generals*, Congdon & Lattes, New York, 1981.

Jones, Vincent, *Operation Torch*, Ballantine Books, New York, 1972.

Lewin, Ronald, *Ultra Goes To War*, McGraw Hill, New York, 1978.

Liddell-Hart, B.H., *History of the Second World War*, G.P. Putnam's Sons, New York, 1971.

MacDonald, Charles, *The Mighty Endeavor*, Oxford University Press, New York, 1969.

Pfannes, C. & Salamone, V., *The Great Commanders of World War II, Volume II—The British*, Zebra Books, New York, 1981.

Pogue, Forrest, *Organizer of Victory*, Viking Press, New York, 1973.

Salmaggi, C. & Pallavisine, A., *2,194 Days of War*, Windward, London, 1977.

Summersby-Morgan, Kay, *Past Forgetting*, Simon & Schuster, New York, 1975.

Weigley, Russell, *Eisenhower's Lieutenants*, Indiana University, Bloomington, 1981.

Bibliography to Chapter Six

Baldwin, Hanson W., *Battles Lost and Won*, Harper & Row, New York, 1966.

Blair, Clay Jr., *MacArthur*, Nelson Doubleday Inc., New York, 1977.

Burns, James MacGregor, *Roosevelt: The Soldier of Freedom 1940-1945*, Harcourt Brace Jovanovich Inc., New York, 1970.

Cannon, M. Hamlin, *Leyte: The Return to the Philippines*, Office of the Chief of Military History, Washington, 1954.

Carver, Michael, ed., *The War Lords*, Little Brown & Co., Boston, 1976.

Clausewitz, Karl von, *On War*, The Modern Library, 1943.

Eichelberger, Robert L., *Our Jungle Road to Tokyo*, The Viking Press, New York, 1950.

Eisenhower, Dwight D., *Crusade in Europe*, Doubleday & Co., New York, 1948.

Falk, Stanley, *Decision at Leyte*, W.W. Norton & Co., New York.

Halsey, William F. & Bryann, J., *Admiral Halsey's Story*, McGraw-Hill Book

Co., New York, 1947.

Holmes, W.J., *Double Edged Secrets*, Naval Institute Press, Annapolis, 1979.

Hunt, Frazier, *The Untold Story of Douglas MacArthur*, The Devin-Adair Co., 1954.

Kenney, George, *General Kenney Reports*, Duell, Sloane and Pearce, 1949.

King, Ernest J. & Whitehill, Walter, *Fleet Admiral King*, W.W. Norton & Co., New York, 1952.

Krueger, Walter, *From Down Under to Nippon*, Combat Forces Press, 1953.

Leahy, William D., *I Was There*, Whittlesey House, 1950.

Long, Gavin, *MacArthur as Military Commander*, B.T. Batsford Ltd., London, 1969.

MacArthur, Douglas, *Reminiscences*, McGraw-Hill Book Co., New York, 1964.

Manchester, William, *American Caesar*, Little Brown and Co., Boston, 1978.

Mayer, Sidney, *MacArthur*, Ballantine Books, New York, 1971.

Mayer, Sidney, *MacArthur in Japan*, Ballantine Books, New York, 1971.

Miller, Francis Trevelyan, *General Douglas MacArthur: Fighter For Freedom*, The John C. Winston Co., 1942.

Miller, John, *Cartwheel, The Reduction of Rabaul*, Office of the Chief of Military History, Washington, 1959.

Morton, Louis, *The Fall of the Philippines*, Office of the Chief of Military History, Washington, 1953.

Potter, E.B., *Nimitz*, Naval Institute Press, Annapolis, 1976.

Romulo, Carlos P., *I Saw The Fall Of The Philippines*, Doubleday, Doran & Co., New York, 1943.

Smith, Robert Ross, *The Approach To The Philippines*, Office of the Chief of Military History, Washington, 1953.

Smith, Robert Ross, *Trimph In The Philippines*, Office of the Chief of Military History, Washington, 1963.

Wainwright, Jonathan M., *General Wainwright's Story*, Doubleday & Co., New York, 1946.

Willoughby, Charles A. & Chamberlain, John, *MacArthur 1941-1951*, McGraw-Hill Book Co., New York, 1954.

Wright, B.C., *The 1st Cavalry Division In World War II*, Toppan Printing Co. Ltd., 1947.